Your Worst Poker Enemy

Your Worst Poker Enemy

ALAN N. SCHOONMAKER, PH.D.

Kensington Publishing Corp.

www.Kensingtonbooks.com

LYLE STUART BOOKS are published by

Kensington Publishing Corp.
850 Third Avenue
New York, NY 10022

All Kensington titles, imprints, and distributed lines are available at special
quantity discounts for bulk purchases for sales promotions, premiums, fund-
raising, educational, or institutional use. Special book excerpts or customized
printings can also be created to fit specific needs. For details, write or phone the
office of the Kensington special sales manager: Kensington Publishing Corp.,
850 Third Avenue, New York, NY 10022, attn: Special Sales Department; phone
1-800-221-2647

Lyle Stuart is a trademark of Kensington Publishing Corp.

First printing May 2007

10 9 8 7 6 5 4

Printed in the United States of America

ISBN-13: 978-0-8184-0720-8
ISBN-10: 0-8184-0720-4

*This book is dedicated with love
to my wonderful grandchildren.*

At the table, your worst enemy is yourself.
—STU UNGAR*

---

* The greatest poker player of all time. Quoted by Nolan Dalla and Peter Alson, *One of a Kind: The Rise and Fall of Stuey "The Kid" Ungar, the World's Greatest Poker Player* (New York: Atria Books, 2005), 282.

Contents

Acknowledgments

Many people helped me write this book. Matt Lessinger, Barry Tanenbaum, Jim Brier, and Dave "Cinch" Hench are very talented writers with whom I have swapped editing for years. They edited these chapters before they were published in other places and then again to revise them into a coherent book. Matt, the author of *The Book of Bluffs*, was exceptionally helpful, making hundreds of suggestions.

Talking to Mason Malmuth and reading his own and his authors' books have greatly improved my thinking. Malmuth also made many suggestions about this book. David Sklansky did not comment directly on this book, but our conversations about these issues have been very helpful. I would also like to thank all the other poker authors whose work has influenced me. As you will see from the footnotes, I have relied heavily on their published works.

The people who participate in the discussions on the Psychology Forum at twoplustwo.com have provided many subjects for my magazine columns, and some of them have been revised and included here. Without their comments I would have run out of ideas a long time ago. Dr. Dan Kessler and Dr. Eric Niler are very active on that forum, and they have helped me with several chapters.

Jan Siroky and Preston Oade are excellent players who see the game differently from me. Discussions with them have helped me to recognize some holes in my thinking.

The Wednesday Poker Discussion Group talks about everything related to poker, and our meetings have been extremely valuable. A spin-off of that group discusses only no-limit poker, and it has helped me to make the transition to that game.

The people who play at RoyalVegasPoker.com's Play the Experts tournaments provided several useful ideas. I'm grateful to the players, especially Cheryl Connors, to my colleagues, Lou Krieger, Matt Lessinger, Barbara Enright, Max Shapiro, Mike Cappelletti, Rose Richie, and Bob Ciaffone, and to Lou Kelmanson and Mike Emmanual for inviting me to play there.

Donna Lane and Sharron Hippe, my personal assistants, have been helpful in more ways than I can count. Sheree Bykofsky, an outstanding agent, introduced me to Richard Ember and helped me organize and market the book. Richard, in turn, has helped me to present my ideas.

Your Worst Poker Enemy

Introduction

Let's not beat around the bush. You wouldn't read this book if you didn't want to answer the critical question: *How can I win more money?*

That's what poker is all about, winning money. Unlike gymnastics, diving, figure skating, and some other competitions, there are no points for style, technical knowledge, fancy plays, and so on. The only thing that matters is, How much money did you win or lose?

Many players are not satisfied with their results. Losing players want to become winners. Small winners want to become bigger ones and to move up to larger games to make even more money. Big winners want to win even more. It's a natural desire, part of our inherently competitive nature.

Even if they are disappointed by their results, most people do not seriously try to improve them. To accomplish that goal, they would have to look hard at themselves and change some of their ideas and habits. Instead, they protect their egos by whining and blaming bad luck. Since I am a hard-nosed psychologist, I will not even try to make you feel better. Instead, I will state my harsh position right now. I agree with Stu Ungar: *YOU are your worst poker enemy*.

Stu wasn't referring to his drug addiction and other personal flaws. He was talking only about being your own worst enemy *at the table*. If that principle applied to him, it certainly applies to you and me. We don't have his immense talent, nor do we have his terrible weaknesses, but we certainly harm ourselves in many ways. Virtually all the poker literature focuses on how to beat other people, but you aren't going to reach your full potential until you beat your own worst enemy: yourself.

This book will describe the ways that we beat ourselves and help you stop doing it.[1] If your *long-term* results are unsatisfactory, you

- Do not know how to play as well as your competition
- Do not apply your knowledge as well as they do
- Have unrealistic expectations
- All of the above

There are no other reasonable possibilities. Of course, you could have been extremely unlucky, but the odds are against it. If you're looking for a shoulder to cry on and an ear to hear your hard-luck stories, I'm the wrong guy.

Should you learn more about poker? Of course, but so should everybody else. *Nobody* ever completely masters our game, and, if you did, your knowledge would soon become obsolete because poker changes so quickly.

I'm a Psychologist, Not a Strategist

For years I've been extremely active on the Psychology Forum at twoplustwo.com. My profile there states: "I'm not a poker expert. I'm a psychologist who plays for moderate stakes and writes about poker psychology. I rarely give advice about playing specific cards because many people can do it better."

That profile fits this entire book. If you want advice on strategic decisions, go to "Recommended Readings." The books there will give you much better strategic advice than you can get from me. This book has very different goals. It will make you:

1. A few chapters (such as the ones about poker's evolution) may not seem to relate directly to being your own worst enemy. But those apparently irrelevant chapters show that your survival as a winning player is threatened unless you resist your own closed-mindedness, arrogance, and complacency.

- More aware of how psychological factors affect the way you and other people play
- More able to use them against other people
- Less vulnerable to these factors' destructive effects[2]

Most poker writers ignore or minimize these factors. In fact, until Two Plus Two simultaneously published Dr. John Feeney's *Inside the Poker Mind* and my *The Psychology of Poker*, there were no serious books about poker psychology.[3] Nearly all poker books described how people *should* play without analyzing why:

- Most people don't play as well as they know how to play
- Some people don't even try to learn how to play well

I think that analyzing these psychological forces is essential. People are not computers, and just giving them information will not necessarily change their behavior. Some people will ignore, misunderstand, or misuse even the best-quality information. If you visit several Internet forums, you will see many effects of psychological factors. Many people who post comments there have read excellent books and *Card Player* magazine, but thousands of posts show that they cannot apply the publications' principles. Some of them:

- Rely upon instincts or skills they don't have
- Deny reality about how well they or other people play
- Blame bad luck for losses caused by their own errors
- Overreact to anger, pride, guilt, and other emotions

2. I coach a few people, and my coaching goals are the same as this book's. If people want to learn how to play, I refer them to friends. I work *only* with people who know how to play, but get disappointing results because of psychological factors.

3. Mike Caro had published an outstanding book on tells, but it is very narrowly focused on reading other people.

- Complain bitterly about other people's mistakes that *add* to their expected value (EV)
- Believe in ESP, luck, and many other silly subjects

The Psychology Forum has provided the material for many of these chapters, which were originally published in *Card Player*, two plustwo.com's *Internet Magazine, Poker Digest*, and *Wednesday Night Poker*. They have been expanded and edited; some titles have been changed; and some series have been condensed into just one or two chapters.

This Book Emphasizes a Logical Approach

This book has several themes: especially that *except for a few, very gifted people, a logical approach works better than an intuitive one.* This belief is based on my graduate work at The University of California at Berkeley and my faculty experience at UCLA, Carnegie-Mellon, and Belgium's Catholic University of Louvain. The scientific departments of all great universities demand logical, data-based research. If you rely on intuition and anecdotes, you will fail.

This book frequently quotes books that emphasize a logical approach and rarely quotes (except to disagree with them) ones that urge people to rely on intuition. Far too many poker books are written by people who essentially say, "Here is what works for me. Just do what I do." However, many readers can't use their approach because it relies heavily on the authors' personal gifts and experiences, especially their intuition. Learning how to apply logic is immeasurably easier than developing intuition.

A logical emphasis irritates many intuitive players and writers. They naturally dislike it because they have a silly belief: *real players don't use logic*; they rely primarily on their intuition. That belief is rarely stated directly because doing so would reveal its absurdity. Instead, people make statements such as these:

"Stick to your *first* impression. Have the courage of your convictions."[4]

"Every poker situation is unique."

"I never read poker books."

"You have to develop your own, unique style."

When winning players make these comments, I respect their position. They have proved that they have enough intuition and other gifts to win without relying on logic. But, when losers or breakeven players make the same comments, I have extreme doubts about their motives and intelligence. They seem to care more about preserving their illusions than improving their results. They want to rely on their intuition and other gifts, even though their results are disappointing.

They may also try to apply a famous player's approach because they don't understand the immense difference between playing and teaching: The author's playing credentials say very little about a book's value. The important point is not the number of tournaments the author has won; it's his ability to teach *you* how to win.

Let me make an apparent digression. A few untrained people (called idiot savants) can multiply two ten-digit numbers in their heads. If you don't have a calculator, should you try to do what they do? Or should you use the step-by-step method you learned in school? The textbook system is not very exciting, but almost anyone can use it. Only a few people can do it in their heads.

The same general principle applies to poker. Some players have a nearly magical ability to read other players' hands. They just *know* that you've got a great hand or are bluffing. In fact, they sometimes know *exactly* what you have. For example, Stu Ungar once called a

4. Doyle Brunson, *Doyle Brunson's Super System: A Course in Power Poker* (New York: Cardoza Publishing, 2005), 431.

huge bluff with a jack high because he *knew* that his opponent had missed a smaller draw. This rare gift enables these "magicians" to make moves that less-gifted people shouldn't even attempt. But don't assume you have these abilities.

Good teachers do not tell you, "Here's how *I* play." They give you a method that *you* can use even if your only gifts are normal intelligence and the discipline to apply it. It is not exciting or original, but it will make you a winning player. If you try to play poker in a way that requires *unusual gifts*, you will probably lose, and you will almost certainly get poorer results than you could get.

You should also understand that logical people naturally resemble each other. We don't want to be unique because the logical method is very clearly defined, and it should usually be applied. Unless the situation is extremely unusual, you should take all the steps, in the proper order, in the proper way. For example, you do not solve math problems or conduct scientific research in unique ways; you *must* use the right methods or pay the consequences:

- If you don't take all the steps, you will probably get the wrong answer.
- If you get the right answer by using the wrong method, any professor would subtract points from your exam score.
- If you don't conduct research "by the numbers," no scientist will take your work seriously, and no journal will publish it. They know that sloppy methods produce had results.

Nearly everyone trained in logical analysis, the sciences, or engineering would agree with these points, but many people reject them. They regard accepting and working within rigorous procedural constraints as signs of a lack of imagination or self-confidence. They also love songs such as "My Way." They want to believe they can ignore the experts' advice, do it their way, and succeed. Unfortunately, if you insist on playing poker *your* way, your results will almost certainly be disappointing.

Who Should Read This Book?

If you are one of the fortunate few with great intuition, you don't need many parts of this book. Your rare gift will let you get away with playing your own way. If you're one of the other 99-plus percent, this book will help you use facts and logic to improve your game.

In addition, even if you have wonderful intuition, you may lack the emotional control needed to survive in poker. If you doubt me, just read *One of a Kind: The Rise and Fall of Stuey, "The Kid," Ungar.*[5] He had incredible gifts, including uncanny intuition, but died young and broke in a crummy motel room. He never learned how to control his impulses or to recognize his limitations, and these flaws destroyed him.

Unfortunately, you probably have *much* less intuition than you believe. It's a critically important difference between idiot savants and poker players. You know you can't multiply ten digit numbers in your head, but you can easily believe that you have great intuition. Your ego and selective memory can make you remember the few times your intuition was right and ignore or forget your mistakes. Since memories are so selective, *don't* assume that you've got great intuition (or any other asset).

Read this book *only* if you already understand strategic principles as well or better than your competition. You need that knowledge more than you need this book. Without it you simply can't play well. This book focuses on the psychological factors that prevent you from:

- Learning as much as you should learn
- Getting the full benefits of the knowledge you do have

A wide variety of factors prevent people from studying strategy. Laziness is one of them because many people play for fun and don't

---

5. Nolan Dalla and Peter Alson, *One of a Kind: The Rise and Fall of Stuey "The Kid" Ungar, The World's Greatest Poker Player* (New York: Atria Books, 2005).

want to work on their skills. That attitude is reasonable as long as they accept that it costs them money. However, even people who take the game seriously probably don't study enough for two major reasons:

1. They greatly overestimate their innate abilities. They say, in effect, "Other people may have to study all those books, but I am so talented that I don't need to study." That statement is true for a handful of very gifted people, but it is self-defeating nonsense for everyone else.

2. They don't understand how subtle and complicated poker really is. Many players want to know the two or three rules for playing each kind of hand, and there aren't any simple rules.

If you don't understand strategic principles, turn to the "Recommended Readings," buy some books, and get to work. Focus more on strategy than on psychology. I made that same point in *The Psychology of Poker*.

If Freud had played poker and ignored the odds and strategic principles, he would have gone broke. He was the greatest psychologist, but the odds and strategy come way ahead of psychology. To play winning poker, you *must* master and apply the odds and basic strategic concepts.[6]

Understanding is necessary, but not sufficient. In fact, you probably don't play as well as you know how to play. You doubt me? Then just answer a few questions. Do you sometimes:

---

6. Alan Shoonmaker, *The Psychology of Poker* (Henderson, NV: Two Plus Two, 2000), 5.

- Play hands on third street or before the flop that you *know* you should fold?
- Go too far with hands, *knowing* that the pot odds don't justify calling, but hoping to get lucky?
- Keep playing when you *know* you're off your game because you're losing and want to get even?
- Let anger, fear, or other emotions affect the way you play your cards, even when you *know* better?
- Take many other actions that you *know* are foolish and expensive?

If you answered *"yes"* to any question, you obviously don't play as well as you know how to play. My primary goal is to help you stop making these and other psychologically based mistakes.

Other Themes

This book insists that psychological factors damage your play and distort your perceptions about yourself, other people, and the game itself. You probably

- Know less about the game than you think you know
- Are less talented than you think you are
- Let pride, anger, and other emotions adversely affect you
- Don't seriously try to maximize your profits, despite anything you may say
- Don't fully accept responsibility for your decisions and their consequences
- Expect greater profits than your talents, knowledge, and personality can produce
- Don't analyze yourself thoroughly and objectively

Some friends told me, after reading this material, that I was too hard on my readers. Perhaps I am, but my job is to help you, not make you feel good. Poker is a brutal game. Since your opponents will exploit every weakness, you had better understand and correct them. Otherwise, you can't reach your potential.

Because you lack objectivity about yourself, you should get feedback from other people about your knowledge, skill, and self-control. You can get it from friends, Internet forums, or professional coaches, and I repeatedly recommend that you do so.

A final theme should be discussed separately because it's not as directly related to the bottom line: *don't take poker too seriously*. It's just a game, and games should be played for pleasure. Of course, you should do whatever will improve your play, but don't let poker take over your life. That principle applies even if you play for a living; don't let poker (or any other job) become an obsession. You'd risk much more than your money. You could destroy your work, studies, health, and important relationships. In addition, if you let poker take over your life, you're *much* more likely to go on tilt. Instead of shrugging off the inevitable bad beats and losing streaks, your self-concept may be threatened, making you act irrationally.

All these themes have a common element: the focus is on you, not the other players. Most of the poker literature focuses on how to read and adjust to situations and other people. That emphasis is certainly reasonable; you must understand them to play winning poker. But the most important person to understand is yourself. You must ruthlessly analyze yourself, and most players just don't want to do it. So they never reach their potential as players or people. As the title states, *you* are your worst poker enemy.

My Definition of the Word "Players"

Players and writers sometimes disagree about the meaning of the word "players." It can mean everyone who plays poker, or just the ones who know how to play or just the ones who play regularly, and so on. To avoid confusion, I will have only one definition: "players" means everyone who plays in cardrooms, including online ones—the pros, wannabe pros, beginners, regulars, tourists, perpetual fish, and everyone in between. It does *not* include "kitchen table" players. There are three reasons for this definition:

1. Most psychological forces affect everybody from pros to novices. People like to think that "they" have this or that weakness, but "we" don't. Nonsense. We may have more or less of a certain psychological flaw, but we probably have some of it.

2. I don't know anything about kitchen-table players.

3. The house's charges dramatically change everyone's economics, especially at the lower limits (because they are proportionately larger). The average players will break even in kitchen-table games, but will lose in a cardroom. If you do not play significantly better than the average player in your game, you will lose. Since it is so much harder to beat cardroom games, you must understand these psychological factors.

How This Book Is Organized

This book is organized and based on a simple premise: because poker is a game of incomplete information, *information management is the critical skill*. If you manage information well, you will win. If you manage it badly, you will lose.

Egotism causes many information-management errors, and you must constantly guard against its destructive effects. In addition to making you overestimate your abilities, your ego can cause a huge mistake on an extremely important information-management decision: *will you emphasize logic or intuition?* This decision is discussed in part one because it affects everything you do at a poker table.

Part two: "Evaluating ourselves and the opposition" comes so early because it has such extreme effects on your results. Many players overestimate, not just their intuition, but also their skills, knowledge, and other talents. The same ego-driven desire to think well of themselves causes them to underestimate the competition. These mistakes are extremely expensive. If you do not accurately compare yourself to the competition, you will play in the wrong games against the wrong people. You will also play hands you should fold because you think you can outplay your opposition.

Part three: "Understanding Unconscious and Emotional Factors" distinguishes between how people *should* play and how they *do* play. If you look objectively at what actually happens at poker tables, you will see that "irrational" forces *must* be operating. How else can you explain all the stupid mistakes?

Part four: "Adjusting to Changes" is essential because our game is constantly changing. For example, draw and five-card stud were once the primary games, but hardly anyone plays them today. Even seven-card stud, which was very popular just a few years ago, is being supplanted by hold'em, especially no limit. Poker has always had Darwinian evolution, "the survival of the fittest." If you don't understand and adapt to the way poker is changing, you'll slowly be left behind, and you may not survive as a winning player.

Part five: "Handling Stress" states that you must learn how to handle it because poker is intrinsically stressful and frustrating. Our interests directly conflict because we want to take each other's money. Someone always loses, and we often lose enough to hurt both our wallets and our egos. Everyone has bad beats, bad nights, and bad weeks. If you can't handle them, these stresses can severely damage your enjoyment, attitudes, and results.

Using This Book

As I said earlier, this book's primary purpose is to help you win more money. The more sensibly you use it, the better return you will get on the time you spend reading it.

This book is both a textbook and a reference manual. It teaches you principles and suggests ways to get more information. Many of these references are in footnotes. If you want to know why I've taken various positions or want to have more information, read the footnotes.[1] If you don't care to read further, just ignore them.

If you just want help with certain kinds of problems, the traditional poker literature is almost useless. For example, most poker books don't tell you what to do when you:

- Lose night after night
- Can't control your emotions
- Think of quitting forever

These problems and many others really bother some people, and they don't know where to get help with them. If something is severely troubling you, don't read this entire book, at least not immediately. Just look in the table of contents and index, and then focus on the one or two chapters that relate directly to your problem.

You may find exactly what you need. If you don't, go to an Inter-

---

1. Most poker books have hardly any footnotes. I think the authors have made a huge mistake. If you need more information, they should tell you where to get it. Many of my footnotes are for articles you can easily find at cardplayer.com, an outstanding source of poker information.

net forum, especially the ones at cardplayer.com and twoplustwo. com. Many forums have a search function; just type in a subject, and you may find that I or someone else has posted something that solves your problem. If you don't find anything, send me an e-mail at alannschoonmaker@hotmail.com. I may answer your question, send you an essay that is not in this book, or refer you to some other writer's work.

Because some chapters are designed to help you with specific problems, there is considerable repetition. The same principles apply to a wide variety of problems:

- *Thinking logically* instead of relying on intuition is this book's central theme, and I constantly urge you to do so.

- *Studying* helps with almost everything, and I repeatedly recommend it.

- *Overestimating yourself and underestimating the opposition* are major problems. I will frequently warn you about their wide-ranging effects and urge you to be objective.

- *Diversifying your life* provides the balance you need to cope with poker's frustrations.

- *Participating in Internet forums* provides information and advice you can't get anywhere else. In fact, you can learn more from exchanging ideas with informed people than from any book, including this one.

- *Getting coaching from a professional, a friend, or a discussion group* is probably the best way to improve your skills, perspective, and evaluations of your competition and yourself. You need an outsider's objectivity to reach your potential.[2]

---

2. It can be hard to find someone to provide feedback, but it's worth the effort. You will develop much more rapidly with feedback than without it. So do whatever it takes to get it.

My goal is to help you think logically about psychological issues that most poker writers have ignored or minimized. These issues have an immense impact on your bottom line, and they will continue to harm it until you fully understand them. You will gain the most by reading this book critically, challenging my positions, discussing them with friends and a coach, and going to Internet forums to debate these issues with other people and me.

I hope you enjoy this book and that it helps you to cope with the stresses and challenges of our exciting but frustrating game.

PART ONE

Logic Versus Intuition

Introduction

Doyle Brunson, Layne Flack, and some other great players are intuitive geniuses, "artists at the poker table." They share with the late Stu Ungar a natural feel for the game and an uncanny ability to read their opponents.

The ancient Greeks, Carl Jung, and many other eminent thinkers contrasted intuition and logic, and scientists have recently discovered that they occur in different parts of the brain. Intuition takes place in the right half, the seat of artistic abilities, while logic occurs in the left half. These halves are often called the right and left brains.

This long series of chapters will describe both, review historical trends, discuss each one's advantages and disadvantages, and suggest ways to develop your ability to think logically. I will not suggest ways to develop intuition because—like most scientifically trained people—I rarely rely on it.

Intuition

My dictionary defines intuition as "the process of coming to direct knowledge without reasoning or rational thought." Given that definition, intuition cannot be taught in the same way as logic. I once believed that either you have it or you don't. However, David Sklansky, Prof. Arthur Reber, and others helped me realize that intuition can be developed, but only by a very difficult and poorly defined process. The problems of developing intuition will be discussed in the next chapter, "Which Is Better?"

"Feel" is the word many people use for intuition, and many right-brain thinkers do not even try to analyze it. In fact, since analysis is a logical process, it directly conflicts with the essence of intuition. You do not take a series of steps to reach a conclusion; you just *feel* it is right, and you cannot explain exactly why you feel that way.

In *Doyle Brunson's Super System*, Brunson wrote: "Whenever I use the word 'feel'... I recall what happened.... Even though I might not *consciously* do so... I recall that this same play came up (or something close to it) and this is what he did or somebody else did. So I get a feeling that he's bluffing or that I can make a play here and get the pot. But, actually my subconscious mind is reasoning it all out."[1]

Brunson and many other right brain thinkers do not know *how* they know. Flack frankly admitted it: "I seem to have an intuition in poker that is amazing. I think I have a sixth sense.... I don't read books.... I don't want to be influenced by what others do or say. I don't discuss hands with other people.... It can't be taught or written down."[2]

The intuitive players have a gift, and it is as natural to them as Michael Jordan's miraculous moves were to him. When someone unexpectedly blocked him, he responded instantly by switching hands, twisting his body, and shooting the ball a little higher with a little different spin. He could never tell you how he did it; it was just by feel or instinct.

Some great poker players have that gift: they remember how you played a certain hand or they see a look in your eye or they sense something from the way you handle your chips, and they make exactly the right play. If you ask why they did it, they probably can't say. It just felt right.

After studying and teaching psychology for many years, I am still amazed by some people's intuition. I once worked with someone for

1. Doyle Brunson, *Doyle Brunson's Super System: A Course in Power Poker* (New York: Cardoza Publishing, 2002), 430.

2. Allyn Jaffrey Shulman, "Layne Flack", *Card Player*, March 16, 2005, 54.

months. After meeting him for two minutes, my wife said, "He's a crook; don't trust him." I later learned that I should have listened to her, but she never could tell me how she knew; she just did.

Logic

My dictionary contains several definitions, and many of them contain words such as "formal," "reasoning," "definition," and "principles." The critical point is that conclusions are drawn using clearly defined methods that you can see and explain to other people. That is, logical thinking is "visible," while intuition is not.

Chris Ferguson, the World Series of Poker Champion (WSOP) in 2000, David Sklansky, and Mason Malmuth are logical thinkers. They break the decision process into a series of steps, explicitly state their premises, and can clearly state how they reach a conclusion. The title of his column, "Fighting Fuzzy Thinking," clearly demonstrates Sklansky's commitment to formal, explicit logic, and the books he has written by himself and with Malmuth, Ray Zee, and Ed Miller are rigorously logical.

In *Getting the Best of It*, Sklansky answered the question of the relative importance of "playing your cards" or "playing your people" by saying: "There is a third factor that is more important than the other two ... logic. . . . When I speak of logic, I [mean] . . . the formal type of reasoning that is characterized by frequent use of words 'if . . . then.' "[3]

The decision-making process is broken into steps, which are taken in order. The premises are extremely explicit. The reasoning is a series of "if . . . then" statements. Probabilities may be assigned to each alternative, and these probabilities are added to make an overall assessment of risks and rewards. If you are thinking logically, you may say to yourself, "If I raise, there is an X percent chance that I will win the pot immediately, a Y percent chance that I will get a free card,

3. David Sklansky, *Getting the Best of It* (Henderson, NV: Two Plus Two, 1997), 67.

and a Z percent chance I will draw out. Not one of these outcomes justifies the raise, but since the combination of them all has a positive expectation, I should raise."

At all times Sklansky and his co-authors urge readers to think logically, to make their premises explicit, and to know *why* they make a decision, rather than just responding to feelings. An excellent bridge partner had the same idea when he told me, "As long as you can tell me *why* you made a bid or played a card, I will never get angry with you because I can straighten out your thinking. For example, if you tell me that you played the queen of clubs because you thought the king was on your left, I can review the bidding and show you why you should have realized it was on your right. But, if you just played the queen without thinking, I'll get mad." It was some of the best advice I have ever gotten about cardplaying or anything else. By making my thought processes explicit, I can improve them.

It's a Continuum, Not a Dichotomy

Although I have clearly contrasted intuition and logic, there are not just two approaches; there are a whole range of them. The purely logical approach is at one end of the continuum, and the purely intuitive one is at the other end.

INTUITION $\longleftrightarrow$ LOGIC

Ungar	Malmuth
Flack	Sklansky
Brunson	Ferguson

Most people use both, and hardly anyone *ever* just uses either logic or intuition. Note that neither group of experts is at the very end of the continuum. Even the most rigorous logicians—such as Malmuth, Sklansky, and Ferguson—occasionally respond to their gut feelings or make decisions they cannot fully explain. Even the most

intuitive players—such as Ungar, Flack, and Brunson—will sometimes use logic. Although everyone uses a somewhat mixed
approach, I'll simplify this discussion by ignoring the overlaps to contrast the approaches more sharply. Don't forget that this simplifica-
tion is somewhat artificial.

The Historical Trend

Some great players will live and die by their feel, but the historical trend is unquestionably toward logic in poker and many other
competitions. Let's discuss a few of these other "games." Until fairly
recently politics was dominated by people with a great feel for the
voters. Today no serious politician would make a major campaign decision without extensive logical analysis, using polling, focus groups,
and other analytic tools.

The same trend has occurred in marketing, corporate planning,
warfare, and other competitions. The process is broken into elements; formulas are developed, tested, and revised; and the resulting
strategy is as clearly defined as the experts can make it. If you proposed that a major organization make an important decision on feel
alone, you would be ridiculed as a hopeless amateur.

The Internet poker forums illustrate this shift toward logical, explicit analysis. Everything from playing ace-jack suited to adjusting to
shorthanded games to the differences between tournaments and ring
games is thoroughly dissected, and facts, probabilities, and logic are
emphasized. If you argued that a certain position just felt right, you'd
get a lot of heat.

Or take a very intuitive subject, *tells*. Some players just *know* intuitively what opponents have, but Mike Caro showed that even tells
can be analyzed logically. He does not say, "Trust your gut feeling." He
describes many specific cues (such as glancing at chips, nervousness,
shuffling a hand, and double-checking one's cards), and states what
these cues usually mean. He uses the same kind of "if . . . then" logic

as Sklansky. For example, "Caro's Law of Tells #9" states, "If a player looks and then checks instantly, it's unlikely that he improved his hand."[4]

Does that historical trend mean that the great players of the future will all approach poker logically? Of course not. Some top players will always be "artists," but they may not be pure ones. They will rely on their feel, but they will also use logic, probabilities, computer simulations, and other analytic tools. These definitions and historical trends may be interesting, but they just lay the foundation for your real interest: getting better results. The chapters here will discuss the advantages and disadvantages of both and suggest ways to develop your logical abilities.

4. Mike Caro, *The Body Language of Poker: Mike Caro's Book of Tells* (Hollywood, CA: Gambling Times, 1984), 280.

Which Is Better, Logic or Intuition?

Don't expect a simple answer to a question that has been debated for more than 2,000 years. Both have substantial advantages, and like so many poker questions, *it depends on the situation.*

The Advantages of Logic

The three major advantages of logic are that it is *correctable, easily teachable, and additive.*

Advantage No. 1: Correctable

If you make a mistake, you and other people can see why you made it because the entire process is visible. If your basic premise is wrong, you can change it. If your reasoning process is faulty, you can retrace your steps, see *exactly* where you went wrong, change your method, and get it right. Nearly all scientific journals demand a detailed report of methodology so that readers can see how results were obtained and how conclusions were drawn.

Because intuition is not clearly defined or visible, it is often hard to say why a mistake was made, which can make you repeat your mistakes. However, some intuitive people feel that *something* is not right, and they adjust, even though they may not be able to say exactly what went wrong.

Advantage No. 2: Easily Teachable

The process is broken down into a series of small, clearly defined steps that other people can easily learn and duplicate. It took extraordinary genius for Archimedes to discover the principles of leverage and water displacement, but we learn them as children. In college many of us learn basic scientific methods, and we may use some of them without even knowing we are doing so. They have become natural parts of our thinking.

I once believed that intuition could not be taught, that you had to be born with it. Sklansky, Prof. Reber and others convinced me that intuition could be learned, but the process was poorly defined, and it was far from easy.

> When someone asks me what kind of favorite hand A is over hand B, my gut reaction is usually much closer than others. And that is because I have studied and practiced my subject. Intuitiveness about something does not come solely from subconscious memories about similar situations. It can also come from learning and practicing how to solve problems in that field. People who do that are much more likely to come up with a good guess on the spur of the moment than the vast majority of others even if they have a lot of "experience" but never learned the right way to get the precise answer.[1]

People learn intuition in widely varying ways,[2] and it usually requires gifted students and exceptional teachers. For example, Johann Sebastian Bach taught some of his children to be successful composers. They had inherited their father's genes, and he spent countless hours teaching them.

Contrast their learning pattern with the way children learn geometry. It took Euclid, a genius, many years to develop geometry, but

---

1. David Sklansky, e-mail message to author.

2. "Reading and adjusting to players" in my next book, *Your Best Poker Friend* (New York: Lyle Stuart, forthcoming), describes a simple system for developing "feel," which is a form of intuition.

children learn it easily and quickly in high school. In addition, the way to learn it has not changed much in over 2,000 years. We cannot understand how Mozart wrote his music or Rembrandt made his paintings, nor can we do what they did. They had an indescribable gift called "genius." I couldn't write *Hold'em Poker for Advanced Players*, but I can follow its reasoning and apply its principles.

Some intuitive writers don't understand how little value their advice has. They essentially say, "Here is what works for me," but it can't work for someone who lacks their gifts. In fact, if nonintuitive players try to apply their recommendations, they will probably lose.

Advantage No. 3: Additive

Because logic is correctable and teachable, it is also additive. We can build on the works of earlier people. Sir Isaac Newton, one of the two greatest physicists, said it best: "If I have seen further than other men, it was by standing on the shoulders of giants."

You and I know much more about physics, chemistry, and every other science than specialists of previous centuries, and we take for granted airplanes, television, computers, and other inventions that would have appeared magical to them. Almost everything in our world has been slowly developed from the work of previous scientists and engineers. Today's sciences and engineering are incomparably superior to those of the past, but there has been much less progress in the arts. Hardly anyone would argue that today's artists are better than Beethoven, Rembrandt, and the other immortals.

To summarize, intuition cannot—by itself—provide the three major benefits of logic: it is not correctable, easily teachable, or additive.

The Advantages of Intuition

Intuition has three great advantages: it can go beyond logic, it is much faster, and it can utilize logic and its products.

Advantage No. 1: Going Beyond Logic

Despite its immense advantages, logic is limited. It is a slow, controlled process that builds gradually on the past, but it cannot go far beyond known facts and theories. To make the great leaps, you *must* have a special gift.

These leaps usually, but not always, occur in the arts. No amount of logic would produce the Mona Lisa or Handel's Messiah. Great leaps of imagination have also occurred in science, and the process has been just as mysterious. For example, a dream about a snake with its tail in its mouth helped a chemist see that the benzine molecule was circular. Einstein discovered relativity by imagining how the world would look if you could ride on a light beam. Logic alone could never make such leaps.

Some poker players go far beyond logic. For example, John Duthie won the British "Poker Million" by making four brilliant bluffs, and at least one was incredible. Tony Bloom raised about $35,000 with K-2 offsuit, and Duthie made a questionable call with Q-J offsuit. The flop was A-2-3, and Bloom bet about $50,000. The only logical decision was folding, but Duthie moved all-in for about $160,000. Bloom folded. His other three bluffs were almost as amazing, and I doubt that he can say exactly why he made them. The only explanation I've heard is that he "sensed weakness," and this feeling helped him win one million British pounds.

Advantage No. 2: Acting Much Faster

Intuition is a nearly instantaneous process. Judgments and decisions can be reached without going through a series of clearly defined steps. At times speed is absolutely essential. Let me give two apparently irrelevant examples:

First, when a baseball outfielder hears the crack of the bat and sees the ball starting to rise, he almost instantly knows that it's going to be a long fly ball in his direction, and he starts moving. It's literally impossible for him to do the equations. The ball is rising at this angle, at this speed, and soon. Somehow, his mind works out where that ball is going and when it'll get there. He couldn't articulate the process, any more than some poker players can articulate how they "knew" that somebody was bluffing or had a big hand or was setting a trap.

Second, Michael Jordan uses a similar process when he makes *extremely* complicated decisions. As I noted before, in less time than it takes for you to make a simple decision such as whether you should hit the brakes, he decides whether to pass off or to shoot, and, if he will shoot, whether he will use his right or left hand, how he will twist his body, how high he will throw the ball, and how much spin he will put on it. Such a complicated decision could never be made logically in such a brief time.

This speed can be valuable in poker. You don't have much time to make most decisions. If you have to rush through all the steps, you will probably make some mistakes. In addition, taking extra time for analysis gives your opposition important information. They can see that you have a difficult decision and can make inferences from it. If John Duthie thought logically before making those bluffs, he would have acted more slowly, and his opponents would have been more likely to call him.

Advantage No. 3: Utilizing Logic and Its Products

Even though intuition is a right-brain activity, it can benefit from logic, numbers, scientific theories, computer simulations, and anything else that the left brain can produce. For example, today's composers use computers and synthesizers to write their music and hear the way it will sound before it gets played.

The old-timers had to rely on their feel for cards because they had no hard data. For example, nobody had put starting hands into ranked groups, and you couldn't run a computer simulation of pocket aces against one, two, five, or more opponents. Today virtually all serious players, even if they have great intuition, have memorized some odds, have known some results of computer simulations, and have studied many of the best books.

This ability to combine right- and left-brain thinking is the biggest edge that intuitive people have over logical thinkers like me. Because their gift is inherent and hard to develop, *they can easily borrow from us, but we usually can't borrow from them.*

Understanding and Exploiting Our Own Gifts

That last sentence is depressing unless we understand and exploit our own gifts. Despite spending years developing my left brain, I don't have that intuitive gift, and I may never get it. What should I do? More importantly, what should *you* do? All of us should take three steps:

1. Appraise ourselves honestly.
2. Select games that fit our natural gifts.
3. Develop and use those gifts.

Should *You* Emphasize Logic or Intuition?

Although some people insist that you should always use one approach or the other, the answer is the same as the one to most poker questions: it depends on the situation. Base your choice on a careful appraisal of yourself and the game you're playing.

Appraise Yourself Honestly

Honest self-appraisal is a central theme of my work, and I keep harping on it because so many poker players pay a high price for kidding themselves about their abilities. Regardless of whether you emphasize logic or intuition, understand and work within your personal limitations. Otherwise, you won't do as well as you should. You'll play in the wrong games and use the wrong strategies.

The first step is to keep records. Otherwise, your selective memory can make you remember winning a few big pots by reacting to your instincts but forget the dozens of times they caused expensive mistakes. You see it all the time. People brag about the great decisions they make by their marvelous feel. "I knew he was on a flush draw." But they forget the times they were equally sure the opponent was on a draw, but he really had a big made hand. So keep track of how often you're right and wrong about various decisions.

Of course, you should record your overall results and where and how you got them. These records will improve your game selection. For example, if you win steadily in limit games, but lose at pot- and no-limit games, you probably lack the skills and other qualities needed for big-bet poker. Perhaps you can develop them, perhaps not, but you don't have them *now*.

The second step is to work with skilled players who will give you honest feedback. You need an outsider's objectivity because *nobody* is completely objective about himself. Ask them to criticize your game, and don't be offended when they tell you things you don't want to hear. The more a statement offends you, the more you need to hear it. Learning the truth about yourself may not be pleasant, but it's the essential starting point for any development plan.

One question to ask them and yourself is: Which is more natural for you, intuition or logic? Do you have the gift of intuition, or (like most of us) should you rely on logic because it is much easier to develop?

When to Emphasize Logic

Emphasize logic unless you have clear evidence that you really have the gift of intuition. In addition, even if you have great intuition, combine it with logic. The combination of both is more effective than either one. Logic is particularly important in limit games, especially low- and middle-limit ones. In those games *being right frequently* is much more *important* than making great plays.

Logic and the discipline to use it consistently will give you a little edge here and a little edge there, enabling you to make the right decisions often enough to do well. Logical play will win in the long run because so many players act illogically.

In fact, some people lose money by being too creative. You have probably played with "creative geniuses" who lose because they make fancy plays that nobody understands. Then they get angry at the "idiots" who beat them and at the tight, straightforward, logical players who just sit there, unimaginatively grinding out a profit.

When Should You Emphasize Intuition?

First and most important, don't rely on intuition unless you have solid evidence—meaning good records—that you have it. If you don't have good intuition, some books can actually *cost* you money. For example, in *Doyle Brunson's Super System 2* Brunson recommended that "once you decide what a man's most likely to have—especially in no-limit—you should never change your mind. You'll probably be right the first time, so don't try to second-guess yourself. Have the courage and conviction to trust your instincts."[1]

Because Doyle has great instincts, he should trust them. Unless you have *proof* that you have great instincts, don't follow his advice. His position is as silly as telling a young basketball player to develop Michael Jordan's reflexes. Those reflexes are a gift that he will probably never have. He should work with the abilities he has, just as you and I have to work within our own limitations.

Unfortunately, many people overestimate their abilities, especially hard-to-measure ones such as intuition. They may rely on intuition they don't have instead of learning how to think logically. I'm reminded of those television shows with highly skilled professionals doing crazy stunts on skis, motorcycles, and skateboards. Sometimes they warn viewers, "Don't try these stunts yourself." Despite the warnings, many less-skilled people try those stunts, and some of them cripple or kill themselves. Relying on intuition you don't have won't kill or cripple you, but it can cost you lots of money.

Second, intuition becomes more important as you move to higher stakes in limit games, and it is particularly important in pot- and no-limit games. As the stakes get higher, more players know the odds and strategy, read the books, and act in a logical, disciplined way. You therefore need something extra, and intuition can be the critical difference between winning and losing.

1. Doyle Brunson, *Doyle Brunson's Super System 2: A Course in Power Poker* (New York: Cardoza Publishing, 2005), 551.

Intuition can be particularly valuable in pot- and no-limit games because the bottom line often depends on making great plays. You can lose many pots, but end up winning because you won the big ones, perhaps just one or two of them.

In addition, logical people tend to be predictable, which can be deadly, especially in pot- and no-limit games. If you always act in a rigidly logical manner, the better players will soon learn how to read you and beat you. If you don't use game theory and other approaches to become less predictable, an excessively logical approach can become counterproductive against expert players, especially in big-bet poker.

Labels and Decision Rules

Logical and intuitive people have completely opposed attitudes toward labels and decision rules (such as "Don't cold call raises in early position with medium, suited connectors"). Logical people usually like them, while intuitive people detest them. This emotional reaction has caused many people to rely too heavily on them or to reject them automatically. Both extreme reactions are destructive. It is as foolish to rely excessively on them, as it is to reject them completely.

The Values and Dangers of Labeling Systems

Some people love labels so much that they label almost everything and act rigidly. They say to themselves, "This is a group three hand (or a type X player or a type Z situation), and the manual says that I should . . ."

Others have such loathing for labels that they insist that every person, hand, or situation is unique, and you must always consider all the factors that make this situation different from that one. For example, Sklansky's Hold'em Hand Groupings have been attacked as "training wheels" that prevent players from developing judgment and cause them to act rigidly. My two-dimensional grid for labeling players and games has received similar criticisms.

A fascinating aspect of these attacks is that we have repeatedly stated that our systems should *not* be used mechanically. Some intuitive people hate labels so much that they refuse to hear our warnings about their limitations.

In fact, the starting hands actually move up and down the hand rankings depending on the circumstances. Because of that it can be a mistake to rigidly adhere to the hand rankings.[1]

Rate players and fit them into a grid. Expect them to play about the same as other people with similar ratings, but look for and adjust to other information.... Use the grid cautiously, and accept that there is no substitute for knowing how this particular player is feeling and acting *now*.[2]

A labeling system is nothing more than a starting point. By labeling people, hands, games, and so on you get a *preliminary* idea of what to do, but you should consider as much information as possible before acting.

Everybody Uses Labels and Decision Rules

Anyone who says, "I don't use labels and decision rules because every situation is unique," is kidding himself. *Nobody* can function without using them. You, Sigmund Freud, poker champions and everyone else put information into groups, label these groups, and have rules for dealing with different types of people and situations.

Take Doyle Brunson, the most respected intuitive writer. He insists that we should rely on feel and first impressions, but *he* uses many labels such as "weak players," "strong players," and "trash hands," and *Super System* states the decision rules for each.[3]

The question is not whether you use labels and decision rules. It is whether they are clear, explicit, and logically organized, or vague,

1. David Sklansky and Mason Malmuth, *Hold'em Poker for Advanced Players, 21st Century Edition* (Henderson, NV: Two Plus Two, 1999), 14.

2. Alan Schoonmaker, *The Psychology of Poker* (Henderson, NV: Two Plus Two, 2000), 75.

3. Brunson, *Super System*.

intuitive, and disorganized. If you use explicit labels and decision rules in a systematic manner, you gain the benefits of logic: you can correct your errors, learn new strategies, and improve your game slowly. Conversely, relying entirely on your intuition and treating every situation as unique makes it very hard to improve your skills.

How Simple Should a Labeling System Be?

The simplicity of a labeling system depends on what you want to do and how long you have to make decisions. The simpler the system, the easier it is to use, but the more information will get lost or ignored. People *love* to label and propose rules for dealing with different types of individuals. They have been creating systems for thousands of years. The ancient Greeks had four types based on earth, air, fire, and water. Freud wrote endlessly about oral, anal, and other types of personalities. The American Psychiatric Association has a huge manual with hundreds of categories, subcategories, and subsubcategories.

Any good system can help you make decisions about what to do with various "types" of people, and no system—no matter how complicated—can cover all the possibilities. Psychiatrists may spend hours with a patient and give him or her a dozen tests, but find that none of their hundreds of categories exactly fits *this* patient.

So what should you do? If you have great intuition, you can go with your "gut feelings." If you don't have that gift, you had better find or develop a system for labeling and adjusting to different types of players, games, and situations.

Is my grid too simple? It depends on who you are and how much time you have to make a decision. If you're a psychiatrist and can spend hours with patients and give them many tests before diagnosing them, any two-dimensional grid is absurd. If you're an advanced player with a gift for reading people, you don't need my grid. You already have some system, even if you can't say exactly what it is.

But if you can't understand why some players act the way they do and you don't know how to adjust to Tom, Susan, and Charlie, you need a simple system *now*. Maybe later, when you've developed further, you can throw away the labels and deal with each unique player and situation differently, but until you've got that "feel," you need an explicit, logical system.

If you try to consider all the factors that make this player or situation unique, you will become confused and indecisive, and indecisive players haven't got a chance. Poker is a very "now" game. When the action gets to you, you have to do *something*. You can fold, check, call, bet, or raise, but you cannot take much time to analyze the situation—and, unlike contestants on audience-assisted game shows—you cannot ask anyone for help. You have a few seconds to make a decision, and every mistake theoretically costs you money. An explicit system—even a simplistic one—can reduce the number of mistakes you make. Unless you have great "feel," take three actions:

1. Learn how to label players, games, starting hands, and other "things."
2. Master the decision rules for each type.
3. Learn how and when to adjust these decision rules.

As you develop better instincts, you can experiment with more complicated labeling systems and bend the decision rules, but at this stage in your development, keep it simple.

How Should You Prepare Logically?

The next three chapters will provide an overview of how to prepare, play, and review logically. You will find more specific information in several other places.

Logical players could learn something from the Boy Scouts. Their motto is "Be prepared," and it certainly applies to us. When it is our turn, we must act quickly. Although we have only a few choices, many decisions are quite complicated, and nearly all of them involve risks and rewards. If we have not prepared well, we will probably make costly mistakes.

Intuitive people have much less need to prepare. They can just trust their instincts, a nearly instantaneous process. Logical people need to prepare because we depend on labels and decision rules. We have just a few seconds to assess these nine factors:

1. The cards that we hold
2. The other players' probable cards
3. The probability that we have the best hand
4. The probability that other hands will improve enough to beat us
5. The probability, if we are behind, that our hand will improve enough to win
6. The odds being given by the pot
7. The potential costs and profits of future betting rounds
8. The other players' likely actions
9. The relevant strategic principles

When You Should Prepare

Because it is literally impossible to make all those preceding assessments in just a few seconds, there are certain times we should prepare. Of course, we can take a bit more time, but we usually want to act quickly. Pressure from the other players is one reason, and hesitating to remember these facts or principles can give away valuable information. To hide our uncertainty, we may act without fully considering important factors. We have all done it and then wondered, "How could I make such a stupid mistake?" To prevent those mistakes, we should prepare at all these times:

1. Long before the game
2. On the way to the cardroom
3. Before taking a seat
4. While playing a hand
5. After folding our cards
6. After finishing the session

Hardly anyone is that thorough, but the closer we come to this ideal, the better we will do.

Time No. 1: Long Before the Game

Our goal should be to master the odds and strategy so completely that we don't have to think about them long before the game. Applying strategic principles should be almost as automatic as tying our shoelaces. To create that automatic reaction, we should buy and study some good books, participate in forums, attend seminars, and treat poker the way good doctors and lawyers treat their professions.

A few winning players brag that they have never studied a book (just as a few successful people brag that they never cracked a schoolbook). However, studying will greatly improve *your* results. Sklansky wrote:

I contend that no more than one percent of those who try to make it as poker players without serious study succeed. On the other hand, I think about 10 percent of serious students succeed. But since the first group is much larger than the second . . . we wind up with about equal numbers of successful players from each group.[1]

It is no secret that many successful poker players have learned little or nothing from poker books or articles. However, that doesn't mean that reading about poker is of little value. The fact is that many of the superstars are freaks. They have an inborn talent for the game as most champion athletes do.

With proper coaching, practice, and study [many people] can frequently surpass people who have much more talent, but don't want to study and practice the fundamentals.[2]

In other words, unless you have immense, natural talent, you had better study carefully. Unfortunately, many people overestimate their abilities and don't understand how much their poor preparation costs them.

Some intuitive players detest study and other forms of preparation. They regard them as a mechanical, unimaginative approach, similar to "painting by the numbers." They say, in effect, "You simpletons need to prepare, but smart people like me are beyond it."

I'm reminded of an English professor's comment: "Some aspiring authors insist that they don't need to learn the rules of composition because James Joyce violated them in his greatest book, *Ulysses*. But he didn't break them until he mastered them in his earlier works." Exactly the same principle applies to poker. We should master the rules, not to apply them mechanically, but to ensure that we know them so well that we don't have to think much about them.

1. David Sklansky, *Poker, Gaming & Life* (Henderson, NV: Two Plus Two, 2000) 11.

2. Ibid., 25f.

Time No. 2: On the Way to the Cardroom

While traveling, most players don't think seriously about the game. Their minds are on jobs, family, traffic, dinner, and other subjects. If they think of poker, it is usually in a vague, hopeful way: "I sure hope I win tonight." Winners use this time to prepare mentally. They may review their recent play and decide how they will play differently tonight. They may also "psych themselves up" just the way professional athletes do. They purge their minds of distractions, such as problems at home or a meeting at work, to get ready to *win*.

Time No. 3: Before Taking a Seat

If a seat is open, many people just take it and start to play, but winners look over the entire room, see who is playing at each table, review mentally what they know about these players, look for other signs such as laughter or large pots, and then pick the table that offers the best prospects.

After choosing a table, winners keep preparing. For example, they size up the unknown players and see whether familiar players are acting differently from usual. They may note that a normally conservative player is playing wildly or that someone is drinking heavily. They use all this information to plan their strategy. They also choose their seat carefully. Because it helps to be to the left or right of various players, they take or plan to take the best seat. Losers don't think seriously about seat selection, or they pick a seat for superstitious or other silly reasons.

Time No. 4: While Playing a Hand

Many people focus their attention on their own cards and ignore almost everything else. When the action is to them, they may not know the size of the pot, how much it will cost to call or raise, who is in the pot, what each player did, and what the other players' bets mean. Since they must make rapid, complicated decisions without enough information, they may just guess or rely on simplistic formulas. For example, if they have a pair of aces, they may automatically raise, regardless of the situation.

Because they prepare, winners don't have to guess or rely on formulas. They automatically count the pot. They mentally record who is involved, how they play, and what each one has done on every betting round. They get enough information in advance to make good decisions.

Time No. 5: After Folding Their Cards

After folding their cards, many people lose interest in the game. They check the baseball scores, make small talk, think about lunch, or just relax. Winners use this time to prepare for later actions. They look at every revealed card, review the other players' betting, and make inferences about their strategies, strengths, and weaknesses.

They also review their own play. What have they done well or poorly? Why are they playing this way? They may even write notes about themselves and other people. From time to time, logical players put together all this information and make some important decisions:

- Should they change their strategy?
- Should they change tables? The game that appeared attractive may be tougher than anticipated, or it may have changed.
- Should they change seats to improve their position on certain players?
- Should they just go home? If they are not playing well and the only games available are too tough, it is probably the best decision.

These decisions require more careful analysis than they can make while playing a hand. If they are unsure of what to do, they take a break, carefully review their mental or written notes, and then make an informed decision.

Time No. 6: After Finishing the Session

After playing, many people forget what has happened and shift their attention to other matters. If they think of the game, it is of how much they won or lost, or what bad beats they took, not what lessons they can learn. Winners review the session, analyze their own play (especially their mistakes), and prepare for later sessions. We will discuss this subject in "How Should You Review Logically?" on page 51.

What Should We Study?

We certainly have enough choices. Not too long ago there were hardly any good books, magazines,[3] and videos, but now there are many of them, plus several Internet forums. In fact, so much information is available that your problem is selecting the materials that will give you the best value for your time and money. Two logical principles can help you:

1. Select books that explicitly state the evidence on which conclusions are based.
2. Analyze yourself to determine what you need to learn.

Principle No. 1: Stating the Evidence

Virtually all scientific journals demand that writers provide the evidence and a description of the methods used to collect it. If the evidence is not collected properly, false conclusions can easily be drawn. The description of methodology allows readers to challenge conclusions, and some challenges succeed. That is, because the evidence is not collected properly, the conclusions cannot be trusted.

The mass media have much lower standards. Because reporters often fail to check the facts or do not know how to evaluate evidence,

---

3. Although there are many magazines, I must say that *Card Player* is—by a huge margin—the best one. Of course, I'm prejudiced, but no other magazine has remotely as many top writers.

they frequently mislead the public. Take, for example, cold fusion. A few years ago, some crackpots claimed they had found a way to produce it, and the media proclaimed it would solve all our energy problems. When other investigators used better-controlled methods, they could not replicate their results. After wasting millions of dollars and lots of time, cold fusion suddenly disappeared.

We see the same sort of nonsense all the time in poker. Many authors do not provide any evidence at all; they essentially say, "Trust me. Do what I recommend, and it will work for you." Whenever I am asked to take something on trust, I get suspicious. If, for example, a poker writer says something works for him, but does not say why, I want to know, Did it really work for him? More importantly, will it work for *me*?

Since some of the "trust me" writers are great players, their principles are obviously valid for them. So what? I'm not them, and neither are you. If a principle or system works only for highly gifted people, it's worthless or destructive for less-gifted players.

Principle No. 2: Analyzing Yourself and Your Choices

You should take a hard look at yourself, decide what you need to learn, and then find the information that fits your real needs. Far too many poker books try to appeal to an impossibly large audience. I have read claims that a book can improve the game of everyone from a beginner to an expert. Nonsense! No math book would try to cover everything from addition to calculus, and no poker book can satisfy the needs of beginners and experts. If a book is not written for a clearly defined audience or if you are not a member of that audience, do not waste your money and time.

For example, if you're a beginner, don't read books written for advanced players. You won't understand them. In fact, trying to make advanced plays can actually *cost* you money because you'll mess them up. Conversely, if you're an advanced player, don't waste your time reading beginners' books. Find books that fit your real needs, and then *study them thoroughly*.

Final Remarks

Because they dislike preparing, most people don't do enough of it—not for poker or anything else. But careful preparation will improve your results—even if you play intuitively. If you play logically, good preparation is even more important. You probably can't get good results without it.

How Should You Play Logically?

It is much harder to act logically while playing than while preparing or reviewing. We have much less time, and our emotions can become aroused. These pressures have caused all of us to act illogically, sometimes even irrationally. We make foolish mistakes and then wonder: "Why did I do that?"

Recommendations

Here are some recommendations that should help you:

Recommendation No. 1: Take your time.

Intuition is almost instantaneous, but logical thinking takes time. If you rush it, you will probably make mistakes. Poker is not like chess with a timer. If you take a few extra seconds, you will not get penalized. Do not take too much time because it suggests that you have a hard decision, but a brief delay can greatly improve your decisions in two ways.

1. You will remember more information and improve the way you process it. You will use facts or principles you may overlook if you hurry.

2. You may get additional information because players behind you telegraph their intentions For example, you may be in middle position, intending to limp with A♥ 6♥ before the flop, but see that several players will fold. You can raise to

steal the blinds or go heads-up with good position against the blinds' random cards.

Recommendation No. 2: Control your emotions.

Emotions can make you ignore or minimize important information or select the wrong decision rules. Instead of realistically assessing your EV, you may react to your hopes or fears. For example, if you want to call, you may ignore evidence—including quite obvious signals—that you are drawing dead. If you are scared, you may ignore equally obvious cues that you should raise.

Recommendation No. 3: Talk to yourself.

Do it silently, of course. You don't want to appear crazy or to let people know your thoughts. Putting your ideas into words, preferably in complete sentences, will show you how you make decisions. Here are three examples:

1. Which information did you consider?
2. How did you interpret it?
3. Which decision rules did you apply?

You may realize that some decisions make no sense at all! For example, you may decide that someone is bluffing, not because of the evidence, but because a bluff is the only thing you can beat! You don't really think he is bluffing, and the pot odds don't justify your call because he almost certainly has you beaten. You have let your foolish hopes overwhelm your logic.

Recommendation No. 4: Mentally record the critical facts.

Automatically mentally record facts such as the pot's size, each player's actions, and that player's style. Every time a bet is made, add it to your running total and make a mental note of any relevant facts: "His $10 call plus the blinds and two other limpers makes the total pot $45. Although he's very loose-aggressive, he did not raise."

Recommendation No. 5: Constantly ask "why?"

The other steps lay the foundation for answering this critical question. You need to know why people have taken or failed to take certain actions. In that last example, the obvious question is "Why didn't he raise?" The obvious answer is that he probably has a weak hand.

A Few Examples

These examples *aren't* designed to teach strategies. You may object to them and feel that there are better ways to play these hands, and I won't argue. All I'm doing is illustrating logical thinking.

Example No. 1: The third heart comes on the turn, and the button is very loose-aggressive.

You are the big blind and bet your queen-high flush draw on the flop. Two players call, and he does not raise. The third heart makes your flush; you bet, everyone folds to the button, and he raises. What do you do?

Reraise! Your verbalization should go something like this: "Because he is very loose-aggressive, he would have raised with an ace- or king-high flush draw."

Example No. 2: The third heart comes on the turn, and the button is very tight-passive.

Three players limp, the small blind folds, and you check in the big blind with J♣ J♠. The flop is 10♥ 6♣ 5♥. You bet, the other limpers fold, and the button raises. You just call. The turn is the J♥, giving you top set, but making a flush possible. What do you do?

Bet. Your verbalization might be "Because he is very tight-passive, he would not raise on a draw, especially heads-up. He probably does not have a flush. Because he is so tight-passive, I cannot check for a raise; he would probably just check behind me."

Note that both examples require considering the player's style. The loose-aggressive player probably does not have a bigger flush because he would have raised on the flop, and the tight-passive player probably does not have a flush because he would not have raised with a flush draw.

Can you be certain? Of course not. People do act out of character, or you may have misunderstood a player's style. But to develop yourself, you need enough confidence in your judgment to back it up with money.

Example No. 3: Should you go for a check-raise?

Two players limped in and then the button, a loose-passive player, raised before the flop. You called in the big blind with

The flop is

giving you the top two pair. What do you do?

Check-raise. Your verbalization could go: "I am way ahead, and he will probably bet. A loose-passive player would not have raised with a weak, steal-type hand. Even if he would have raised with pocket tens or nines, there is only one possible pair of each since two tens and two nines are accounted for. He probably has an overpair or a hand such as ace-king or ace-queen that he will bet.

Final Remarks

Although it is often difficult to think logically when you have to act quickly, you should constantly strive to do so. If you apply these principles, you will slowly develop a more logical way of playing, and slowly improve your decisions and results.

How Should You Review Logically?

Because most players don't review their play carefully, they keep making the same mistakes. Thoroughly and logically review your play to expand your database and update your decision rules. It will yield three benefits:

1. Reduce denial about your results and abilities
2. Prepare for future sessions against the same players
3. Develop your skills

Reduce Denial About Your Results and Abilities

This denial is quite common and extremely destructive. In fact, people who don't faithfully keep and carefully review good records usually lie to themselves, and it costs them dearly. They may pretend to be winners or "just a little behind," but really lose heavily. Because memories are selective, they naturally remember their big wins and ignore or minimize their losses.

Because luck has such extreme short-term effects, it's even easier to kid yourself about your abilities. You can believe that your winning nights came from skill, but your losses were caused by bad luck. You may remember your great plays, but forget your stupid ones. You may bore people with bad beat stories, but forget the times you drew out to win huge pots. Your selective memory lets you believe you'd do much better if you weren't so unlucky.

The best way to prevent denial is to keep good records and then review them carefully and frequently. If possible, use a computer program such as Card Player Analyst (CPA), StatKing, or Excel because they show patterns more clearly. Ask yourself three questions:

1. How have I done?
2. What caused the results?
3. What should I do differently?

You may find, for example, that you do much better in short sessions or in the first few hours of long ones than you do in the later parts of long ones. That pattern clearly suggests that you get tired or bored. Unless you can correct these reactions to long sessions, play only short ones.

Your records should show how well you do in shorthanded versus full games. If you do much better in full games, either learn how to adjust to shorthanded games or avoid them. Fortunately, you can get excellent advice from many of the books in the "Recommended Readings." If you can make the adjustments, fine. If not, avoid shorthanded games and the places and times they occur such as tournaments and very late at night. This example indicates another benefit of thorough reviews: learning what to study. Because there are so many books, you should know not only which books to study, but also which pages.

Let's consider a different problem. You may love wild games, but your records show that you do poorly at them. Once you see the pattern, you can make an intelligent choice. You can adjust your strategy or avoid wild games or decide that the excitement is worth the price. With good records, it's easy to make a logical decision. Without them, it's almost impossible.

Prepare for Future Sessions Against the Same Players

Unless you have an extraordinary memory, you can't remember how every opponent plays. In addition, their play changes when they get tired, are winning or losing, have had too much to drink, and so on. Pretending you can remember all that information is just a fantasy. Yet many people flatly refuse to take notes about hands and players. They seem to believe that "real players don't take notes."

This belief is based on denial about our own limitations and ignorance about what good players actually do. Do you think that Dan Harrington is not a real player? He is the most successful player of recent years in the World Series Championship, with four final tables and a first-place finish. He is also the primary author of three extremely successful books. He knows what the best players do.

> In top-class poker you will encounter many players who, after each session, go home and write down everything they've seen at the table. . . . There are players with enormous written notebooks on the habits of hundreds of other players.[1]

Unless you think you are smarter or have a better memory than Harrington and the people he plays against, stop pretending that you don't need notes.

Don't even wait until the session is over. When you see something important, or if you just feel confused and unsure of what to do, take a brief break to make mental or written notes, or use a dictating machine. You may think written notes and a dictating machine are overkill, but lawyers, doctors, and other professionals use them because they don't trust their memories. Your memory is no better than theirs. Your notes should cover two subjects:

1. The way they play
2. The best strategy to use against them

---

1. Dan Harrington and Bill Robertie, *Harrington on Hold'em: Expert Strategy for No-Limit Hold'em,* vol. 1, *Strategic Play* (Henderson, NV: Two Plus Two, 2004), 179.

Subject No. 1: The Way They Play

Your notes should include their general pattern of play; their tells, if any; and when and how their play or tells change. For example, someone might normally be tight, be moderately aggressive, and have no tells, but you just learned that he gets much wilder and telegraphs his intentions when he is losing heavily. Write it down before you forget it.

Subject No. 2: The Best Strategy to Use Against Them

Begin with the two most important topics:

1. Should you seek out or avoid this player?
2. Where should you sit?

These two decisions will have a much greater impact on your results than any other strategic adjustments. Let's say, for example, that you know that two players are extremely loose-aggressive, but one of them telegraphs his raises, while the other is unreadable. You want the "telegrapher" on your left so that you can take advantage of his signals, and you want the other one on your right so that his frequent raises don't surprise you.

Also record how often and in what kind of situations various people bluff or can be bluffed, when and how they make mistakes, such as chasing with weak hands and any other specific habits. That sort of information is the purest gold, but you'll often forget it. If you take frequent notes, you'll see many patterns that tell you how to play next time.

Develop Your Skills

Developing your skills is the most important and difficult task, and it requires intense introspection, preferably with help from other people. Thoroughly review your play, writing down a description of the hands you played poorly or well, commenting on your good and bad plays, and specifying the changes you should make.

Look at the larger picture.
Although analyzing your play of various hands is useful, go beyond the specifics and look for patterns.

- What are your strengths and weaknesses?
- How can you get the maximum value from your strengths?
- How can you overcome or minimize your weaknesses?
- What kind of games should you select?
- What books should you study?

Every large corporation spends millions of dollars on periodic performance reviews because people need that information to develop themselves. Exactly the same principle applies to you.

Get a coach.
Many performance reviews include a coaching session with the boss, and they are often the most valuable part of the process. We all need a coach because we lack objectivity and have "tunnel vision" about ourselves. We need feedback from someone who impartially looks at us from a different perspective. Coaches are so important that the best players in many other games use them. Since Tiger Woods and Andre Agassi have coaches, you could obviously use one. Select someone with the following characteristics:

- *Able to play well.* The better he plays, the more you will learn.

- *Constructively critical.* You need someone who will tell you things you don't want to hear, but do it in a helpful way.

- *Trustworthy.* He must respect your confidence and not use this information against you.

- *Willing to spend serious time coaching you.* Ideally, your coach should review and comment on your notes, and observe and comment on your actual play. Direct observation is extremely desirable because a coach will see things you do not cover in your notes. You may not notice them, or you may minimize their importance—deliberately to protect your ego or carelessly because you don't recognize their importance. Some coaches charge a fee, and—if you take the game seriously—it is an excellent investment.

  Other alternatives are to swap coaching with another player, join a poker discussion group, or post questions on Internet forums. You can swap coaching by periodically observing each other's play or comparing notes. Discussion groups and forums are essentially ways to swap coaching with a larger number of players. They will provide a much wider range of opinions than you can get from any coach. However, since they cannot observe your play, they are not as helpful as a good coach is.[2]

Of course, a coach can't help you much unless you're open-minded, and many people don't really want honest feedback. They want to stay in their comfortable "cocoons of denial," blaming bad luck for their results, instead of accepting responsibility for them, criticizing themselves, and making uncomfortable adjustments. Honest feedback can destroy your cherished illusions, but that's part of the price of developing yourself.

---

2. All of these ways to get help are discussed extensively in my next book, *Your Best Poker Friend* (New York: Lyle Stuart, forthcoming).

Afterthought

This section has been long and has covered many topics because the choice you make between intuition and logic affects everything you do at the poker table and elsewhere. Let's close with three recommendations:

1. *Accept that, if you don't have great intuition, you* must *rely on logical thinking.* If you have great intuition, take advantage of it. However, even intuitive players can benefit from logical thinking. You will encounter unfamiliar situations that your intuition can't handle. For those situations there's no substitute for logical analysis.

2. *Don't assume that you have great intuition.* Unfortunately, you may think that you have it, but be utterly wrong. The next section states that many people overestimate their abilities, particularly their intuition. This error occurs because memories are selective; we naturally remember the times that our feelings were right, but forget our mistakes.

    Before deciding that you have great intuition, get an objective appraisal of it. For example, keep records of how often your gut feelings are right and wrong. You may find that your batting average is much lower than you think. Unless you have convincing evidence, assume you don't have it.

3. *Develop your ability to think logically.* Even if you have good instincts, you should work on this ability. It is extremely

valuable, and our educational system does *not* usually develop it well. Students learn how to memorize material so that they can pass multiple-choice exams, but—except in engineering, mathematics, and scientific programs—they may not learn how to think logically. If you have not been trained in analytic methods, ask a professor or librarian to suggest ways to develop that skill.

PART TWO

Evaluating Ourselves and the Opposition

Introduction

The biggest reason for disappointing results is *overestimating* how well you play compared to your opponents, and *almost everybody does it*. Nearly all of us overestimate our own abilities and underestimate our opponents.

That pattern is most obvious in bad players, but it can be seen everywhere—from the smallest kitchen-table games to the ones for enormous stakes. Part three will discuss the unconscious and emotional causes for these errors. Now I will consider some other causes, but focus primarily on effects of overestimating your own play or underestimating the opposition, especially choosing the wrong games.

"Once you reach a certain level of competence at poker, your most important decision by far is game selection."[1] If you choose the wrong games, your results will be much poorer than if you choose the right ones. It really is that simple.

You cannot make this decision well without objectively evaluating yourself and your opposition, and most players are not objective. "Your success at poker depends, not on how well you play, but on how well you play in relation to your opponents. . . . This presents a significant problem. . . . almost all players put themselves closer to the front of the pack than they deserve to be."[2]

This tendency affects our beliefs about countless subjects. We may believe that we are better than we really are at work, school, par-

---

1. Mason Malmuth, "The Best Game," *Poker Essays* (Henderson, NV: Two Plus Two, 2004), 122.

2. Roy Cooke, "A Great Game?" *Card Player*, May 10, 2002, page 14

enting, dancing, sex, conversation, and so on. But its effects are particularly strong in poker because, as I have said, luck has such huge short-term effects. We can easily believe that our wins come from our skill, but our losses come from bad luck. Our desire to preserve that belief causes the bad beat stories we tell so often. We bore our friends because those stories reinforce our silly delusion: "I'm a good player, but so unlucky."

Many people don't admit that their losses are caused by their own weaknesses. They blame bad luck, refuse to work on their game, keep trying to beat superior players, and continue to lose. Some losers continue this pattern for decades, hoping their "luck will change."

Even very good players ignore their limitations. They could beat most games, but insist on playing against better players. For example, hundreds of hometown champions have built a bankroll and challenged Las Vegas. Nearly all of them go home broke, but many of them try repeatedly. Do they believe that they aren't good enough to beat our games? No, they insist that they have been cheated or "ran bad." The logical conclusion, "You aren't good enough," is just too painful to accept.

The poker world has a wonderful saying: "It's no good to be the tenth best player in the world if the other nine are at your table." The problem, of course, is that all ten think they are the best. I've heard, but couldn't confirm, that this tendency caused an amusing deadlock at the first WSOP. A small group of invited experts played many types of poker and then voted for the best player. They couldn't select a champion because everyone voted for himself. To break the tie, the tournament director had them choose the *second*-best player.

We all make similar mistakes because we have a natural desire to think highly of ourselves. We tend to believe what we want to believe, not what the evidence indicates. The benefits of logical thinking are particularly great on this issue. An intuitive person can deny evidence and insist that he plays better than various other people. How does he know? He just *feels* that he does, and he proudly has "the courage of his convictions."

Occasionally, readers demonstrate how badly they can delude themselves. One reader objected to my articles on "Are You Really 'Running Bad?'" He insisted that my claim that losing for months was a sign that you don't play well indicated a lack of "self-confidence"! I resisted the impulse to tell him that his position was based on defensiveness, not self-confidence.

A logical person would not have the self-confidence to insist that he played well despite losing for months. He would ask, "What do the facts say?" Then he would keep records to answer that question. If those records indicated that he had poorer results than Harry or Joe, he would draw the painful conclusion: he probably doesn't play as well as they do.[3]

As I stated earlier, one of the logic's greatest advantages is that you can correct your errors. These corrections are especially important on this issue. If you do not objectively and accurately evaluate yourself and the competition, you will not just choose the wrong games, but you will also make the following errors (and perhaps some others):

- Choose the wrong seats
- Focus on the wrong players
- Make the wrong strategic adjustments

Choosing the wrong seats is less costly than choosing the wrong games, but it is still expensive. In fact, Ray Zee, a great player and author, said it was one of the ten most important reasons for losing.[4] If you don't accurately appraise how well you and others play, and you don't understand how your style relates to those of the other players,

3. Whenever I make that point, someone says, "But Mason Malmuth, Mike Caro, and others have argued that you can lose for a long time just from variance." Of course they did, but a long losing streak is *much* more likely to be caused by poor play and game selection than by random variance.

4. Ray Zee, "Ten Top Reasons You Lose," TwoPlusTwo.com, May, 2005.

you'll have position on the wrong people, and the wrong people will have position on you. You want the predictable and weaker players to your left, and the unpredictable and better ones to your right. You will then get fewer surprises and will be outplayed less frequently.

Focusing on the wrong players is an extremely common error. Most people focus on the loose-aggressive ones because they are so visible. Although they should be watched closely, they may not be the most important opponents. Highly skilled, tricky players are much more dangerous, and you should watch them very carefully.

Making the wrong strategic adjustments covers a variety of errors. For example, millions of dollars are lost every week by people who play poor cards or chase when they are beaten. They deceive themselves about the cost of doing so and believe that they are so far superior to the competition that they can get away with it. They essentially give the competition a head start in a series of short races because they believe that they can run fast enough to catch up and pass them.

Let's get to the bottom line. You *don't* have to be an excellent player to win. If you are honest about your abilities, carefully select your games and seats, and make the right strategic adjustments, you can win consistently—even with limited skills. All you have to do is play against weaker players, but your assessment must be correct.

Denial About Ourselves
and Our Opponents

The gambling industry is based on denial of reality. Without it the entire industry would collapse immediately. Casino managers sell dreams and fantasies, and many foolish people buy them.

You can't beat craps, roulette, keno, and most other casino games, but countless people keep playing, hoping to "get lucky" or to find a winning system. Despite that reality, slightly more than half of the people surveyed by Mississippi State University said they gambled "to make money." Walk into many large bookstores, and you'll find several useless books on how to beat those games. The stores wouldn't stock them if people didn't buy them. People believe what they want to believe, not what the mathematicians and gambling experts tell them.

Poker is beatable because you are not playing against the house and do not have to beat a systematic, mathematical house edge. You just have to have enough edge over your competition to overcome the house's charges. Since these charges are substantial (especially at the lower limits), most cardroom players lose.[1] A major reason for the winners' success is that they are more realistic. They exploit the losers' denial (just as the casinos do).

---

1. Nobody has published good statistics, but most experts say that over 85 percent of all cardroom players lose. A few experts believe that fewer people lose.

Denial Has Only a Small Relationship to Knowledge

Many people know much more about how to play poker than you'd think from watching them play. They don't apply their knowledge because they deny how much it costs them to play foolishly. This denial has only a small relationship to knowledge. For example, virtually everyone knows that he shouldn't play weak hands, but many people still play them. In fact, the single most common error is playing too many hands, followed closely by chasing without pot odds.

Do many people *know* that they shouldn't make those mistakes? Of course they do, but they keep making them. They give all sorts of rationalizations to justify their foolishness:

"I feel lucky."

"I'm on a rush."

"I'm due."

"I'm advertising, improving my table image."

"I'm so good, I can win anyway."

I don't correctly apply all the theory I know, and you probably don't either. Therefore, acquiring more of it may not cause large changes in our play. We may act foolishly—not because we don't know better—but because delusions are more pleasant than reality. We would rather kid ourselves than face up to unpleasant truths.

We see the same pattern in almost every area of life. People constantly disregard information they know to be true, even on matters of life and death. For example, we all know that being overweight causes or aggravates many health and social problems, but more than half of all adult Americans are overweight.

Even experts deny reality. I vividly recall a picture in a news magazine. Hundreds of doctors were listening to a lecture with pictures of lungs destroyed by smoking, but they were sitting beneath a cloud of smoke. Those doctors not only had all the information, but they were trained to understand it. Still, they denied reality and foolishly believed, "Smoking won't kill *me*."

Some friends have told me that the doctors did not deny reality; they just made a trade-off because the immediate pleasure was more important to them than the long-term danger. Some of those doctors would make that claim, but I think they would be rationalizing (or extremely stupid). Sensible people would not make that trade-off if they had truly accepted that smoking would certainly damage their health and probably shorten their lives.

This failure to apply information certainly applies to the way we play poker. You and I have much more information about how to play than we regularly use. Therefore, acquiring more of it may not cause large changes in our play. We act foolishly —not because we don't know better—but because delusions are more pleasant than reality.[2]

This chapter could have been placed in part three because denial is an unconscious process. I decided to put it here because denial has such huge effects on our evaluations of ourselves and our opponents.

Our Denial About Ourselves

Our denial about ourselves is extremely costly and common, and it affects every aspect of our self-perceptions and play. We believe all sorts of nonsense about ourselves, especially that we play well, but bad luck prevents us from getting the results we deserve. In fact, most of us do not play remotely as well as we think we do. Our selective memories let us delude ourselves. We remember our brilliant

---

2. Every psychotherapist knows that merely providing information to patients has almost no effect. After a few sessions, a therapist can usually tell patients what they should do, but they just won't do it.

moves, but forget our mistakes. We whine about bad beats, but forget the times we drew out.

Deluding ourselves is so common and important that Sklansky discussed it on the very first page of his classic book, *The Theory of Poker*. "From the expert's point of view, the veneer of simplicity that deludes so many players into thinking they are good is the profitable side of the game's beauty.... Losers ... return to the table again and again, donating their money and blaming their losses on bad luck, not bad play."[3]

At times the tendency to overrate skills is pathologically strong. For example, Nolan Dalla asked readers of *Card Player* magazine to respond to a statement: "If I get heads up at the final table [of the $10,000 buy-in World Championship event] and am even in chips with a top pro, I believe I have just as good a chance to win as he does." Forty-four percent of the respondents agreed, even though the professional is an immeasurably better player.[4]

Hardly anyone would agree that he had an equal chance against a golf or tennis pro. Luck has such huge short-term effects in poker that most people can deny reality about the odds. Because the blinds are huge and luck is so important, they may have some chance against a top pro, but they are certainly not close to being an even money bet.

Luck reinforces our denial. As mentioned earlier, it has such enormous short-term effects that stupidity is often rewarded, and our selective memories let us delude ourselves about our skills. Bad players can win for a session, a tournament, or even a few months. Instead of realizing they have been extremely lucky, they congratulate themselves on their skill and keep playing, but lose in the long run. Most people don't admit that their losses are caused by their own weaknesses. They blame bad luck, refuse to work on their game, keep trying to beat superior players, and continue to lose.

3. David Sklansky, *The Theory of Poker* (Henderson, NV: Two Plus Two, 1999).

4. Nolan Dalla, "Chasing Dreams: Player Goals and Expectations at the World Series of Poker—Poll Results," *Card Player,* July 16, 2004.

Our denial about ourselves has its amusing aspects. Malmuth originally wanted to call their book *Professional Hold'em*, but Sklansky recommended *Hold'em Poker for Advanced Players* because "everyone thinks he is an advanced player."

The worse people play, the more likely they are to deny reality about themselves. For example, we have all been forced to listen to unwanted lessons from terrible players. The same sort of denial occurs everywhere, not just at the poker table. An excellent article stated that the *less skilled* people are, the *less aware* they are of their own limitations.

People tend to hold overly favorable views of their abilities.... This overestimation occurs, in part, because people who are unskilled... suffer a dual burden: Not only do these people reach erroneous conclusions and make unfortunate choices, but their incompetence robs them of the metacognitive ability to realize it. Across four studies, the authors found that participants [whose]... test scores put them in the 12th percentile... estimated themselves to be in the 62nd.[5]

That is, even though their scores put them in the bottom eighth, they thought they were well above average.

Several analyses linked this miscalibration to deficits in metacognitive skill, or the capacity to distinguish accuracy from error. Paradoxically, improving the skills of participants, and thus increasing their metacognitive competence, helped them recognize the limitations of their abilities.[6]

5. Justin Kruger and David Dunning: "Unskilled and Unaware of it: How Difficulties in Recognizing One's Own Incompetence Lead to Inflated Self-Assessments," *Journal of Personality and Social Psychology* 70, no. 6 (December 1999): 1121–1134.

6. Ibid.

In other words, as they became more skilled, they became more aware of their own limitations.

This study has huge implications for poker. Weaker players don't know enough to realize how bad they are. *Studying not only increases your skill, it also increases your ability to recognize and correct your weaknesses.*

However, even some good players deny their limitations. They could beat most games, but insist on playing against better players. Winners accept the reality about their limitations, but losers deny it. Arnold "The Bishop" Snyder wrote: "Poker players . . . continue to go up the ladder until they find themselves pitted against players they can't easily beat, and that's where they stay. Poker players who could make a comfortable living in $20–$40 games struggle to survive in $100–$200 games."

People who try to beat superior players also deny their own motives. They may claim to be trying to increase their profits, but other motives are involved. They may want to prove that they can beat the best or to have the status of being big game players, even though their results say they aren't good enough.[7]

Many people also deny their motives for playing at all. They may claim they want to make money, and a handful of people do win a lot of it. But most people play for many other reasons such as the thrill of gambling, the enjoyment of competition, the socialization with other people, and just the desire to pass some empty hours. Because these other motives are seen as irrational or undesirable, they deny them.

As I will say repeatedly, you *don't* have to be an excellent player to win. If you are objective and accurate about your own and the competition's abilities and use this information to select your games care-

---

7. Las Vegas and other gambling towns brilliantly exploit this desire to be treated as a high roller. The biggest fish at pit games such as craps are called "whales," and they are given whatever they want (suites, food, airline and show tickets, even hookers). They could buy the things they are given for a tiny fraction of their losses, but they gladly pay for the "status" of being treated like big suckers.

fully, you can be a consistent winner—even with limited skills. If you play only against weaker players, you will win.

Our Denial About Our Opponents

The unconscious forces that cause us to overestimate ourselves are closely related to the ones that make us underestimate our opponents. Most of these forces will be discussed in part three. Now I will discuss only two of them: our prejudices and our own limitations.

Our Prejudices

Because we must quickly assess new players, we naturally rely on cues such as their age, sex, race, appearance, the way they dress, and the way they talk. Our prejudices often distort these assessments. We may think that people like us are better than others, and some prejudices áre just silly. Many young people look down on older ones, and vice versa. Men and women often have unreasonable contempt for the way the other sex thinks and acts.

It may be politically incorrect to say so, but there are huge differences between young and old, men and women, and so on. These differences refer to groups, not individuals. For example, the average man is much more aggressive than the average woman, at the poker table and in most other places. However, some women are much more aggressive than some men. You should use every bit of information you have—including stereotypes—to make a preliminary assessment of every stranger, but you must keep your mind open to inconsistent information.

Unfortunately, once we label someone, we tend to ignore or deny any conflicting data. Even psychiatrists—who certainly should know better—may stick to faulty diagnoses long after their mistakes should have been obvious. To test how quickly psychiatrists would correct an incorrect diagnosis, several psychologists[8] went to a men-

8. Psychiatrists have an M.D. degree, while psychologists have either a Ph.D. or a D. Psy.

tal hospital and complained of hearing voices, a schizophrenic symptom. Even though they had no other symptoms, they were diagnosed as schizophrenic. They then stopped claiming to hear voices and acted normally. All the psychiatrists stuck with their diagnoses long after they should have recognized their mistake.[9] If psychiatrists can jump to conclusions and deny clear evidence, so can you.

In poker you have to make quick judgments, but don't close your mind to new information. For example, a well-dressed, middle-aged woman probably plays more conservatively than a young man with green hair and a pierced tongue. If they are both at your table, you should start by giving more respect to the woman's bets and raises. However, keep your mind open and watch the way they play. The woman may repeatedly bluff the prejudiced, closed-minded people, and they may continue to treat the kid as a wild player long after more open-minded and observant people realize he is rock solid.

That same closed-mindedness can affect almost any belief. For example, after labeling someone as a weak player, we may deny that his game has improved immensely, even if other people can see he now plays well.

Our Own Limitations

Denial about our opponents is just the flip side of our denial about ourselves. Malmuth wrote: "In the poker world, very few players will admit that someone plays better than they do. I have even been told about all the 'suckers' who have won major tournaments."[10]

He wrote those words long before so many poker tournaments were televised. Now that so many poker tournaments are on television, these criticisms are everywhere. I've heard weak players insist that a world-famous player is just lucky. They don't understand that

---

9. David L. Rosenhan, "On Being Sane in Insane Places," *Science* 179, no. 407. (January 19, 1973): 250–258.

10. Mason Malmuth, "Evaluating Yourself and Your Opponents," *Poker Essays* (Henderson, NV: Two Plus Two 2004), 16–17.

they see only the lucky draws outs and great bluffs because the television shows are heavily edited to show the most dramatic moments. More importantly, they don't understand how a great player must adjust to conditions that are *extremely* different from their games. Their criticisms say more about their own limitations than they do about the televised players.

"Very sophisticated plays can look bad to someone who doesn't understand them."[11] An expert may make a play that seems foolish to a nonexpert because the expert bases his decisions on so many more factors. If an expert makes a play *you wouldn't make,* he probably knows something *you don't know.* Instead of criticizing him, try to understand his reasoning.

David Sklansky once showed me that I did not analyze a situation correctly. His approach is based on assigning probabilities to many possibilities, and I had not considered enough of them. We were discussing his apparently irrational call on the turn with only an overcard ace and a gutshot draw to a wheel. Since the pot was small, the odds of making his straight did not justify the call. He missed his draw, but won with ace high after his opponent checked and he checked behind him. If I had been his opponent and did not know him, I might have concluded that he was lucky, but dumb.

Our discussion made me see that I had not considered all the possibilities:

- If his opponent might be on a draw, that meant his ace high could be good on the turn.

- Even if he were behind, David could make the winning hand on the river with a straight or a pair of aces.

- If they both missed, there was a significant probability that his opponent would not bluff on the river because David had called on the turn. In fact, his opponent later said,

11. Ibid., 16–17.

"When you called on the turn, I knew you'd call on the river." He was wrong.

- If he had bet, David would have folded. He and other experts understand and adjust to players immeasurably better than you and I do.

The various ways that David could miss his hand, but still win the pot, when added to the other ways he could win, made a questionable call into a good one.

This example illustrates a critical difference between experts and nonexperts: they consider the additional variables that make a seemingly irrational play into a correct one. Less dramatic examples of this process occur all the time. I have heard countless criticisms of players—including big winners—for apparently "senseless" plays. Of course, some of those plays were mistakes, but some were based on extremely sophisticated thinking.

When you see a winning player make a play you wouldn't make, don't automatically assume that he's stupid, "weak-tight," "a wild man," or any of the other labels that are used so often and so carelessly. Try to understand *why* he made it. You may learn something that will improve your game.

Conclusion

In the article mentioned earlier, Mason went right to the bottom line: "If you have trouble admitting: (1) that you don't play as well as you think you do, and (2) that some of your opponents play very well, perhaps even better than you do, then you are simply costing yourself money."

Your goal should *not* be to build your ego; it should be to build your bankroll. To build it more quickly, you should stop denying reality about yourself and your opponents.

Are You Really "Running Bad?"

You will often hear people complain about "running bad," but many of them are just whining and denying reality. Don't follow their example. If you blame bad luck for your results, you will feel like a helpless victim, and victims can't win at poker. To be a winning player, you must *stop blaming bad luck* and *accept responsibility* for your results.

When people complain about running bad, I often ask, "What are you doing wrong?" Many whiners insist, "Nothing! I'm just running bad. I'm a good player, and I'm playing my A-game, but I have been unbelievably unlucky." They may tell me how often their aces and kings have been cracked, how many runner-runner flushes have been made against them, and how they have missed draw after draw.

But I won't listen because I'm a psychologist, not a bartender. If you want sympathy, walk over to the bar, buy a drink, tip the bartender, and tell him your troubles. My job isn't to give sympathy; it's to help you get better results. And you won't get them without accepting that *everybody* has hard-luck stories. But winners don't waste their time telling them.

The whiners never have solid evidence that they are unluckier than others; they just claim that the only reason for their disappointing results is that they are "running bad." So they keep whining and keep losing. It may make them feel good, but blaming bad luck virtually guarantees that they won't solve their problem. You won't either if you think you're just "running bad."

Why Do They Believe It?

Players believe that they have been extremely unlucky for three main reasons:

Reason No. 1: They Overemphasize Bad Beats

They are extremely frustrating, but they don't cause long-term losses. By definition, a bad beat occurs when you are a large favorite, but lose to someone who draws out on you. If people are putting their money into the pot as huge underdogs, they are *adding* to your profits, not subtracting from them. It just seems that you are losing money because you see only the hands that beat you.

For example, a post on an Internet forum stated: "The past month or so I'm down about 130 big bets, 85 percent of which are from people hitting four-or-fewer-outers or having their 7–2 hit a Q-7-2 flop vs. my K-K."

His position is absurd, but many people—perhaps including you—have said essentially the same thing. When the underdog doesn't make a winning hand, he usually mucks his cards, and you never see them. But when he beats you, you see and remember them. Since you don't know the bets you win from the underdogs, but vividly remember the pots you lose to them, you can easily think you lose money because of bad beats.

To determine how much you win or lose to underdogs, you must count the bets you win from them as well as the ones you lose when they draw out on you. Since you can't count the bets you win, but are painfully aware of the ones you lose, any calculations are nonsense. The simple fact is that EV is the *only* determinant of long-term results. If people are making enough negative EV plays against you, you'll *certainly* beat them over the long term. If your long-term results are disappointing, the *only* reasonable cause is that you are making too many negative EV plays.[1]

---

1. This chapter deals only with *long-term* results; if you think you're "running bad" for a night or two, this chapter is irrelevant.

When I make that point, some whiners get very angry. "Don't give me that long-term BS, people are always sucking out on me." But over the long term, your results will be approximately equal to your EV. If you can't accept that fact, don't play poker.

Reason No. 2: They Are Denying Reality

As an earlier chapter stated (see p. 51), denial is extremely common, and blaming bad luck for their results contains a great deal of denial. Of course, bad luck may have affected their short-term results, but it probably didn't cause a *long* period of poor results. Even though I wrote about denial elsewhere, it deserves discussion here because it causes so much confusion about bad luck versus bad play. But let's not talk about people in general; let's focus on you and look at two other types of denial:

Denial Type 1: You don't play as well as you think you do. How can I make such a flat statement without knowing you? Because it applies to nearly everyone. In fact, research in many other areas proves that most people overestimate their skill and performance. For example, hundreds of studies show that employees at every level believe they should get better performance appraisals than their bosses have given them. Teachers know that students think they deserve better grades than they receive or merit.

This type of denial is particularly common in poker, because luck has such a huge and obvious impact on short-term results. So before blaming bad luck, ask a few talented, objective people to assess your skill. You will probably find that it is significantly lower than you think it is.

When I suggest that bad results are caused by playing poorly, I may get my own words thrown back at me: "Didn't you write that Mason Malmuth and other authorities have said a player could play well, yet still lose for a long period of time?" Of course I did, and perhaps you're playing well, but are having an extraordinarily bad run of luck.

If your results have been bad for weeks or months, there are three possibilities:

- You have had extremely bad luck
- You're not playing that well
- You're playing in the wrong games

The first possibility is much less likely than the other two. It's simple math. The odds against luck being the only cause for a long losing streak are quite high, and most people deny reality about themselves. In addition, you should focus on your play and game selection because you can do something positive about them. If you focus on your bad luck, you will make yourself miserable, and that feeling will damage your play.

You may believe that your feelings don't affect your game, but it's just another type of denial. If you feel sorry for yourself, you will become tentative and timid. You will check when you should bet, call when you should raise and fold when you should call. The bets and pots you lose from playing timidly will worsen your results, making you even more convinced that you are running bad.

Whining about your bad luck can also cause other players to sense and exploit your vulnerability. You may give away valuable information and encourage them to take shots at you. Feeling sorry for yourself can make you play and be treated as a loser.

Denial Type 2: You select the wrong games. If you don't know how well you play, you can easily select games you can't beat and then blame bad luck for your losses. Ask the people who evaluated your talent to help you pick games you can beat. In fact, the simplest, most obvious action to improve your results is to pick weaker games—including smaller ones than you're now playing.

Some people object that their cardroom spreads only one game at their preferred limits. But if you're losing steadily, seriously consider moving down, and there are usually more games at lower limits. If the brick-and-mortar cardrooms don't provide enough choices, play online.

But here again, we see denial in action. Many players insist that they can't beat lower-limit games because people won't respect their raises, will play any two cards, and will do all those other idiotic things that cause bad beats. But to improve their EV in those games, they must make the right adjustments.[2] If they don't know what these adjustments are, their denial may hold them back here as well.

Reason No. 3: You Expect Too Much

Many people expect to win even though they don't play well enough to overcome the rake. It takes a great deal of money out of the game. To win, you must be more skilled than your opposition. In fact, just to break even, you must win $10 or more per hour, which totals thousands of dollars per year.

If you play well and select the right games, you can have a good time and make a few dollars. Unfortunately, you may expect to make serious money. Many mediocre players have told me they expect to win one big bet per hour, and a few have said they should win even more. They seem to believe that they have almost a "constitutional right" to win that much. If they don't win that much (or, God forbid, they lose), they may claim to be running bad.

Don't be so silly. Adjust your expectations to the harsh realities of cardroom poker. Hardly any other recreational activity offers you the same combination of pleasure at a low cost or with a slight profit. Golf and tennis can cost serious money; skiing is often even more expensive; and boating can be a bottomless pit. But with a modest amount of work, a poker player can net a small profit.[3]

---

2. See Ed Miller, David Sklansky, and Mason Malmuth, *Small Stakes Hold'em: Winning Big with Expert Play* (Hendenon, NV: Two Plus Two, 2004) for discussion of these adjustments. Adjusting to these games is the theme of the entire book.

3 See Mason Malmuth, "Playing for Minimum Wage" in *Poker Essays, Volume III* (Henderson, NV: Two Plus Two Publishing, 2001), 26.

Changes in Long-Term Winners

When I published the first part of this chapter as a magazine column, some readers challenged its conclusion that their bad results were caused by their own limitations and mistakes. They insisted that they had won nicely year after year, while still playing in the same games, but had done poorly for six months or longer. Then they asked—sometimes quite angrily—"Doesn't the combination of my previous track record and recent results prove that I am running bad?"

Absolutely not. Their track record proved only that they once had the ability to beat that game. Perhaps they still had it and were just running bad, but they might have lost their edge. When they heard that, some people became furious. They insisted that they had not overestimated their abilities or chosen the wrong games and that their old track record proved they were running bad. Nonsense! There are four possibilities:

1. They have had horrible luck.
2. Their edge may have disappeared.
3. Their performance may have declined with age, as everyone's does.
4. Their games may have changed.

The first alternative is improbable, the second is predictable, and the third and fourth are near certainties. I have already discussed the low probability that only bad luck has caused the problem and won't belabor that point. Let's look at four other points that can cause poor results.

Point No. 1. All human performance varies substantially.

Many players and writers have said that you should always play your A-game, and every one of them denies a central reality: it is absolutely impossible to do it. Thousands of studies prove that performance varies on virtually every task such as adding numbers, driving a car, and programming a computer.

Some of these variations occur from minute to minute or day to day, but there are also long-term fluctuations. For example, in sports everybody's batting average, points per game, foul-shot percentage, and so on, change from year to year. Why should you assume that similar variance for poker results must be caused by bad luck?

You probably do it because you want to deny a painful reality: you aren't playing that well. So stop whining and concentrate on learning what you're doing wrong.

Point No. 2: Their edge may have disappeared.

The critical issue in poker is the difference between your skill and the opposition's. If you play as well as you did last year, but the competition has gotten tougher, your edge has been reduced, and it may have disappeared or become negative. Your opponents may be playing better than you are. This issue will be discussed in part five.

You must also realize that the line between winning and losing is very thin. Even if you are winning that one big bet per hour, it is only a small percentage of the total amount wagered. Since you normally risk over twenty bets per hour, that one big bet is less than 5 percent of the total amount wagered.

Since your winning edge is so tiny, a small decline in abilities plus a small increase in the game's demands could easily convert a winning player into a loser *even if the cards break even.* You can seem to "run bad" forever without being unlucky.

Point No. 3: Their performance may have declined with age, as everyone's does.

Since I'm getting old, I don't like to accept this reality, but it's unquestionably a fact. You can see it most clearly in sports; all the top athletes are young. But the same process occurs—albeit more slowly and less dramatically—in purely mental competitions.

I and the other people my age aren't as sharp as we once were—

not just at the poker table, but everywhere. For example, I'm a two-time Jeopardy champion, but I won't even watch the show now. It's too painful to be repeatedly reminded that I don't think fast enough to win today.

To win at poker, you must analyze complicated situations very rapidly, and the ability to do so declines slowly after the age of thirty or so. Thousands of studies have shown that most mental abilities peak in the twenties or thirties and then gradually decline. This weakening occurs so slowly that you may not notice the loss, but—if you're over forty—you probably aren't quite as smart as you were just a year ago.

Take chess, a game of pure skill. Virtually all the greatest players are under fifty. The former champions haven't gotten unlucky; you can't run bad at chess. They still play very well, but not quite as well as they once did. If you won for many years, but think that you have run bad for a long time, your play has almost certainly deteriorated.

Some friends have objected that only idle minds weaken, citing the old saying, "Use it or lose it." It's another form of denial. Mental and physical exercise, food supplements, eating properly, and a few other things can slow down the deterioration process, but absolutely nothing can stop it.

Point No. 4: Their games may have changed.

Poker has changed very rapidly. Part five describes some of these changes and the need to adjust to them. Unfortunately, many people ignore them, continue to play the same old way, and then blame their results on bad luck. Poker is changing everywhere, even in your game. Some of the weak players have quit and been replaced by new people, and others have improved their play.

The most dramatic changes have occurred in no-limit hold'em. Most games now have a maximum buy-in, and the games are extremely different from those of just a few years ago. For example, until recently many hands were won before the flop, and most contested pots had only two or three players. Big pairs and high cards were the best hands, and hardly anyone played small, suited connectors. Now eight limpers may see the flop, or three or more players may call huge pre-flop raises with mediocre hands. These changes affect every element of the game. If you play the way the older books recommend, your results will be disappointing.

Seven-card stud games have gotten much tougher because so many weak players have shifted to hold'em. Games that were once easy to beat may now contain mostly tough players. All the changes in poker increase the effects of any reduction in abilities. New situations demand new kinds of thinking, but virtually everyone becomes more rigid with age.

Older people naturally rely more on formulas and habits and less on thinking quickly. Their thinking becomes less flexible, and their actions become more predictable. But poker demands flexibility and situational thinking. If you ignore this reality, your results will probably be disappointing, making you think that you're unlucky.

Aging also reduces our ability to adjust to situations and makes us become more predictable. The other players may be able to read us better than we can read them. I don't adjust to new situations as well as I once did, and the same grim truth applies to many older people.

What Should you Do?

Many poker players will always complain about their bad luck, but you should definitely not copy them. Instead, I recommend that you take seven simple actions:

Recommendation No. 1: Stop whining.

You may want sympathy, but you won't get it. Ours is a ruthlessly predatory game, and showing weakness will just result in contempt and poor results. You will feel like a victim and will be treated as one, and victims can't win at poker.

Recommendation No. 2: Accept responsibility for your results.

When you focus on your bad luck, you become helpless. You essentially transfer the control of your results from yourself to the poker gods, fate, luck, or whatever you choose to call it. Since nothing you can do will change the cards you get, you can't solve your problem without accepting that responsibility.

Recommendation No. 3: Accurately compare yourself to your opposition.

If you don't play better than they do, you are going to lose. It really is that simple, and bad luck has very little effect on your long-term results.

Recommendation No. 4: Compare your recent and your earlier play.

What are you doing differently? If your current results are worse than your historical average, you're probably doing something wrong, and your critical task is to learn what that is. If you play online and use a data-recording system such as Poker Tracker, meticulously compare your play for different periods. Regardless of where you play, if you can't identify any differences, ask some other people to comment on your play.

Recommendation No. 5: Look for changes in the games.

Changes may occur so slowly that you don't notice them. You may therefore continue to play in an outdated way. Step back from deciding how to play this particular hand and look for long-term patterns. Have the games become looser or tighter? More passive or more aggressive? Are there any other changes? Then, of course, ask whether you've adjusted well to any changes. Finally, modify your strategy to fit the current games.

Recommendation No. 6: Work on your game.

Study the books, criticize your own play, discuss strategy with other people, and do whatever else it takes to improve your play.

Recommendation No. 7: Lower your expectations.

If you have more realistic expectations, you won't be so disappointed. You will then enjoy poker more, and bad luck will affect you less. Unless you need a regular income from poker, regard it as a game, and remember that games are played for pleasure. Do not make yourself and others miserable by complaining about your luck, accept responsibility for your results, work on your game, and reduce your expectations. You will feel better and play better.

Male and Female Advantages

Until fairly recently cardroom poker was primarily a man's game. Fifty years ago hardly any women played in cardrooms. The number of women players has steadily increased, and the current explosion is accelerating that trend. However, there are still three huge differences between the sexes:

1. Far more men play in cardrooms.
2. Far more men than women play as the stakes get higher.
3. Far more men excel at tournament poker.

Although not many people will disagree with these points, I've never read a good explanation for them. I hesitated about writing on this subject because it might offend some people—both male and female. As some of these chapters illustrate, I don't mind offending people when I'm sure I'm right. But now I'm not so sure.

Most of my points are supported by research conducted outside of poker, but applying this research to poker can get quite speculative. My positions should therefore be regarded as just opinions, not facts. Some men and women will emphatically disagree, but this issue is worth discussing. Since male-female differences at home, work, schools, and almost everyplace else have been discussed very frequently, I wonder why they have not been seriously discussed for poker.

More Men Play in Cardrooms

The most important reason that more men play in cardrooms is that, until recently, women were not welcome or comfortable in many of them. Cardrooms were often "men's clubs." Many of them were in bad neighborhoods, and they were often dirty, smoky, and disreputable. Until the early 1980s, a few cardrooms actually refused to let women play! Even the women who loved playing at home and in private clubs wouldn't go to cardrooms; it just wasn't done. Today's cardrooms are much nicer and more welcoming places, which has encouraged more women (and more men) to play in them.

Men Unquestionably Dominate Tournaments

Since there are no good statistics for cash games, nobody knows how well men and women do. I suspect, but cannot prove, that most of the big winners and big losers are male (because they play more aggressively, are more macho,[1] and drink more while playing). I have no idea whether the average male does better than the average female.

Most cash-game professionals are men, as are nearly all the top tournament pros. *Card Player's* October 24, 2003, issue reports tournament records on page 134. In "Overall Player Standings," the top nineteen players are male. The top ten players for limit hold'em, Omaha, and seven other games are listed. A few players appear on more than one list, and I cannot tell a few players' gender. However, of these nearly ninety players, only two names are clearly female; that is, over 95 percent of the top tournament pros are men. The same general pattern appears month after month.

---

1. A later chapter discusses machismo's destructive effects. See p. 187.

Why Men Dominate Tournaments

If a corporation had such an imbalance, there would be massive lawsuits claiming discrimination or a "glass ceiling." Since the rules don't favor either men or women, discrimination can't cause this imbalance.

However, since nearly all the tournament pros are men, the percentage of top winners who are male may not be higher than the percentage of entrants into the major tournaments. Why don't more women join the "tour?" I don't know. Some may think they can't succeed, while others may not want that lifestyle. The same factors (plus others) probably influence the numbers of men and women who choose to play professionally.

Some of my politically correct friends insist that women can do as well as men, but they don't want the tournament pro lifestyle. I think they're wrong. Many women have chosen a similar lifestyle by joining the golf, tennis, and bowling tournament circuits, but there's one huge difference: they compete only against other women, while most poker tournaments are open to both sexes. If they had to contend with men, hardly any women would enter golf, tennis, and bowling tournaments.

There are poker tournaments, even in the WSOP, for women only, but no major tournaments just for men. It's politically correct to discriminate *for* women, but intolerable to discriminate *against* them. Some people have very strange definitions of that Civil Rights term "equal opportunities."

Because they discriminate against the best players, women's events are *much* easier than open ones. Many women have won titles in women's events, but have never done well in open ones. In the 2004 WSOP championship event the highest-ranking woman finished ninety-eighth,[2] and no woman has ever come close to winning it.

---

2. The highest-ranking woman that year was Rose Richie, my friend and colleague at RoyalVegasPoker.com.

I therefore believe that more women avoid the poker tournament circuit for competitive than for lifestyle reasons. To put it bluntly, they don't think they can win, and they're probably right.

Let's look at two possible reasons for men's greater success. The first reason is quite obvious: men invented the game, and its rules and culture favor them. The second, probable reason for the greater number of male players is that they like math and aggression, but dislike emotionality. The term "poker face" has become part of the general vocabulary, and it is used—even by nonplayers—to describe someone (usually a man) who tightly controls his feelings and expressions. In fact, men are proud of their ability to control their feelings and facial expressions, and women often criticize them for doing so.

Research on Males' Advantages

Thousands of studies in an extremely wide range of settings have given a clear picture of three major advantages: aggression, emotionality, and mathematical abilities. These studies refer to averages, not individuals. These three and most other characteristics are distributed as bell-shaped curves, and there is immense overlap between the distributions for males and females. For example, the average male is much more aggressive than the average female, but many females are much more aggressive than the average male.

1. *Aggression:* As I mentioned earlier, males are unquestionably more aggressive than females, at the poker table and in most other places. The primary cause is almost certainly testosterone (the male hormone), but there are also huge differences in social training. Boys are taught to be tough and competitive, while girls are taught to be sweet and cooperative. That pattern continues indefinitely; for example, employers and society in general often reward aggressive men, but punish aggressive women. As socialization pat-

terns have changed, differences in aggression have decreased, but males will *always* be more aggressive.

Some radical feminists insist that socialization causes *all* differences in aggression, but their position is ideological, not scientific. Results of countless studies show that very small boys are much more aggressive than girls, and that very young male lions, horses, cats, dogs, and virtually all other mammals are more aggressive than females. Those differences could not be caused by socialization.

Todd Brunson is not a researcher, but he is a great player, and he expressed a position that many people believe: "Women have a harder time becoming successful in poker because they don't have the killer instinct. . . . They're nicer people."[3]

Brandie Johnson countered that female lions do the hunting while the males sit on their butts. She's right, and Poker Babe noted that mothers defending babies are utterly ferocious. So females can be more aggressive when something important is at stake, but males get into far more fights over dominance, territory, and mates—all that macho nonsense. In addition, men have started virtually all wars, and hardly any serial killers are women. Perhaps poker's goal of winning money is not important enough to arouse most women's aggressive impulses, while many men love to prove how tough they are.

2. *Emotionality:* Daniel Goleman, author of *Emotional Intelligence*, reviewed the research literature and concluded that "women, on average, experience the entire range of emotions with greater intensity and volatility—in this sense,

3. Lisa Wheeler, "Todd Brunson: His Own Successful Path," *Card Player*, February 26, 2006.

woman *are* more emotional than men."[4] They are also much worse at controlling and hiding their emotions, which are extreme liabilities.

Perhaps because of their greater emotionality, women are much better than men are at reading and manipulating other people's emotions, which are formidable assets. However, as I will discuss later, their emotionality costs them, but they don't take full advantage of their greater perceptiveness and manipulative abilities.

3. *Mathematical abilities:* Males score much higher on math tests. Some researchers believe these differences are primarily biological, but there has been a recent and very dramatic reduction in the differences between math scores. Changed socialization patterns almost certainly caused this reduction. Women were once discouraged from studying math, but this pressure has decreased sharply. There is, however, one exception to the trend: males make nearly all the top scores.

Only young people take almost all these tests—especially the SATs. Hardly anyone takes tests or studies math after completing formal schooling, and adults' math abilities and attitudes rarely change. Changed socialization patterns may therefore have had little impact on older players, but will probably affect younger ones. Since poker has become extremely popular among college students of both sexes, tomorrow's champions will probably include more women.

---

4   Daniel Goleman: *Emotional Intelligence* (New York: Bantam Books, 1995), p. 132. Throughout the book he cites several research studies supporting that assertion.

Implications for Poker

Poker is a mathematical game that rewards rationality and punishes emotionality.[5] It also rewards aggression, particularly during tournaments. Nearly all tournaments are won by aggressive players, and nearly all the top tournament players—whether male or female—are aggressive.

Since men are better at math, less emotional, and more aggressive, they obviously have a huge natural advantage. There are, of course, exceptions. Some women are unemotional math whizzes, and everybody has played with aggressive women. Virtually all female professionals are aggressive, unemotional, and mathematically competent, which is very different from the feminine stereotype. To put it bluntly, to succeed at poker a woman must act in *nonfeminine ways*.

Research on Females' Advantages

Females test higher on verbal and social skills. Verbal skills are not important in poker, but social skills—especially the ability to read and manipulate other people's emotions—can create a *huge* edge. Women are much better at reading and manipulating men than vice versa.

Many women use their reading ability well, but a surprising number of them are reluctant to use their manipulative abilities. They seem to believe that it's wrong to use the so-called feminine wiles at the poker table that they use so effectively in other places. That is, they seem to feel that—since they're playing a men's game—they have to play it on men's terms.

I believe that this inhibition is foolish. Men use their aggression, math abilities, and emotional control without any qualms. If you're a woman, why shouldn't you use whatever you can to give you an edge? Poker is not about "being nice." It's about making money. Use whatever works.

5. See "Destructive Emotions," p. 138.

Let me go a step further: your natural advantages are much more effective in brick-and-mortar games than online. You will get nonverbal cues, and you can read them much better than men do. And it is certainly much easier to manipulate men face to face. *So play in the games—and against the kinds of men—that you can read and manipulate.*[6]

6. My thanks to Linda Johnson, Jan Fisher, Poker Babe, Brandie Johnson, and Mary McGuirk for their comments. Of course, none of them agrees with everything I wrote, and they have no responsibility for this material.

We Are All Magoos

Several friends have said that I'm too serious and professorial, and they're right. Once I sit down at the computer, I get heavy handed, even boring. So I have decided that this book should have one light-hearted chapter.

Years ago my friend, Jesus "Zeus" Marrero, said, "That man plays like that cartoon character, the nearsighted Mr. Magoo. He can't even read his own cards, and he certainly doesn't know what to do with them." Zeus liked the term so much that he started using it for any form of stupidity, and it became a common, but friendly, insult in the Atlantic City cardrooms.

We would call each other "Magoo!" and it even became an adjective and a verb. You might say, "That was a Magoo thing to do" or "He was really Magooing last night." Matt Lessinger and I brought it to Las Vegas; Dave Adams took it to San Diego; and Lessinger took it on to Berkeley. Other people have probably taken it to Reno, Phoenix, and many other places. You may have heard it in your local cardroom.

I'm a Magoo

Occasionally, I do something spectacularly stupid, the sort of mistake that a beginner shouldn't make. For example, I was once dozing in the big blind; somebody limped under the gun; and everyone folded. For some reason I thought I was the small blind, and I asked the limper if he wanted to chop. When he said, "No," I threw my hand away instead of taking the free flop.

That mistake was funny, but I've made worse. One was so bad that

I sent an e-mail describing it to friends with this subject, "I'm the King of Magoos." In fact, it was so bad that I won't tell you what I did, but the poker gods took pity on me. They must have thought, "This guy is such a Magoo that he needs a miracle card," and they gave it to me. My e-mail cracked up Howard Burroughs, and he greeted me as "Your Majesty, the King of Magoos."

Everyone Is a Magoo Sometime

You may think that you and the people in your game would never make really dreadful plays, but occasionally everybody is a Magoo and does something extremely stupid.

You don't believe me? You think that you and your friends are too smart to be Magoos? Are you smarter than Hellmuth? He has won Ten WSOP bracelets and many other major tournaments, but he admitted making a *terrible* mistake. Even beginners know that they should check their cards, but Hellmuth didn't do it, and it cost him over $27,000. He thought he had a flush and then learned that "I had just called off all my chips with nothing! Talk about bad plays."[1]

Are you smarter than the people who make the final table of the "Big One" at the WSOP? I doubt it very, very much. Yet they make an occasional Magoo play. For example, once the action stopped for a couple of minutes while they waited for a player to act. He suddenly realized they were waiting for him because he had forgotten that he had live cards! If two top players can make such silly mistakes, so can you and everyone you know.

How Does This Relate to Being Your Own Worst Enemy?

How can not admitting your mistakes relate to being your own worst enemy? More directly than you may think. Everyone makes

1. Phil Hellmuth, "Never give up—Part II," *Card Player*, February 28, 2003, 22.

silly mistakes, but winners—like Hellmuth—admit and learn from them, while losers deny or cover them up. If you say you have never been a Magoo, I am certain of one thing: you lie to yourself and other people.

If you lie about this subject, you probably lie about others, and those lies really cost you. You may be extremely skilled and win very consistently, but you will not reach your full potential until you get honest with yourself.

Let me get serious for a moment and make a central point: A critical difference between winners and losers is that winners accept reality—including their weaknesses—while losers deny and distort reality to fit their hopes, fears, and dreams.

What Should You Do?

I have three ways to help you admit your mistakes and turn them into positives.

First, once in a while look in the mirror and say to yourself, "I'm a Magoo." Then prove it by remembering the times you deserved that title. What really dumb plays have you made? Why did you make them? What parts of you are "Magoo?" What can you learn from being harshly self-critical?

Second, ask one or more trusted friends to point out how and when you've been a Magoo. They have probably seen things you overlooked or have forgotten (perhaps deliberately).

Third, don't beat yourself up too badly for your mistakes. Accept that it is human, not shameful to be a Magoo once in a while. If Hellmuth can admit a dreadful mistake to all his readers, admitting your mistakes is not that big a deal. You should be ashamed only if you lack the courage to admit it and to do something to correct it.

Why Bother?

Why should you bother to take such unsettling actions? Isn't it better to insist that you're not a Magoo? No, no, no. There are four reasons for admitting it:

1. It is very healthy to accept your weaknesses and even laugh at your own mistakes. Trying to cover them up wastes a lot of energy that could be used more productively.

2. It will improve your game. If you accept yourself as you are, you can change. If you don't accept yourself, you'll keep making the same old mistakes.

3. It will reduce your chances of going on tilt. One reason I don't go on tilt is that I can laugh at myself and remember that I'm a Magoo. If I start getting angry because someone sucked out on me, I remember my King of Magoos play (and similar errors) and being saved by miracle cards.

4. It well allow you to be more fun to play with. If you can laugh at yourself and let other people do the same, the tourists and other weak players will want to play with you. If you're too serious, defensive, or irritable, they will go someplace else.

So, repeat after me, "We are all Magoos."

Is It Time to Quit?

We've all asked ourselves that question, and we have all regretted giving the wrong answer. We play too long, sometimes for very silly reasons, and it costs us dearly. Then we may angrily ask ourselves, "Why didn't I stop sooner? I wouldn't have lost all that money." If we don't know why we kept playing, we'll probably make the same mistakes again.

Good Reasons to Quit

At some point in many games, we know we have good reasons to quit. But the stay-or-go decision is often made emotionally. We may keep playing even when we are sure we should stop. Then we may pretend that we stayed because it was a great game or we were playing well or many other rationalizations. To make the right decision, we should ask a critical question: "*Why* am I thinking of quitting?"

You should obviously quit if you have an important commitment, but many people do not do it. Countless serious problems have occurred because people did not pick up their wives or children, or they did not keep an important business appointment, or they lost so much sleep that they did not work well the next day, and so on. They got so involved in the game or so desperate to get even that they kept playing.

In addition to causing family or work problems, they were probably distracted, played poorly, and lost money. Don't be so stupid. If you have to go someplace important—including to your own bed—don't even think about staying. *Quit!*

If you are a recreational player and a game isn't fun, quit. Many people stay in games they dislike, getting upset, grumbling about the players or the smoke or the noise, and asking, "Why am I playing in this crummy game?" If you feel that way, quit, take a break, or change tables.

Although you should consider those factors, I will not discuss them further. I will focus only on how the stay-or-go decision affects your profits. From that perspective, the *only* reason to stay is that you expect to win. Ignore everything else, especially whether you are ahead or behind. As Sklansky put it: "You should not allow the fact that you are winning or losing to affect your decision to stay or quit a game. From a money-making point of view, the only criterion for playing is whether you are a favorite or an underdog."[1]

Hitting and Running

If you "hit and run," you break that rule, and you may not even think about it. You leave quickly when you get ahead, but when you get stuck, you may play on and on, trying to get even. This pattern nearly guarantees poor long-term results.

You hit and run primarily because you don't want to give back your profits. You may even have a formula such as, "Quit when I've doubled (or tripled, or quadrupled) my buy-in." These formulas are just rationalizations to justify your desire to lock up a win. They are based on the implicit, but illogical, assumption that luck has to change. Nonsense! Cards are random, period.

Hitting and running but staying on to get even is exactly backwards. If you're going to let winning or losing affect this decision, then you should stay when you're winning, but go when you're losing.

Winning suggests (but certainly does not prove) that you are a favorite, while losing suggests that you are an underdog. In addition,

1. Sklansky, *The Theory of Poker*, 7.

winning or losing can become self-fulfilling prophecies. If winning makes you and the other players believe you have an edge, your play will improve, and theirs will deteriorate. You will probably play more confidently, decisively, and aggressively, and they will respect you more. Conversely, when you are losing, you will probably play more timidly and passively, and you will have a weaker image.

You should therefore be *much* more willing to stay when winning than when losing. "Quitting early when you are winning often means quitting when you are playing your best and your image is at its most effective, enabling you to win more easily. . . . your win rate is likely to be at its highest."[2]

How Do You Know That You're a Favorite?

Are you a favorite? Many of us would agree with Sklansky's principle, but not be able to answer that question. Pride, denial of reality, and other factors may cause us to overestimate ourselves and underestimate the competition. We may sincerely believe that we are big favorites when we are really huge underdogs.

Denial is especially common when we are losing. Since we do not want to believe that the competition is better than we are, we emphasize our bad luck and their weaknesses. For example, you have probably said to yourself, "I would be even or ahead if I had made my flush in that big pot or he hadn't rivered me with that two-outer or these people played well enough to respect my raises."

We can often recognize denial more easily in other people than in ourselves. For example, you may have been asked to loan money to people who just went broke. They say, "It's a great game, and I know I can beat it." When you look at the table, you realize that your friend is hopelessly outclassed and shouldn't go near it. Or he may be play-

2   John Feeney, "The Hit and Run Follies," *Inside the Poker Mind: Essays on Hold'em and General Poker Concepts* (Henderson, NV: Two Plus Two, 2000), 58.

ing terribly, but not see it. Although we can easily recognize that our friends are outclassed, we may be unable to recognize that we're the underdog.

Our *selective memories* greatly increase denial. We may think, "If they hadn't sucked out on me to win those two large pots, I'd be ahead." But we forget the pots we won by sucking out. Deceiving ourselves about why we're losing helps us rationalize decisions we make for emotional reasons. Since everybody denies reality occasionally, my primary purpose is to suggest ways to minimize denial and its effects. Your critical task is to assess objectively your own and the competition's play. These assessments should consider three issues:

1. How do your usual skills compare to theirs?
2. How well are you playing *now*?
3. How is the game changing?

Denial can occur about all three issues. *Most* people overstimate their own abilities and underestimate the competition, and they also ignore evidence that they are playing worse than usual or that their competition is playing better than usual.

Using Stop-Loss Formulas

Stop-loss formulas say that you should quit when you've lost a rack, thirty big bets, two racks, or some other amount. Although I dislike relying on formulas, they are useful if you can't objectively compare yourself to the competition. In addition, some of them are based on solid reasoning. As I said before, losing suggests that you're an underdog, and it can become a self-fulfilling prophecy. It can cause you to play worse, weaken your image, and encourage others to take shots at you.

The biggest danger is going on tilt. You may become so desperate to get even that you take a huge loss. Even if it does not put you on tilt, a large loss can make you more tentative or weaken your play in other ways. You may be unable to play your A-game when you are losing badly, and the further behind you get, the worse you may play.

A stop-loss formula will prevent you from playing too long when you're an underdog. Once your loss gets to a certain number, that rule clearly says, *"Quit!"* Of course, some people set stop-loss limits and then violate them, but that's a different problem.

Evaluating the Competition

Many of us do it before choosing a table. We may walk around the cardroom or roam around the website, checking out the tables, and then pick the game or games (if we are multi-tabling) that seem best. We may continue this process when we first sit down, trying to get a reading on other players, wondering whether we should change tables, or deciding how to adjust our strategy. However, after playing for a while, we naturally focus on how to play the current hand. This narrow focus can prevent us from seeing that the game is gradually changing. In fact, we may barely notice that two players have left and been replaced by very different ones.

In addition, if we're card dead, we may lose interest in the action. We just fold, fold, fold and tend to ignore what the other players are doing. We have to fight these tendencies, see how the game is changing, and ask ourselves constantly, "Am I a favorite *now?*"

Setting a Fixed Time

With some coaching clients, I emphasize making reports to me to help them become more aware of their own motives. Many poker players are anti-introspective; they don't like to look at themselves. Being "forced" to explain their decisions to me (or to anyone else) makes them much more aware of their real reasons—including the emotional ones—for making decisions. They can't get away with the sloppy thinking that all of us use so often.

One client's records showed that his results were much worse after 2 a.m. than they were before it. Because he usually played after working a full day, he just got tired. We jointly decided that he had to leave at 2 a.m. or call me to explain why he chose to continue. He knew that I would be skeptical and that I would ask probing questions to ensure that he was not rationalizing. He and most other people—including me—are very good at giving rationalizations for actions we take for foolish reasons.

This extremely simple system had two benefits: First, he usually left before his play and results deteriorated. Second, if he did stay, he had solid reasons for doing so. For example, if he was playing exceptionally well, and the game was weaker than usual, he would keep playing.

I didn't accept his word on either point. He had to prove it with solid evidence and arguments. You don't need a psychologist or professional coach to use this system. Any friend who is willing to ask hard questions will do.

Dr. Dan's Monitoring System

Dr. Dan Kessler is a clinical psychologist whom I often consult about emotional and impulse control issues. He suggested making this simple reporting system more structured. If a player wanted to play after his originally set time, he had to rate five issues on a 1–10 scale every half hour:

1. Quality of the game
2. Quality of his own play
3. Awareness of his own wakefulness
4. Awareness of his own emotional state[3]
5. Number of bets he was up or down[4]

---

3. This scale was included to make people examine their own emotions. Without encouragement, many people would ignore their emotions.

4. Results are included because winning or losing affects so many players.

If the numbers indicated that a client should continue, he was free to do so. If the numbers were not positive, he had one of two choices:

1. He could go home
2. He could call me to explain why he was taking an apparently foolish action. If I was not home, he had to explain his decision to my answering machine.

Making these ratings and having to explain his decisions helped him focus on issues he may have ignored and reduced mistakes made for emotional reasons. For example, having to rate the quality of the game may make him realize that the game had become much tougher than he thought. Rating his wakefulness, emotional state, and play could help him see that he was playing poorly because he was tired, angry, or bored.

These ratings cause people to consider more factors and to think more rationally about them. Having to explain decisions to someone else accelerates that process. You may think that having to explain yourself would have little deterrent value, but most people do not want to explain their decisions, especially when they are unsure of them. When the listener is smart and skeptical, apparently plausible rationalizations often fall apart, and someone may realize how badly he is thinking.

In fact, after explaining his decision to keep playing to my answering machine, one client realized how badly he was thinking. He then changed his mind and went home.

The Two-Mistakes Rule

As I noted earlier, most of us cannot accurately evaluate our own play. My friend, Jerry Flanningan, taught me a new way to do it. He was clearly superior to the competition in a soft game, but he suddenly quit. When I asked him why, he replied, "I just made my second mistake for the day and that's my limit." He later explained that two mistakes are a "trip wire" warning that he is off his game.

When we discussed this issue, *Card Player* columnist Barry Tanenbaum added that "mistake" should be defined carefully. It should be a serious error that you would not have made when you first sat down. That sort of error indicates that your play has deteriorated, which is exactly the kind of trip wire you need.

Stop-loss limits are also trip wires, but "the two-mistakes rule" is much better. It shifts the focus from results to decision-oriented analysis. Please note that this rule does *not* say anything about how much you are winning and losing. It refers only to how well you are playing. When we focus on our decisions, we make better ones and develop our skills.

If you can look objectively at your game, you will be way ahead of most people. Let me quote Jerry again. "It is more significant that I take corrective action than simply acknowledge a mistake. Certain basic principles govern my play, and I will not knowingly violate them. On this day I did! By the way, I did correct the problem causing those two frightful mistakes, but remain sensitive to any recurrence."

Looking hard at your decisions isn't fun. It's much more pleasant and natural to deny reality and react emotionally. The stay-or-quit decision should be based on an objective comparison of yourself and the competition. When you've got an edge, stay. When you're an underdog, *get out fast.*

Afterthought

To win at poker, you must objectively compare yourself to your competition, and most people don't do it well. Because of our egotistical nature, most of us overestimate our own abilities and underestimate the competition's. If you fall into this trap, you will:

- Play in the wrong games
- Select the wrong seats
- Make the wrong strategic adjustments
- Hinder your self-development
- Cost yourself a lot of money

If you are thinking of moving up, you should make a separate comparison to the competition in any game you intend to join. For example, you may understand strategic principles better than the players in your current game, but not as well as the ones in the bigger game. To beat that bigger game, study strategic principles.

While playing, constantly compare yourself to the competition on dimensions such as your knowledge, skill, and intensity. If you find yourself at a disadvantage, leave the game.

For your longer-term development, systematically compare yourself to the competition on more dimensions. I will briefly describe a few of them and suggest some questions to ask yourself. Assume that the words "compared with the competition" are part of each question.

If you play different games (such as stud and hold'em) or for different stakes, make a separate comparison for each one. For example, you may read cards much better than the competition does in the $10–$20 game, but not as well as the $15–$30 players.

1. Write your answers in the blank space.
2. Write your answers to any other questions you think are important. Use extra paper if necessary.
3. Ask someone you trust to criticize your answers. You could do the same for him, which would help both of you.
4. Listen carefully to that critique. It may be more accurate than your own answers.

The Understanding of Strategic Principles

If you don't understand these principles as well as they do, nothing else matters much. You probably won't win if you don't know at least as much—preferably a lot more—than your competition.

How well do you understand these principles?

Which principles do you understand particularly well?

Why do you think you understand them well?

Which principles do you need to study?

Why do you think you need to study them?

What books should you study?

What can you do besides just studying to increase your understanding of strategic principles? For example, you can discuss strategy in online forums and with a coach or discussion group.

The Ability to Apply These Strategic Principles

Some people understand strategic principles, but can't apply them well because they lack discipline, love action, are indecisive, think slowly, get distracted, or have other weaknesses.

Which principles do you apply well?

Why?

Which principles do you apply poorly?

Why?

How can you increase your ability to apply strategic principles?

Card-Reading Skill

Since hands have only relative value, this skill is critically important. If you can't accurately put people on hands, you probably can't beat anyone except extremely weak players.

How well do you read cards?

What are your reasons for making that assessment?

How can you increase your card-reading skill?

People Reading Skill

Since the meaning of any bet or other action depends on the person making it, you must be able to read and understand his style, moods, and motives.

Warning: Most people overestimate their ability to read people. Check with others before claiming you read people well.

How well do you read people?

Which kinds of people do you read particularly well?

Which kinds of people do you have trouble understanding?

What are your reasons for making that assessment?

How can you increase your people-reading skill?

Deception

If other people can read you accurately, they have a huge edge over you. You must be able to deceive them about your cards, intentions, and overall strategy.

How well do you deceive other players?

Are there any kinds of people you can deceive easily?

Are there any kinds of people who see right through you?

What are your reasons for that assessment?

How can you become more deceptive?

Intensity

Intensity is hard to measure, but critically important. In fact, if other things are equal, the more intense competitor will usually win. He will work harder, remain more focused, and do whatever it takes to win.

How intensely competitive are you?

What are your reasons for that assessment?

How can you become a more intense competitor?

Style

Because most of my book, *The Psychology of Poker*, focused on styles, this book rarely discusses them. However, I'll do it now because you should understand how your style compares with the competition's. Your style has an immense impact on your results, and its relationship to the competition changes as you move up. Bigger games are generally tighter and more aggressive. Therefore, if your style remains the same as you move up, you will slowly become looser and more passive than the competition, which is exactly the wrong direction. Let me quote my book briefly:

> *If you play the wrong style, you are going to lose.* It is as simple as that. You can read the books, memorize the odds, even make an occasional brilliant play, but you will end up losing.
>
> The word "style" refers to a consistent *pattern of habits.* Everybody's style contains two basic dimensions, tight-loose (*how many* hands you play) and passive-aggressive (*how much* you bet or raise on different kinds of hands). Many people confuse these dimensions, even though they are quite distinct.
>
> *To win consistently, you* must *develop a tight-aggressive style.* The key to winning is to decrease your losses on your losers while increasing your profits on your winners. . . . And the best way to do these things is to become tighter and more selectively aggressive.
>
> *Nearly all successful professionals are* both *tight and selectively aggressive.*[1]

Compare yourself with the competition in every game you play by circling the appropriate number:

Much tighter   Equal   Much looser

1   2   3   4   5   6   7   8   9

What are your reasons for that assessment?

---

1. Schoonmaker, *The Psychology of Poker* (Henderson, NV: Two Plus Two, 2000), 18–19.

Much more passive				Equal		Much more aggressive		
1	2	3	4	5	6	7	8	9

What are your reasons for that assessment?

Should you become more tight-aggressive?

How can you become more tight-aggressive?

Final Remarks

This list of dimensions could be greatly expanded, but these are among the most important: If you can accurately compare yourself with your competition on all of them, you will have a far clearer picture of yourself than most players do. That picture will help you select games, adjust your strategy, and develop your skills.

Since my primary goal is to improve your long-term development, we should consider an extremely common error: many people work, not on what they need to develop, but on what they enjoy doing. For example, some people have studied so many books that they can't apply the theory. They have so many conflicting ideas floating around in their heads that they don't know which one to use. So what do they do? They buy more books! They enjoy studying, even though it won't solve their problem.

Other people are extremely deceptive because they refuse to study theory and play almost any two cards. What do they do next? They try to become even more deceptive by *raising* with almost any two! You would be much better off assessing your comparative strengths and weaknesses and then working on your weaknesses.

PART THREE

Understanding Unconcious and Emotional Forces

Introduction

Hardly any poker writers have systematically discussed unconcious and emotional forces, even though they affect every player. Poker writers naturally focus on strategy and rarely use words such as "unconscious," "emotional," or "irrational" except to describe other (and usually weaker) players. They apparently assume that their readers think and act rationally, which means trying to maximize their long-term profits. They tell readers how to play and essentially assume that they will do whatever will win the most money.

But look at what poker players actually *do!* How often have you played at a table that everyone tried to win the most money? More importantly, don't *you* occasionally act irrationally (in the profit-maximizing sense)? For example, haven't you made countless decisions that you *knew* reduced your EV? You played cards that you should have folded or joined a game that was too big or too tough for you or kept playing when you knew that you were too tired or tilted to play well. You, I, and everyone else often act for unconscious and emotional reasons.

If you ignore these forces, you cannot possibly understand the way people act at the poker table and everywhere else. If we were as rational as some people assume, we could not possibly act so stupidly. Please note that I said, "we," not "they," because we all act irrationally at times. If we cling to the idea that people are rational, a great deal of human behavior becomes inexplicable.

Just turn on the news tonight, listen to the stories of murder and mayhem, and then ask yourself, "How can rational people act that way?" The answer is quite simple: rational people can't and don't act that way. They don't kill themselves and other people, nor do they ruin their lives for trivial reasons. Since you can see the evidence of irrationality everywhere, you should realize that these unconscious and emotional forces have immense effects on *everybody*, including you and me.

We have already discussed some important irrational forces such as denial about ourselves and our opposition. Now we will consider more of them and a wider range of their effects.

We will start with Freud since he focused on the unconscious. When he proposed his theory, he was severely criticized, and many people still regard his work as "psychobabble." The idea that unconscious forces control us is so frightening that some people have to ridicule it. Although Freud has had countless critics, he is unquestionably history's most influential psychological thinker. Even his critics borrow—often unwittingly—from his positions.

Although I will begin with Freud, intelligent people have known for thousands of years that people have a variety of motives, including irrational ones. Poets and playwrights frequently wrote about them, and even average people did not deny their existence. Unfortunately, philosophers and economists focused so intently on how people *should* think and feel that they ignored or minimized what they actually did. They refused to consider motives, thoughts, and impulses that reduced profits or had other undesirable consequences.

The same pattern appears everywhere in the poker literature. In fact, that literature overlooks a central fact of poker: *most players lose.* How can anyone claim that poker players are trying to maximize their profits when most of them lose? There must be other forces involved.

Some of the profit-reducing motives the writers ignore are quite conscious and socially acceptable such as the desires to socialize, to test ourselves, or to be gentle toward weak players. Others are hidden or socially unacceptable such as the desires to show off, to gain sympathy, or to get revenge.

These articles focus on you, on the way that these forces affect your beliefs, thoughts, and actions. Exploiting them in others is covered in a few other places, but is never emphasized.[1] My focus is on *you* and the way you defeat yourself. If you want to get the best results, you have to understand these factors. Then you can reduce their effects on you, but you can *never* eliminate them.

1. The next book in this series will say a lot more about how to use these forces against other players.

Psychoanalysis and Poker

Freud never played poker, but understanding his psychoanalytic theories and methods can really improve your game. He emphasized unconscious, irrational forces, while most of his predecessors and peers focused on conscious, rational thinking. They assumed that people were rational, while Freud insisted that everybody is driven by unconscious, irrational thoughts, feelings, and impulses.

The same assumptions are made today by most poker writers and players, even though Freud's ideas have affected nearly everyone's thinking. People use terms such as libido, death instinct, defense mechanism, and repression without knowing that he coined or popularized those terms.

He also used free association and other techniques to get past rationalizations and other defense mechanisms that prevent you from understanding yourself. When he first used these techniques, they were vehemently criticized. Today people who have barely heard of Freud use them. Simply talking freely often allows you to see how you and others really think and feel.

If you look at the way people play, it's obvious that these irrational impulses affect everyone. Some people are crippled by them; they are literally incapable of acting rationally. Others act logically most of the time, but everybody—even the greatest poker champion—occasionally yields to these unconscious forces. How else can you explain all the stupid things we see and do every night? People know better, but still take self-defeating actions.

Unfortunately, most people don't admit that these drives affect them. You probably do it frequently. You rationalize, giving good reasons for your actions, not the real ones. You say, "I called that bet or raised or joined this game or didn't take that little old lady's last chips (or whatever else you did) because I expected to profit from it." You don't admit, not even to yourself, that you really don't know why you did something or that you did it because you were bored, angry, ashamed, guilty or just felt like it.

The best way to reduce these forces' impact on you is to understand what causes them and how they affect you and other people. This knowledge will also help you to comprehend, predict, and manipulate other people, but they are secondary benefits. The most important player to understand and control is yourself.

The Structure of Personality

Freud said that personality contains three components: the id, ego, and superego, and they constantly battle each other. Most people grossly misuse these terms, especially ego. In fact, they often use ego in exactly the wrong way. When someone says, "He's got a big ego," I want to say, "Oh, no he doesn't." In fact, most "big ego" actions are really caused by the ego's weakness.[1]

The *id* is the first part of the personality to develop. It is entirely unconscious, and it contains our primitive, biologically based instincts and urges. It operates on the *pleasure principle*, demanding instant gratification of all its desires and immediate relief from discomfort. It is completely unreasonable, accepting no limitations or delays. A baby is pure id, demanding immediate satisfaction of all its demands, ignoring all constraints. Every parent knows that you can't reason with a baby, and part of us never outgrows that primitive demand for instant gratification.

The id causes many stupid actions. For example, it doesn't want to wait for good cards; it wants to play *now*. It also wants to punish peo-

---

1. Thanks, "Cinch" (Dave Hench), for getting me started with your e-mails about "the role ego plays in poker."

ple, show off, and get the kick of wild gambling. If you can't harness these impulses—and nobody can control them completely—you will reduce or eliminate your edge.

The *ego* is the rational part of your personality. You slowly learn that the world is not part of you, that it does not do what you want it to do, and that you must adjust to it and obey its rules. Because the ego operates on the *reality principle*, it is able to understand and relate to the external world. It is much weaker than the id, which is the exact reversal of the common belief that people are primarily rational. The rationalists—including most poker writers—may reluctantly concede that irrational forces occasionally affect people, but they would never agree that these forces dominate our logical minds.

The debate between the Freudians and rationalists has lasted for more than a century, and it will probably never be resolved. I side with the Freudians.[2] In fact, as mentioned earlier, I wonder how anyone can watch the evening news and see how often people slaughter each other and destroy themselves but still insist that we are primarily rational. If you look at the news or at all the crazy things people do at the poker table, you should realize that *irrationality is the norm, not the exception*.

The *superego* starts as part of the ego, but slowly separates itself and becomes a demanding and punitive censor, our "conscience." It operates on the *morality principle*, insisting that we obey the rules of our parents and society, creating strong, often self-defeating feelings of guilt and shame. It can have an immense impact on your play because poker is so predatory, devious, and deceptive. If your superego makes you feel guilty when you bluff, sandbag, exploit a drunk, or bust someone, you're at a tremendous disadvantage. You can't do some of the things that others will do.

In fact, if you are as skilled as your opposition, but feel guilty

2. Although I agree with the Freudians on this issue, I emphatically disagree with them on many other issues.

about being deceptive and predatory, you probably can't win. The rational ego may tell you to do something, but the moralistic superego will stop you or cause you to act clumsily. For example, you may know people who can't bluff well because it embarrasses them, others who won't take someone's last chips, and others who tell weak players how to protect themselves. In fact, you've probably done some of those things, but never even recognized that—from a profit-maximizing perspective—they're clearly irrational.

The stronger your superego is, the more inhibitions you will have and the less effectively you will act. Poker is a predatory game; the strong eat the weak. If your superego prevents you from taking advantage of every opportunity to exploit weaknesses, you are at a tremendous disadvantage against more ruthless players.

Unlocking the Unconscious

You obviously can't analyze your unconscious thoughts and feelings in the same way you analyze your conscious ones. You bury these thoughts and feelings precisely because you don't want to understand or accept them. You want to think that you're rational and moral, and your drives are frequently both irrational and immoral.

Unfortunately, burying them doesn't stop them from affecting your behavior. In fact, it has precisely the opposite effect. They can't be controlled until you understand them, and your mind has powerful barriers to prevent their becoming conscious.

Psychoanalysts use several methods to unlock the unconscious, and the most common and easiest to use is *free association*. It means saying whatever comes into your mind, without worrying whether it is rational, senseless, moral, immoral, and so on.

You may have used a technique based on free association called brain storming. It is usually done in groups, and it often lets the group think of new and unexpected ways to solve problems. It can easily be used to help you understand why you played a hand a certain way or how you have made other decisions. Just let your mind and words flow freely.[3] You may discover possibilities that you would not normally consider.

Who Cares?

A close friend and successful pro told me that he disliked what I said above because Freudian psychobabble has no relationship to poker. I obviously disagree. Freud's ideas have had an immense impact on modern thinking. In fact, countless people use his concepts or variations on them without even recognizing that they came from Freud. Insisting that they have no relationship to poker is essentially assuming that poker players are different from everyone else. Since there are millions of us from all parts of the population, we obviously *can't* be different. And our personalities don't change when we sit down to play.

The evidence clearly indicates that everyone acts irrationally at times, and that these unconscious forces drive these actions. If you don't understand the forces that affect you and other people, you can't play your best, no matter how skilled you are. You cannot understand how these drives affect other people. More importantly, you will take foolish actions for unconscious reasons.

Recommendations

Several actions can reduce the destructive effects of the unconscious, irrational part of your mind:

1. Accept that you need more ego, not less. If you really want to win. This action is most important. I'm using ego in the

3. To keep a record of your thoughts, talk to a dictation machine. Or if you can type quickly, you can use a variation of free association called thinking at the computer (TACing). Just let your thoughts flow and your fingers input whatever crosses your mind.

Freudian sense. His ego deals with reality, while ego trips deny or distort it. To win at poker, you must avoid ego trips and constantly try to apply the reality principle.

2. Accept that you can't increase the ego's control unless you understand how your id and superego affect your play. You should therefore examine *why* you have taken actions. The poker culture is extremely anti-introspective. Instead of analyzing why we do things, many people just assume that people are rational profit maximizers. In fact, most of the poker literature looks as though it were written before Freud identified these unconscious forces.

   Since there's no rational reason not to apply the well-known principles of winning poker, unconscious and irrational forces *must* be operating. Ignoring them doesn't make them go away. It just increases their destructive effects.

3. Discover how your own and other people's minds actually work, not how people say they should work. All psychoanalysts spend years in analysis learning how these forces affect their own thoughts and actions. I'm certainly not suggesting that you undergo psychoanalysis or any other therapy, but examining your own thinking processes will help you to:
   • Get into other players' heads
   • Understand why you act the way you do
   • Reduce the effects of your unconscious drives

4. Try to free associate whenever you can't think of why you or someone else took an apparently irrational action. Just say to yourself, a dictating machine, or a trusted friend whatever comes into your mind. Some of the things you say may surprise you, and they can provide an entirely different way of looking at yourself and other people.

It isn't fun or natural to examine your own motives and thinking processes. You may want to pretend that your only motive is to maximize your profits, that you think rationally, and that all you need to succeed is to learn new strategies. But you already know much more than you apply well, and something is preventing you from getting the full benefit of all that knowledge. So take a hard look at your unconscious. You may find that it's doing a lot of damage.

Why Do People Play So Badly?

Because I'm a psychologist, people often ask me the question, "Why do people play so badly?" Of course, many of them are not really asking for my professional opinion. They just want to whine about losing money because of somebody's mistakes. After pretending to listen to me, they tell me a hard luck story.

Despite their dubious motives, it's a good question, and I will try to answer it, not for other people, but for you. If you are playing badly, you probably have one or more of these weaknesses:

1. You don't know how to play.
2. You have the wrong motives.
3. You lack certain essential traits.
4. You can't handle poker's confusing feedback.

There is substantial overlap between these four, and they often reinforce each other to cause mistakes and problems.

You Don't Know How to Play

Obviously, if you don't know how to play, you can't play well. Despite that fact, many people don't even try to learn how to play— even if they are playing for serious money. My friends who play fairly big games tell me they are constantly surprised by how clueless some of their opponents are. Jim Brier, a *Card Player* columnist and co-author of *Middle Limit Holdem Poker*, told me, "Sometimes I think the biggest difference between the $4–$8 and $80–$160 games is the color of the chips."[1]

Some people don't try to learn how to play, even when they have a chance to become rich and famous. Because I was associated with RoyalVegasPoker.com, I met some online qualifiers from several websites before the 2004 WSOP. They had won the $10,000 buy-in to the World Championship and would have a chance to win millions of dollars and immortality. Naturally, I expected them to prepare carefully, but most of them did little or nothing to get ready for the world's richest and toughest tournament. My conversations with several of them went something like this.[2]

ALAN: What books have you read since qualifying?

OLQ (online qualifier): None or Very few.

ALAN: Why not?

OLQ: I won my qualifying tournament without reading any books. I don't think I need them. I've always been good at games, and I have a feel for poker.

ALAN: You're going to be up against every great player in the world, and all of them excel at games and have much better feel than you do. Nearly all of them have carefully studied the good books again and again.

OLQ: Maybe, but books cost money, and experience is the best teacher.

ALAN: But the top players have much more experience than you, and many of them have said that various books really helped them. Don't you think it's a good idea to study?

1. Bob Ciaffone and Jim Brier, *Middle Limit Holdem Poker* (Saginaw, Michigan: privately printed, 2002).

2. A few of the online qualifiers I met worked much harder, and I'm sure that many of the ones I never met took this opportunity much more seriously.

OLQ: Maybe you're right, but I didn't want to spend the money or the time.

ALAN: Have you talked to serious players about your game?

OLQ: No.

ALAN: Why not?

OLQ: I don't know any serious players. My friends and I just play for fun.

ALAN: Have you participated in any forums at CardPlayer.com, Two PlusTwo.com, RGP,[3] or any other place?

OLQ: No. (Several people did not even know that these forums existed.)

ALAN: Do you realize that virtually all professionals regularly discuss strategy with each other and that some of them pay for coaching?

OLQ: They do?

ALAN: Sure, they do the same thing as Tiger Woods and most professional athletes. They get help with their game. Don't you think it would be a good idea to get some coaching?

OLQ: Maybe, but I don't want to spend the money.

ALAN: Let's change the subject. How many live tournaments have you played?

OLQ: None or one or two.

ALAN: Have you played in any large buy-in events?

OLQ: No.

ALAN: Why haven't you played in the only tournaments that can prepare you to play against great players?

---

3. RGP is Recreational Gambling Poker, a large forum.

OLQ: I didn't want to spend the money. A few said that Chris Moneymaker won in 2003 without playing in any major live tournaments.

ALAN: But you're going to play against the world's greatest players. You can't get experience against them in any other place. Don't you need to learn how to play against them?

OLQ: I guess so, but my prize was just the entry fee and travel expenses. I don't want to spend any of my own money.

None of my conversations went exactly like that, but several qualifiers essentially said, "I'm here to enjoy myself, and if I get lucky, I can win something." Since luck (plus, of course, *some* skill) got them into the world championship, they naturally hoped their luck would continue. And if it didn't, "Oh well, at least I had a good time in Las Vegas."

Recommendation

Accept that—no matter how talented you are—you probably can't play poker well without working hard. Therefore, if you want to become a really good player, you have no realistic choice but to take all the learning activities I've repeatedly recommended: study good books, read *Card Player* magazine, post on Internet forums, discuss strategy with serious players, critically analyze your own play, get coaching, and never, never, never think you know enough.

You Have the Wrong Motives

I certainly don't object to tourists wanting to enjoy themselves. If they weren't willing to pay for their fun, Las Vegas would dry up and disappear. But I had expected that people with a once-in-a-lifetime chance for wealth and fame would take the game much more seriously. If you play for fun and don't care much about your results, copying their lighthearted attitude is quite reasonable. But—since you have read this far—you probably want to improve your game. If so, you really must invest serious time and energy, plus some money.

You must also recognize that reading alone will not make you into a good player. Many people read good books, but still play badly. Malmuth told me, "We've sold over 250,000 copies of *Hold'em Poker for Advanced Players* and almost as many copies of *The Theory of Poker*, but only a small number of people apply the lessons well." I've studied both books many times and talked repeatedly to the authors, but I don't play as well as I should, and you probably don't either. We aren't stupid; we can understand the books we read. *So why don't we play as well as we know how to play?*

Many knowledgeable people play poorly because *they don't have a strong enough desire to play well.* They may claim to play poker to win money, but they don't really mean it. They yield to other motives such as the desire to gamble or socialize or prove their machismo, even when they know that it will cost them money. The unpleasant fact is that for most people—perhaps including you—*it's more fun to play badly than well.*

Many poker writers and players seem to assume that people are driven by the profit motive, but the evidence is overwhelming that other desires affect most actions. As mentioned earlier, we may claim to want to maximize our poker profits, but our actions contradict that claim.

"Psychoanalysis and Poker" on p. 118, discussed the effects of unconscious factors, but many of the reasons for bad play are right out in the open. Let's look at a few extremely common mistakes. If we were really trying to maximize our profits, these mistakes could not occur so frequently. There *must* be other motives at work.

Mistake No. 1: Playing Too Many Hands

Anyone who has read a poker book knows that he should play tightly, but most of us play too many hands, and virtually everyone occasionally plays one he knows he should fold. We have read repeated warnings, but still do it. Why?

Because it's *boring* to fold hand after hand. So we "take a shot," playing a weak hand. Sometimes it pays off, and we kid ourselves that we don't have to follow those silly rules; we can profitably play hands that less-talented players should muck. We may even congratulate ourselves for our "courage" or "flexibility." When playing a weak hand is too costly, we may vow, "Never again," but we soon find an excuse to break that vow.

Mistake No. 2: Chasing

We chase for the same reason, plus the self-defeating desire to "protect our investment." We throw good money after bad. Sometimes we catch a miracle card to win a large pot, and we remember it long after forgetting all the bets we wasted. Of course, if the pot is large enough, chasing is justified, but we *know* that chasing without the right odds is foolish. Yet luck and our selective memories let us pretend that we can get away with it.

Mistake No. 3: Playing Too Aggressively

We know that the top players are aggressive, and an aggressive style works well in shorthanded games and some other situations. When we know we should not do it, but play too aggressively anyway, we are trying to satisfy some other need such as expressing our anger, getting revenge, or trying to impress people.

Instead of recognizing our mistakes, we may remember the times that everyone folded, letting us win a small pot, or we sucked out to win a large one. We may ignore all the bets we wasted or rationalize that they are "advertising" so that we get action when we have a monster.

Mistake No. 4: Playing Too Passively

If we prefer to play passively, we can easily find excuses for it. We remember the times we saved money by not betting or raising, ignoring the pots lost by giving away free or cheap cards, or insisting, "Nothing I could do would get those idiots to fold."

Mistake No. 5: Showing Cards

Almost everyone does it occasionally. If we make a good bluff or fold, we want people to know how smart we are. If we see someone is afraid we were bluffing, we may relieve his tension by showing our winner. If we have aces cracked by someone playing trash, we may want sympathy. We may know we shouldn't give away information, but we can find a good excuse for violating that rule "just this once."

We may also claim that showing cards manipulates our opponents, but it is often just a rationalization. We cannot be sure how people will use the information that we have foolishly given away. Perhaps some people will be manipulated, but others will use it against us.

Mistake No. 6: Playing in the Wrong Games

We have all joined games that were too tough for us, and we probably did it for one of two reasons:

1. We didn't honestly evaluate our competition and ourselves, a subject I've already discussed.
2. We wanted to prove something about ourselves (such as that we are good players or macho gamblers).

Choosing the wrong game is a serious mistake, but staying in one after that mistake becomes clear is much worse. Yet most of us have done it. Perhaps we couldn't stand losing to players we don't respect, or we wouldn't admit that the game was too tough for us. Our pride or other foolishness cost us money.

Miscellaneous Mistakes

I won't discuss all the mistakes caused by antiprofit motives. They include trying to beat a specific person and showing off. Earlier I said, "It's more fun to play badly than well," but perhaps fun is the wrong word. I defined it loosely to mean any short-term satisfactions that reduce long-term profits. Something you enjoy may turn me off. The important point is that we will pay a high price for fun.

Because we get pleasure from different sources, you and I make different kinds of mistakes, but they must be caused by something other than the desire to maximize profits. Despite the evidence, many people insist that people strive to win as much as possible. If you believe that you want to maximize your profits, ask yourself two questions:

1. Have you made many of these mistakes, not just when you were a beginner, but the last time you played?
2. Do you know better?

If the answer to both questions is "yes," you must have some "irrational" (in the profit-maximizing sense) motives. Until you understand and control your own motives—including the unconscious ones—you cannot play your best.

Recommendation

Continuously monitor your own motives. Ask yourself, "*Why* did I do that?" If you understand poker theory and did it because you sincerely believed it was the right play, you will slowly improve your game.[4] If you did it for other reasons such as being bored or irritated

---

4. Obviously, this point applies only if you have followed my previous advice. Don't read this book until after you have studied strategy.

or wanting to impress someone or just feeling lucky, you will continue to make the same mistakes.

You Lack Certain Essential Traits

In *Ace on the River* Barry Greenstein listed twenty-five "Traits of Winning Poker Players."[5] I believe he is the first great player to make such a long list in their order of priority. Most of the poker literature focuses on knowledge and skills, but Greenstein thinks that you need these personal qualities to be a winning player.

Many of them overlap with points I've made here or in other parts of this book, but a few surprised me. Note that some of them are socially acceptable (such as empathic, trustworthy, and generous), while others are not (such as manipulative, greedy, and self-centered). The picture he draws of winning players is much more subtle and complicated than many of us believe. His list is in ascending order of importance:

25. The ones with a sense of humor
24. Prideful
23. Generous
22. Outgoing
21. Insensitive
20. Optimistic
19. Independent
18. Manipulative
17. Greedy
16. Persistent
15. Self-centered
14. Trustworthy

5. Barry Greenstein, *Ace on the River* (Fort Collins, CO: Last Knight Publishing, 2005), 56–70.

13. Aggressive
12. Competitive
11. Survivors
10. Empathic
9. Fearless
8. Able to think under pressure
7. Attentive to detail
6. Motivated
5. The ones with the best memories
4. In control of their emotions
3. Intelligent
2. Honest with themselves
1. Psychologically tough

Although I have the greatest respect for Greenstein, I think his list is too short. You also need four other traits (which may be implicit in the ones he listed):

1. *Discipline:* Some of the mistakes I attributed to poor motivation could just as easily be blamed on poor discipline. Knowing what to do and wanting to do it are not enough. You need enough discipline to resist your destructive desires and impulses. You may want to gamble or act angrily or challenge a tougher player, but you have to control yourself. Poker makes such extreme demands that only a few extremely disciplined people play their A-game most of the time, and nobody always plays it. We all get careless or sloppy occasionally, but good players are *much* more disciplined than poor ones.

2. *Patience:* It could be regarded as a part of discipline, but I'll discuss it separately. It takes a lot of patience to fold and fold and fold. Then, when you finally get a good starting

hand, but the flop is bad or the action is too heavy, you have to fold again.

3. *Confidence in your judgment:* You can beat weak players by just playing tightly, but you can't beat good ones without the confidence to back up your judgment with your chips. However, there is a thin line between confidence and over-confidence, and Geenstein put "overconfidence" on his list of negative traits: "Overconfidence will hamper a player's ability to accurately evaluate his edge in gambling situations."[6] So you need to balance confidence with the honesty about yourself that he put second.

4. *Willingness to invest time and money in developing yourself:* This trait isn't on Geenstein's list, but it is close to the top of mine. Most players are not willing to make that investment, but winning poker demands a *lot* of hard work. If you won't make this investment, you can't become a really good player.

Recommendation

Buy *Ace on the River* and evaluate yourself on all of Greenstein's traits plus the four I listed. Because we all lack objectivity about ourselves, ask someone who knows you well to do the same. If you don't know such a person, retain a professional. You may find that your self-image is quite distorted.

After evaluating yourself on all of them, do whatever you can to develop the ones you lack. Without them you cannot reach your full potential.

6. Ibid, 70.

You Cannot Handle Poker's Confusing Feedback

The best way to learn most skills is to practice and get feedback. If you want to learn how to type, you hit the keyboard, watch the screen or page, and correct your mistakes. Slowly, but surely, you type faster and make fewer mistakes.

Alas, this process "does not work *at all* for poker. The immediate results in poker are often divorced from your actions. . . . Sometimes . . . you acted correctly, but your result was terrible. Other times . . . you acted terribly, but your result was terrific. These common 'backwards' results fool your brain's natural learning processes. . . . This is one reason so many people play so poorly."[7]

Poker's feedback not only makes it hard to learn what to do, but it also prevents you from unlearning bad habits. Thousands of experiments have proved that undesirable behaviors that have this sort of apparently random reinforcement are the hardest to extinguish. Because you get an occasional reward (winning the pot), your bad habits will probably persist. Since you learned poker mostly from experience, your bad habits can continue indefinitely, *even if you know they are destructive.*

You may have read and understood books about what you should do, but be extremely frustrated that the apparently correct play fails so often. You raise with your pocket aces, but some idiot cold calls with seven-deuce offsuit, flops a deuce, and rivers a third deuce to win a huge pot. If it happens often enough, you may ignore the theory and yield to all sorts of stupid impulses. Since you will occasionally be rewarded for these mistakes and you will remember the rewards more than the bets you lose by playing badly, these mistakes can persist indefinitely.

7. Ed Miller, David Sklansky, and Mason Malmuth, *Small Stakes Hold'em: Winning Big with Expert Play* (Henderson, NV: Two Plus Two, 2004), 17.

Recommendation

Resist these impulses and develop a detached, unemotional approach that allows you to ignore these frustrations and confusing memories. "The correct way to learn poker is to understand it *theoretically* and make sure you make the right play, regardless of the results."[8] Unfortunately, you may be unwilling or unable to think that way. You may even pride yourself on being "practical," and dismiss this theoretical approach as too academic. If you feel that way, you will probably continue to play badly.

8. Ibid.

Destructive Emotions

Poker writers rarely discuss emotions other than saying that we must not let them affect our play. Unfortunately, emotions can be so powerful that we often ignore that advice. We may believe we are acting rationally, but our emotions can cause a wide variety of mistakes such as playing cards we should fold, joining a game that is too big or too tough for us, or continuing to play when we know we are too tired or tilted to play well.

If we don't understand how our emotions affect us, a great deal of our behavior becomes inexplicable and uncontrollable. Please note that I said, "our," not "their," because we all act emotionally at times.

These effects are increased because we kid ourselves. We deny or rationalize our feelings instead of looking at them objectively. You can probably remember being told, "Calm down," and replying, "I am calm!" when you were really furious.

This chapter will help you reduce these destructive effects by taking three steps:

1. Describing the most destructive emotions.
2. Explaining how they hurt us at the poker table.
3. Recommending ways to control them.

The Most Destructive Emotions

You could easily argue that some other emotions are as bad as the ones listed here, but they certainly do serious damage. Moderate amounts of any emotions are relatively harmless, but when they become too strong, they distort our perceptions, thoughts, and actions, thereby reducing our intellectual control. We may know better than to take certain actions, but we yield to our emotions.

Destructive Emotion No. 1: Hope

Hope (and its close cousin, denial of reality) is the driving force behind most gambling. If people did not hope to win, they would not gamble, and this hope can easily cause us to act foolishly. We know that the odds do not justify calling with these cards but we call anyway, hoping to catch miracle cards. We see that a game is too big or too tough for us, but we still play, hoping to get lucky. To play winning poker, we must be ruthlessly realistic about everything, but our hopes can distort our judgment.

Destructive Emotion No. 2: Love for Action

Some people go beyond just hoping. They love action so much that they deliberately take foolish chances. Many loose-aggressive players are dominated by their love for action. They may claim that this style is best because of A or B or C, but they are just rationalizing. They love to gamble, and they give plausible reasons to justify yielding to their self-defeating impulses.

If we didn't like action, we wouldn't play poker, but it's very expensive to love it. Action lovers call or even raise with hands that more sensible people would fold. They play in games they can't afford because the higher stakes give them a bigger kick. They react, not to a rational analysis of their risks and potential gains, but to a craving to gamble, the destroyer of countless bankrolls and lives.

Daniel Negreanu, one of the world's greatest players, has repeatedly stated in his *Card Player* column that he recognizes and controls his love for action in an unusual way. He enters small, no-limit hold'em tournaments, goes all-in again and again, and rebuys again and again, just to blow off steam. Then he doesn't have any need to gamble when the money is important.

His example illustrates the critical importance of understanding *why* you are taking actions. Because he recognizes that his gambling urges can cause him to act foolishly when the stakes are high, he can control those urges. If he denies his motives or rationalizes that he overplays hands for this or that strategic reason, his love for action will be much more destructive.

Destructive Emotion No. 3: Fear of Risk

This fear is the opposite of the love for action, and it's much less expensive. Fearful players can win if they play against only weak players, but they can't win much. Their tightness gives them an edge against loose players, but their timidity reduces the profits on their winning hands and makes them avoid potentially profitable situations. They may avoid some juicy games or fold some positive EV hands because they're afraid of the risks.

For example, I was once in an early morning game with an utter maniac. He had lost at least nine racks of chips. When we got down to four players, our game was broken up, and he was assigned to a different table from mine. Since I wanted to play with him, I waited a few minutes, and then walked over to his new table.

I was surprised to see that three local rocks (part of the morning shift) refused to play with him. They were waiting for the rest of the morning-shift locals to come in to play their timid game. I asked for and got a change to their maniac's table. He wanted to throw his money away, and I was glad to help him do it.

Timid players may also "save money" in expensive, foolish ways. They save a little by checking when they should bet or calling when they should raise, but the free or cheap cards they give away can cost them the entire pot. Their timidity also makes them easy to bluff, which some players will sense and exploit.

Destructive Emotion No. 4: Fear of Randomness

Many people simply refuse to believe that cards are utterly, absolutely random. Randomness is so frightening that they deny reality. They may accept it intellectually, but in their secret hearts, they believe or hope that they can predict or control their cards. If you look at many poker tables, you will see people using lucky charms, asking for a new deck, switching seats, or refusing to play with certain dealers.[1]

They do these silly things because randomness is too frightening to accept. If they accept that cards are truly random, they are helpless, at least for the very short term. Helplessness is so frightening that they try to control the uncontrollable. They pray to the poker gods and complain when the gods don't answer their prayers.

This fear is increased by the way our brains work. They have such a strong tendency to find patterns that they will find them even when they don't exist. "Most gamblers tend to ascribe meaning to purely random, independent events. Our brains invented all of this nonsense to explain something they clearly weren't designed to understand: completely random events with absolutely no pattern or meaning whatsoever."[2] Cards are random. Period. There's nothing we can do to change them, and denying that reality distracts us from the only thing we can control: our own decisions.

Destructive Emotion No. 5: Aversion to Conflict

Poker is full of conflict. Our goal is to take each other's money, and we keep score by counting the chips we win or lose from each other. It is based on power, aggression, and deception, which can seem wrong or even immoral to conflict avoiders.

These people shouldn't play poker, but some of them do. They usually play badly because they try to be "nice." They passively do whatever the others want, calling when they should fold, checking when they should bet, calling when they should raise, refusing to

1. Some other reasons for this foolishness are discussed in "Luck, ESP, and Superstitions," p. 167.

2. Miller, Sklansky, and Malmuth, *Small Stakes Hold'em,* pp. 39–40.

check raise or bluff, even showing down winners without betting (especially when they are heads-up).[3] Since poker isn't a "be nice" kind of game, they *must* lose over the long term. In fact, this pattern is the worst possible one.[4]

Destructive Emotion No. 6: Anger

The preceding emotions are fairly permanent characteristics of certain players, but anger comes and goes. Nearly all of us have gotten angry while playing, and we often paid dearly for it. We tried to get revenge on someone, played weak cards, or even made "steam raises" with them, became easy to read, missed obvious signals from other players, kept playing when we were on tilt, and took many other foolish, destructive actions.

Anger may be the most destructive emotion, and many people can't control it. Since poker is an intrinsically frustrating game, people who can't control their anger shouldn't play, but many of them do. When the inevitable bad beats and losing streaks occur, their anger can devastate them. Anger has such destructive effects that the next chapter will focus exclusively on managing it.

Destructive Emotion No. 7: Ache to Get Even

Perhaps the dumbest words in poker are "I've got to get even," and many of us say them occasionally. Worse yet, we may follow up these words by taking foolish risks, which can put us deeper into the hole, making us more desperate and foolish.

Losing suggests that something is wrong. Maybe the game is tougher than we thought, or we have been playing poorly. Losing should make us more conservative, but it often has the opposite effect. We may call or even raise with hands we'd normally fold. We

---

3. Even if you are not primarily a conflict avoider, you may have some of these feelings, and they will certainly harm your results.

4. Alan Schoonmaker, *The Psychology of Poker* (Henderson, NV: Two Plus Two, 2000), 184–187.

may even move up to higher limits, despite knowing that the game is tougher. After all, our luck *has* to change, doesn't it?

Wrong! In fact, if we ignore the fact that something is wrong, get more aggressive, and play for higher limits, we can easily wipe out our bankrolls.

Destructive Emotion No. 8: Pride

Moderate pride and its corollary, self-confidence, are *constructive* emotions. When we feel sure of ourselves, we play more decisively, and our table image can damage our opponents' play. However, excessive pride can be extremely destructive. It is related to many other emotions. For example, one reason we ache to get even is that losing hurts our pride, especially if we think the game is easy. We may angrily ask ourselves, "How could such weak players beat *me?*"

Pride also makes us believe we can beat games that are too tough for us, profitably play weak cards, or play well when we're exhausted or distracted. We're too proud to accept our limitations.

How Emotions Hurt Us

The emotions I have described (plus many others) hurt us in a wide variety of ways, but most emotions have three common and destructive effects:

1. We overlook or misinterpret signals
2. We give away too much information
3. We react viscerally rather than logically

Since poker is primarily a game of information management, much more has been written about the first two effects, but some visceral reactions can severely damage our results.

In the introduction to "The Fundamental Theorem of Poker," David Sklansky wrote: "The art of poker is filling in the gaps in the incomplete information provided by your opponents' betting and the exposed cards in open-handed games, and at the same time preventing your opponents from discovering any more than you want them to know about your hand."[5]

Emotions interfere with both these tasks. They cause us to overlook or misinterpret the information from our opponents and to give away too much information about our situation and ourselves. We become less perceptive and more transparent, a deadly duo.

Effect No. 1: Overlooking or Misinterpreting Signals

The more emotional we become, the more subjectively we handle information. We believe, not what the signals suggest, but what we hope or fear is true. We have all made stupid blunders and then said to ourselves, "How could I misread the situation so badly? The signs were so obvious."

We misread other players' hands and delude ourselves about their skill and strategy because our emotions distort our thinking. Anger incites us to ignore signs of strength and attack. Fear makes us overlook or misinterpret weak signals, exaggerate strong ones, and run away. And pride causes a wide variety of distortions.

The effects of emotions are not always temporary; they are often a major part of our style. Tight-passive players are too pessimistic; they are so afraid of losing that they look for excuses to be excessively cautious. They see dangers where none exist, a bear behind every bush.

For example, even though there is no rational reason to believe an opponent has a big full house, they are too afraid to raise with a small full house, losing a profit. If they are really timid, they may think "worst case" all the time. If there are three cards to a flush or straight, they won't bet, even if two of those cards were the turn and river, and the betting pattern clearly suggests that the other player was not on a backdoor draw. Their excessive pessimism:

5. Chapter 3 of *The Theory of Poker* (Henderson, NV; Two Plus Two, 1999), 17.

- Prevents them from getting the full value from their winning hands
- Causes them to give away free and cheap cards that will cost them entire pots
- Guarantees that they can never beat good players

Loose-aggressive players are too optimistic. Because they love action, they make optimistic assumptions that give them excuses to gamble. If someone raises preflop and the flop doesn't have an ace or king, they put him on ace-king. If the flop is ace-queen-seven and they have a small ace, they put him on pocket kings.[6] If the tightest rock in town raises on the river, they hope he is acting out of character, three-bet with a marginal hand, get capped, and lose to the nuts. They simply can't control their optimism, and it causes many expensive mistakes.

Effect No. 2: Giving Away Too Much Information

Poker depends on deception; if our opponents can read our cards, understand our thinking, and anticipate our actions, they will easily beat us. When we become emotional, we often give ourselves away. For example, players often show their cards or tell bad beat stories because they want sympathy. They essentially say, "Look at the wonderful cards I had, but I lost to this idiot!" Of course, they give away valuable information that other players will use against them.[7] The more emotional people become, the more information they give away. You have probably seen normally unreadable players go on tilt and become extremely "transparent." Some people get so upset that they act out of turn or grab their chips long before the action gets to them.

6. Clarkmeister gave this example on a twoplustwo.com forum in a post titled, "What the Fish Put Us On."

7. This subject is discussed in "We Need a Miranda Warning" on p. 171.

You may not be so obvious, but when you get emotional, you probably give away too much information. You may, for example, invite people to bluff by obviously getting ready to fold or disgustedly staring at your cards, nonverbally shouting: "I missed my hand *again.*" Or perhaps you start betting forcefully with strong hands or timidly with weak ones. It does not matter *how* you give yourself away; anything that helps other people read you will cost you.

Effect No. 3: Reacting Viscerally

These reactions are direct and unthinking such as shutting your eyes and moving your head when you see a fist coming toward your face. You don't think about these reactions; in fact, you probably can't prevent them. Your body is hardwired to react automatically to various threats and opportunities; in fact, the brain may not get involved until after the reaction.

But poker is a thinking game, and these reactions can distort our thinking, give away information, directly harm our play, and improve our opponents' play. For example, as mentioned earlier, angry people make steam raises or muck their cards out of turn, even though their busted draw may be a winner. They don't think; they just express their anger, regardless of the consequences.

The Overall Impact of These Three Effects

Poorly controlled emotions may cause us to act foolishly *even when we know better*. They directly damage our play, and they help our opponents to play better against us.

Directly Damaging Our Play

Our mind tells us to raise, but our fears make us call. We know we should fold, but we make a steam raise. Our intellect says, "Go home; this game is too tough, and you're playing badly," but our pride says, "I can beat them," or our hope says, "My luck has got to change."

The type of reaction depends, of course, on which emotions are involved. If, for example, we are angry with someone, we may ignore signs that he has a strong hand, underestimate his skill, blame his success on luck, and attack him at exactly the wrong time. We may ignore the signals that he has the nuts and call or even raise instead of folding. We may then get angrier and more foolish. We say, in effect, "Take that, you rotten SOB," and he takes—not our punishment, but our chips. We may even become so angry that we give our chips, not just to the player who angered us, but to everybody. We play hands we should fold, raise on nothing more than anger, refuse to be "bluffed" when we are obviously beaten, and so on.

Fear has the opposite effect. If we are afraid of someone, we may let him run over us, steal our blinds, bluff us out of our pots, and make us check when we should bet and call when we should raise. We react, not to the signals, but to our fears.

Making Our Opponents Play Better Against Us

We give them information, and they use it against us. Emotions also create vulnerability, and they may sense and exploit that weakness. Poker is a predatory game, and all predators attack vulnerable prey. We can see it most easily in animals such as growling dogs; if you seem afraid or try to run, they will attack; if you seem unafraid, they will probably bark, but keep their distance.

Emotional players are obviously vulnerable, which encourages opponents to attack, *even if they cannot describe it in words*. A few thousand years of civilization have blunted our hunting instincts, but they are still part of our genes. The hunting instinct just increases the effects of a rational rule: attack the weaker hands and weaker players. If we are emotional, we arouse the opponents' hunting instincts, just when we are most vulnerable.

We are playing badly, making mistakes, giving away information, while they are focused on us, are more sensitive to our signals, and are ready to exploit our mistakes. It is a terrible combination. Our bodies are programmed to react in certain ways, but some of these re-actions were appropriate to a primitive life, not the poker table. The automatic fight-flight reaction helps animals, including humans, to survive, but it sure messes up our poker playing.

Controlling Destructive Emotions

The previous discussion laid the foundation for the critical task: controlling destructive emotions. Let's look at a few steps toward that goal:

Step No. 1: Don't kid yourself.

This step is absolutely essential. Until you get honest with your-self, you can't control your emotions. Unfortunately, it is often hard to be honest about our emotions, particularly in poker games. Intense competition makes us want to kid ourselves, and luck's short-term ef-fects make it easy to do so. As Roy Cooke, *Card Player's* senior colum-nist, put it: "Only in love do I see more self-denial, lack of honesty with oneself, and bad decisions based on emotion than at poker."

Step No. 2: Keep good records.

Good records will reduce denial and improve your perspective about bad beats and losing streaks. You can't kid yourself about your results if your records clearly state them, and any win or loss will have less emotional impact. Let's say, for example, you play $5–$10, and you've just had a bad beat in a $200 pot and have lost $600 this week. If your records show that you were ahead or behind $7,000 for the year, that pot and losing streak become much less important and upsetting.

Step No. 3: Play for the right stakes.

You, I, and nearly everyone else have a comfort zone: the stakes that give you the right mix of stimulation and relaxation. At lower stakes, the stakes and the players' limitations may bore you, which may make you play sloppily. The late Stu Ungar, the world's greatest player, once said that he could not beat a $5–$10 game. If you lose, you could become so embarrassed and angry about losing to weak players that you may play even worse.

At higher limits you will probably feel scared. You may become tentative and timid, checking when you should bet, calling when you should raise, and folding when you are bluffed. Since the players will be more skilled than usual, they may recognize your fears and run over you.

The obvious solution is to play only in your comfort zone. Remember, poker is a game, and games are played for pleasure. You can't enjoy being bored or scared, and you certainly won't enjoy playing poorly and losing.

However, you may want to move up to test your skills or develop your game. If you do poorly in the bigger game, don't be too proud to move back down.

Step No. 4: Accept poker and people as they are.

Many emotional reactions, especially anger, come from refusing to accept reality. People complain bitterly about things they can't change such as bad beats, losing streaks, terrible players, and dealers' mistakes. To play your best, you *must* accept the game and people as they are, including everything you dislike about them. Instead of worrying about things you can't change, accept them and focus on the only thing you can control: your own play.

Step No. 5: Depersonalize conflicts.

Accept that poker's conflicts are not personal. As my friend, Phil Dolan, put it, "I like you, Al, but at the poker table I take no prisoners." Phil would bluff, sandbag, or do whatever else the rules allow to beat me, and I would do the same to him. Neither of us takes these actions personally, they are just parts of the game. If you personalize conflicts, you may become so vengeful that you destroy yourself.

Depersonalizing conflicts also increases your freedom. It lets you attack weaker players and use deceptive tactics without feeling guilty or embarrassed. You aren't a rotten person who wants to hurt anyone; it's just the way the game is played.

Step No. 6: Take a walk, change games, or go home.

If you see or even suspect that you're getting too emotional, stop playing *immediately*. First, take a walk to analyze how well you are playing and the effects (if any) of your emotions. If possible, talk to someone who is honest enough to tell you the truth, even if you don't want to hear it. Then decide whether you have a realistic chance to beat this game. Note the word "realistic." The more emotional you are, the less realistic you will be.

If you even suspect that you're "losing it," change games or go home. That decision can be painful, but the more you want to stay, the angrier you are about losing, or the more convinced you are that your luck has to change, the likelier you are to play poorly. Your intense feelings and denial of the evidence that something is wrong suggest that you are losing control.

It is especially difficult to leave a "great game," and you should frequently stay. You don't want to miss the excitement, which is exactly why you must be *very* cautious. If you feel your heart pumping and hate the thought of leaving, *beware*. You may be so emotional about the game that your judgment is weakening. From there, it is just a short step to going on tilt, which can be disastrous.[8]

Step No. 7: Remember your "good beats."

A "good beat" occurs when *you* are the lucky idiot who misplays his hands, catches a miracle card, and wins a large pot. We hear bad

---

8. Going on tilt is the most extreme and destructive emotional reaction. See "Preventing and Handling Tilt," p. 193.

beat stories all the time, but even though we have all had good beats, we rarely hear about them. Why?

A bad beat story gives us an excuse for losing, and we want to protect our egos. But a good beat story raises doubts about our skill: we won because we were lucky, not because we played well. So we bore our friends with bad beat stories and hardly ever tell the other kind. But you know you have had your share of good beats. You may not want to remember them, but it is a mistake not to. If you think only of your bad beats, you will see yourself as unlucky, which can arouse several destructive emotions.

My favorite good beat came when I had:

in the big blind, and the flop was

The small blind bet, and I smooth called, planning to raise on the turn. A player behind raised, and I decided to check-raise on the turn. The turn was 8♦, I check-raised, got reraised, and I capped it, thinking my opponent had three threes with a smaller kicker.

The river was the 3♦. My opponent had pocket eights and had made a full house on the turn. I had misread his hand and overplayed a one-outer, then caught my miracle card. You have had many good beats, including ones that you had to catch two perfect cards. Remember them, especially when things are going badly. You will play better and project a stronger image.

Step No. 8: Say a "mantra."

No matter how well you play, bad beats and losing streaks are inevitable. When you're feeling angry or sorry for yourself, quietly say a little "mantra:" "If the game lasts long enough, I will win, maybe not tonight or this week or this month, but, eventually, I will be ahead." It has always been true, and it always will be true as long as you play well and select the right games and seats. But you won't do those things if you don't control your emotions.

Anger

The term "anger management" appears frequently in the psychological and popular literature, and it's even been a movie title. Many people use books, articles, training courses, and professional counselors to gain control over their anger. It's obviously a common problem, especially at poker tables.

We see angry players all the time. Some of them seethe quietly, but others throw cards, shout at people, and complain bitterly about everything. Their anger creates a vicious cycle: it harms their play and increases their losses, making them even angrier. Despite its importance, the term anger management hardly ever appears in poker conversations, books, or articles. Why is such a huge problem discussed so rarely?

It's just another example of denial. Most people, including you and me, are not always honest about our feelings. For example, I quietly told a bitterly complaining friend, "Don't get mad at me. I didn't do it." She shouted angrily, "I'M NOT MAD!"

Many people also deny anger's effects. They may say, "I'm very angry, but it hasn't changed my play." Nonsense! We aren't machines. Anger negatively affects almost everything we think and do. Pretending that it doesn't is just another form of denial.

Anger's Destructive Effects

The previous chapter, "Destructive Emotions," described the general effects of several emotions. Anger has the same effects, but they are often much more intense. It also has a few others.

Going on the wildly aggressive form of tilt is anger's most visible and serious effect. When someone is acting crazily, almost everyone can see it, except, perhaps, the one on tilt. It is very important, but other chapters discuss tilt. Besides, for every individual who acts recklessly, several people quietly fume, letting anger sabotage their game.

I suspect that far more money is lost from quiet anger than from obvious craziness. The line between winning and losing is so thin that being slightly off balance can shift us from winning to losing. Anger costs us money in the same ways as other emotions, but more obviously and intensely.

We acquire much less information.

Anger is so distracting that we may miss signals, including quite obvious ones.

We misinterpret the information we do acquire.

All emotions cause us to misinterpret signals, but anger's effects are particularly powerful. For example, angry people often see neutral signals as attacks and respond aggressively.

We give away too much information.

Our need to express our anger may make us say and do things that tell others how to beat us. For example, as mentioned earlier, we may stare disgustedly at a missed draw, inviting a bluff. Or we may show our cards and complain about the idiots who did not respect our raise. We hope for sympathy, but tell others how we play.

We become impatient.

We all know that patience is essential, but angry people don't want to wait for good cards and positions. They need to blow off steam *now*.

We show our vulnerability, and other players will exploit it.

When opponents sense vulnerability, they will take advantage of it. For example, they may goad us to make us even angrier and less effective, or they may raise to isolate us, knowing they can read us easily.

We may seek revenge.

Revenge seeking can make us give our chips to the "enemy" and other players. A Chinese proverb is very relevant, "When you set out for revenge, dig two graves, one for your enemy and one for yourself."

Primary Causes

Many people deny the real causes for their anger. They blame bad beats, bad luck, stupid players, incompetent dealers, smoke, noise, or almost anything except themselves. They may walk in angry and stay that way. They may even win the first pot, but complain that it was not big enough. Perhaps they are reacting to something that happened elsewhere; perhaps they are just angry at the world, but their anger is nearly overwhelming. People like that should not play poker, but they do, and they often lose heavily and disrupt the game. Most other anger problems are caused by the following factors:

Low Frustration Tolerance

Some people blow up over events that others barely notice. Low tolerance is deadly for a poker player because the game is intrinsically frustrating. We often lose real money, sometimes more than we can afford. Because we play against so many opponents, we lose far more hands than we win, and the best hand and best player often lose. In addition, losing is worse at poker than at craps or other games of pure luck because it says we don't play well. Many people deny their weakness and say, in effect, "If the world was not such a rotten place, I would be fine."

Bad Beats

They are often the immediate cause for anger, and for some people losing any hand—even when they are underdogs—is a bad beat. We have all seen people erupt because their pocket kings lost to pocket aces or because they "never make a flush."

When someone else sucks out, anger is extremely common. Some people cannot handle such beats, even though they usually occur when other players make mistakes. Since most of our profits come from other people's mistakes, getting angry about them is self-defeating. If nobody made mistakes, the rake and tokes (dealer-tips) would defeat all of us.

Unrealistic Expectations

Many people have extremely unrealistic expectations. For example, they don't know how hard it is to win because of the rake and tokes, especially at smaller stakes. As mentioned earlier, countless people—including some mediocre players—think they should win more than one big bet per hour, and a few even expect to support themselves by playing. When they don't get the expected results, they angrily ask, "How can I be so terribly unlucky?"

Many others can't accept that poker is *gambling*, and bad luck, bad beats, and losing streaks are absolutely unavoidable. If you can't accept that reality, you shouldn't play, but many people keep playing and steaming.

Overestimation of Our Abilities

As I've noted repeatedly, most people don't play remotely as well as they think they do. This misunderstanding makes them play in games they can't beat and then get angry about their bad luck. It's easier to blame luck than to accept the truth about themselves.

Selective Memories

We naturally remember events that support our beliefs and forget conflicting evidence. For example, because we think we are good, but unlucky, we remember and get angry about our bad beats, but forget the times that we played stupidly and sucked out.

Personalizing Conflicts

Since we take each other's money, our game is full of conflict. It's just the nature of the game, but many people take losing very personally, and it costs them dearly. They become so intent on beating certain players that they give away their chips.

Machismo

The tendency to personalize conflicts is particularly strong for macho men (and a few women). Twoplustwo.com's Psychology Forum had two extremely long threads about whether "real men" should beat up people who suck out and then needle them. Such a childish overreaction indicates how serious the anger-management problem can be.

Vicious Circle

Many of these factors reinforce each other. Unrealistic expectations and overestimation of our abilities increase frustrations because we expect to beat games that are too tough for us. Our selective memories reinforce both our overestimation of our abilities and our anger about being "so unlucky." Machismo aggravates almost everything.

Easing the Problem

For many reasons anger will always be a problem. We cannot completely control our feelings, and anger is programmed into our genes. Although it can never be eliminated, several steps will reduce its destructive effects. Since many of these steps were described in the previous chapter, I will just list them here. If you want more information, read the chapter called. "Destructive Emotions" (See p. 138).

- Play for the right stakes.
- Accept poker and people as they are.
- Depersonalize conflicts.
- Remember your good beats.
- Take a walk, change games, or go home.

In addition to these steps, I have provided a few others that are particularly valuable for anger:

Recognize that you have a problem.

You may not blow up, throw cards, shout at people, and so on, but don't pretend that you don't get angry. Mother Nature programmed anger into all of us. You may get angry less often or less visibly than most people, but almost everybody does it, and it usually harms our play. You can't manage your anger until you recognize and understand your own feelings and their effects.

Identify your triggers.

Triggers are the things that arouse your anger, and they are very individualistic. Something that would anger me may not bother you, and vice versa. If you don't identify your triggers, you can't manage their effects.

Whenever you get angry, ask, "Why do I feel this way?" You will see patterns. For example, you may get angry when people are rude, or they talk too much, or the dealer is too slow, but not be bothered much by bad beats and stupid plays. Other people will have a completely different pattern.

Avoid important triggers.

Countless people either haven't identified their triggers or have insisted that they shouldn't occur. They essentially say, "It's not my fault that I'm angry. It's *theirs*, and they have to change." These attitudes are extremely self-defeating. Since the world isn't going to adjust to you, you have to adjust to it.

For example, since rude players really bother me, I often refuse to play with them, even if they're throwing away their money. I'd rather walk away than let them destroy my enjoyment, mood, and concentration. Some friends have said that I shouldn't let rudeness bother me or that I should insist that people act politely. Unfortunately, I can't control my emotional reactions, and I certainly can't control what other people do, but I can easily avoid most triggers. So can you.

Hesitate, and think before reacting.

If you just hesitate briefly and think about why you want to say or do something, you will prevent some extremely stupid mistakes. We have all said and done stupid things while angry, and we have usually regretted it.

Be honest about your motives.

Whenever you take an action, the critical question is, What are you trying to do? If you're just expressing your anger, you're probably making a mistake. You may briefly ease your inner tensions, but pay a high price for doing so. The reaction that felt so good may cost you a lot of money, get you thrown out of the game, or even barred from the cardroom.

Unfortunately, many people rationalize about their motives. They insist that they are trying to solve a problem, but take actions that will aggravate it. For example, they may pretend that arguing forcefully will teach people how to act, but it will often teach them the wrong lessons. Instead of learning how to behave properly, they learn how to push the "teacher's" buttons, manipulating his emotions.

Turn off chat.

The nasty remarks players make online are triggers for many people, including me, but you can easily avoid them. I would love to tune out the nastiness in live games, and there is no reason to "listen" to it online.

Many people get very upset by nasty comments, but refuse to turn off chat as "a matter of principle." The nasty people are the problem, and *they* have to change. This reaction is understandable, but unrealistic. Unless someone is *way* out of line, most websites won't revoke his chat privileges. You can't shut him up, but there's no reason to listen or, worse yet, to respond to him. Just turn off chat.

Remember that winning is the best revenge.

If you find yourself angry for any reason or if you ache to get even with someone, repeat the winning statement. Don't worry about whether you beat your best friend, your worst enemy, or some nameless stranger. Just get the chips.

Arrogance

A great poker paradox is that some excellent players are often broke. Ungar was the most famous example: he was probably the greatest player who ever lived, but he often needed backers, and he died broke.[1] Other fine players frequently need backers, and arrogance is usually a major cause of their problems.

The Meaning of "Arrogance"

My *Webster's International* dictionary defines arrogance as "a genuine or assumed feeling of superiority that shows itself . . . in excessive claims of position, dignity or power or that unduly exalts one's own worth or importance: overbearing pride." That pride can be so great that it creates denial about essential realities such as one's abilities and limitations.

How Can Great Players Be So Stupid?

The absolute essence of winning poker is to wait until you have the edge, then exploit it. Some great players apply that principle brilliantly at the poker table, then ignore it by playing unbeatable games. They ship money from the poker room to craps tables, roulette, and other games they can't beat.

---

1. His drug addiction was only part of the problem. He arrogantly played craps and other unbeatable games, and he lost immense amounts betting sports against experts.

They want faster action than they can get at poker, and they arrogantly ignore the laws of probability. They may never admit it, even to themselves, but in their secret hearts they believe that "those games may be unbeatable for ordinary people, but not for me. I'm so superior that the laws of probability and lots of other rules don't apply to me."

Arrogance also causes some outstanding tournament players to be suckers in cash games. They beat tournaments, but lose heavily because they don't play well for cash. In fact, when some of them make a tournament's final table, their cash game opponents cheer them on. If they have a big payday, their opponents will get a nice piece of it.

Their arrogance prevents them from learning from their past losses. They delude themselves into believing that this time will be different. Their true superiority will allow them to beat games that have repeatedly defeated them.

Andy Beal, the Epitome of Arrogance

His extraordinary arrogance has been recorded for posterity in *The Professor, the Banker, and the Suicide King*.[2] People will be reading about his arrogance and its costs for decades. Nobody but Beal knows exactly how much he lost, but Todd Brunson said, "I figure we won about $40 million over three years."[3] That statement was made before he lost another $10 million.

Beal is unquestionably a very intelligent man and an excellent player, but—like many highly successful people—he neither understands nor accepts his limitations. He arrogantly believes, "I can do anything."

2. Michael Craig, *The Professor, the Banker, and the Suicide King: Inside the Richest Poker Game of All Time* (New York: Warner Books, 2005).

3. Lisa Wheeler, "Todd Brunson: His Own Successful Path," *Card Player*, February 21, 2006, 51–55.

Not only did he take on the world's best, but he gave them the "home court advantage" by playing in Las Vegas. Then he compounded his error by letting them act as a team against him. When one of them got tired or if he had the wrong style for Beal's play, they would switch players. So he was always up against the toughest, freshest competitor, no matter how tired he was.

Of course, they compared notes after every session and discussed ways to improve their strategy. They would decide which player was best for his current state of mind and give that player clear instructions on how to exploit his weaknesses. To play heads-up against any one of the world's best players was incredibly arrogant. To play against a team of them was nearly insane.

How Do These Stories Relate to You?

You may think these stories are irrelevant and don't relate to you. You don't need backers or play craps or roulette, nor are you a tournament champion who can't beat cash games. And you certainly won't play heads-up against the world's best. You may be a steady winner, and your bankroll may have grown nicely for months or years. Yet arrogance may still be a problem. For example, you may play above your skill and bankroll or plan to become a full-time professional.

Playing above your skill and bankroll is extremely common. You, I, and most other people want to believe that we're much better players than we really are. This arrogance can make you play against superior players or for stakes you can't afford.

These two mistakes often go together because larger games normally have tougher players. If you overestimate your skill, you almost automatically underestimate your bankroll requirements. The bankroll needed depends on win rate and variance (standard deviation). If you move to a bigger and tougher game, the win rate (in bets per hour) will usually go down and the standard deviation will go up (in both bets and dollars per hour). You therefore need a *much* bigger bankroll.

Unfortunately, arrogance may cause you to ignore this reality. It may apply to other people, but not to you. If you won one bet and had a standard deviation of X bets per hour at, say, $5–$10, you can easily delude yourself into thinking that you will win one bet and have a standard deviation of X bets per hour at $10–$20. You may therefore believe that you can beat larger, tougher games, even though you don't have enough talent or bankroll.

Even if you avoid playing above your bankroll or against superior players, arrogance can still hurt you. Perhaps your A-game will beat this table, but you may overlook the fact that you rarely play it, and you aren't playing it *now*. An article about tennis stated that nobody ever plays "My Game," the one we see in our minds.

My Game is a composite of the best shots we ever hit. It's the service ace that we blew past the club champion, that great overhead smash that beat Charlie, that wonderful backhand down the line last Tuesday, and that topspin lob that Bill couldn't reach. In fact, our normal game consists of a few good shots and lots of unforced errors.

You may think the same way about poker. You may remember the great bluffs and calls, the brilliant bets for value, and the moves that won a big pot. You certainly remember bad beats because they help you delude yourself. You probably forget the stupid mistakes and lucky breaks because you want to believe that you play much better than your results would indicate.

Arrogance can also delude you about how well you're playing now, especially if you're losing. Instead of concluding that you're doing something wrong or that the table is too tough for you, you may blame bad luck. Or you ignore the fact that you're tired or had too much to drink or are distracted by something. Your A-game may be good enough to beat these people, but if you're not playing it now, you're probably going to lose.

On this point I must take strong exception to the common imperative: "Always play your best game." *Nobody* always plays his best game at the poker table or any other place. Tiger Woods has missed short putts. Roger Clemens has been knocked out of the box in the first inning. Bill Gates has made stupid business decisions. You aren't superhuman, and it's arrogant to pretend that you can always play your best.

Becoming a full-time professional is another arrogant fantasy. Professor Hayano's *Poker Faces* was based on his doctoral research.[4] That research proved that hardly anyone can make a good career in poker, and many writers, including myself, have told readers to keep their day jobs.

My poker discussion group once considered this issue. One successful, high stakes player (with a WSOP bracelet) estimated that only 2 percent of the wannabes make it, and another bracelet holder said only one half of one percent make it. That is, the odds against succeeding were from 50 to 200 to 1.

But several readers are planning to quit their jobs and move to Las Vegas, Atlantic City, or another poker capital to become full-time pros. They have probably read equally pessimistic estimates of their chances, but arrogance makes them think they will beat the odds. Eventually, most of them will go home with their tails between their legs, complaining about bad luck, short bankrolls, or anything else that will help them deny the reality that they just aren't good enough.[5]

4. David Hyano, *Poker Faces: The Life and Work of Professional Poker Players* (Berkeley, CA: The University of California Press, 1982).

5. Because the poker explosion has brought many weak players into the game, many people are now making much more money than "pros" have ever made. They naturally think they are great players, but they are just feasting off the fish. When the party ends—as it *certainly* will—most of these pros will quickly go broke.

What Should You Do?

What should we do to eliminate our arrogance?: First, recognize that arrogance is a ubiquitous problem. You've got it, I've got it, and so does nearly everyone else. We all want to believe that we are special, and the nature of poker supports our pleasant delusions. Luck has such a huge impact on our short-term results that we can easily believe we play better than we really do. When we win, it's our skill. When we lose, it's bad luck.

Second, develop relationships with people who will puncture that bubble of arrogant fantasies. You probably overestimate your own abilities. I certainly do, but my friends tell me the truth. Find someone who will do the same for you.

Third, believe what you hear. I don't like hearing my friends' criticisms, but I know they're trying to help me. If I listen open-mindedly, I usually realize they're right.[6]

Fourth, never forget that arrogance is both natural and destructive. It makes us feel good about ourselves, but we pay a high price for that short-term pleasure. We have to fight constantly against our natural arrogance to gain the greater and much longer-term satisfactions of beating the game.

---

6. I vividly recall bragging about a hand to my friend, Barry Tanenbaum. He showed me that I had made serious mistakes on the turn and river.

Luck, ESP, and Superstitions

Far too many poker players have silly beliefs, and among the silliest is that they can predict or control their cards. They may not express it explicitly, but at many poker tables you will see lucky charms, changes from "unlucky" to "lucky" seats, and rituals for squeezing or holding cards. You will also hear many stories about lucky cards, unlucky dealers, rushes, and cold streaks.

All beliefs that you can affect your cards are utter, absolute nonsense. Whenever I say that, some people disagree, and they often offer "proof" that I'm wrong, usually anecdotes about amazing, inexplicable personal experiences:

- They had a hunch that a miracle card would come, and they got it.
- They *knew* that an opponent was going to suck out, and he did.
- They were convinced they would win tonight, and they won.
- They knew they shouldn't play tonight, and they lost heavily.
- They changed decks or seats, and they went from cold to hot.
- They lost when Joe dealt, but won when Mary did.

They may also insist that millions of people share their beliefs in luck, ESP, and related subjects such as astrology. So what? Everybody once believed that the earth was flat, and the sun revolved around it.

The number of people who believe something is totally irrelevant, and it does not matter that the believers include prominent people.

Nancy Reagan believed in all sorts of nonsense, including astrology, and hundreds of newspapers carry astrology columns. The world's most famous astronomers once constructed elaborate maps of the universe with the earth as its center, but the maps were total nonsense.

Some great players have stated publicly that you will get bad cards if you expect them. For example, Phil Hellmuth, one of the world's best tournament players, once wrote, "When I start whining at the table about being unlucky, I'm in for some really bad luck. When I throw negative energy out there, complaining about my luck and berating other players, watch out, Phil!"[1]

Charlie Shoten wrote the same sort of nonsense. "Your words are magnets that will draw a winning or losing hand depending on their thought content."[2] He said that he got that insight from *The Awesome Science of Luck*.[3] But there is no *science* of luck. Calling it "science" may make Charlie or other people feel good, but their beliefs are just childish superstitions. Some other great players wear lucky hats, demand deck changes, or have other superstitions. Nonsense is nonsense no matter who says it or how many people believe it.

Television has greatly increased the belief that some players are naturally lucky. Millions of people have seen a few players win repeatedly with terrible cards, and some viewers have tried to emulate them. They don't realize that the television directors show the most dramatic hands. If the best hand beats trash, they probably don't show it because it's not dramatic, but they show the times that long shots and garbage beat much better hands. If someone gets

1. "Attitude, Attitude, Attitude," *Card Player*, October 11, 2002.

2. Charlie Shoten, "Here's Your Choice: You Can Create Incredible Good Luck or be a Victim of Reverse Luck," *Poker Player*, May 29 2006, 38.

3. Peter Ragner, *The Awesome Science of Luck* (Asheville, NC: Roaring Lion, 2005).

lucky a few times on television, gullible people believe he is a "card magnet."

Interestingly, I have heard (but can't confirm) that some of the players who are believed to be supremely lucky are broke and in debt. They got away with taking foolish chances for a while, but the immutable laws of probabilities caught up with them.

There Is *No* Good Evidence That Luck and ESP Exist

The only worthwhile evidence comes from carefully controlled, scientifically acceptable research. If you don't rigorously control the way you gather and analyze data, huge errors are almost inevitable. For example, you cannot purchase a prescription drug unless it's been very carefully tested because sloppy testing (or none at all) has convinced millions of people that junk is useful and safe.

Charlatans and drug companies complain bitterly about the cost and delays of the FDA's rigorous testing procedures, but these tests have protected millions of Americans from useless and dangerous drugs. Similar testing agencies have had the same effects in other countries. Because the FDA does not test them, you can see ads on television for copper bracelets, magnetic amulets, and a host of other useless junk.[4] Gullible people swear by them, but they have absolutely no value. I wish we had an agency like the FDA for lucky charms and similar garbage. Alas, there is nobody to protect the public from the frauds who peddle it or the pseudo-science on which it is based.

The media have irresponsibly reported much of this pseudo-science, but reporters don't have the training or the temperament to evaluate evidence. For example, over fifty years ago Dr. Rhine of Duke University conducted some research that convinced many peo-

---

4. If you go to roaringlionpublishing.com, the website of the publisher of *The Awesome Science of Luck*, you will see that it sells this kind of junk.

ple that ESP had been proved scientifically. That research has been totally discredited, but a Google search for "ESP research at Duke" got
486,000 hits, including some very recent books and articles.

Dr. Rhine was incredibly sloppy. He strenuously resisted adding
controls because every control weakened the effects. He also committed the most unforgivable sin in research: He discarded data that disagreed with his expectations. "He left out the scores of those he
suspected of deliberately guessing wrong. . . . How did he know they
deliberately guessed wrong? Because their scores were too low to
have been due to chance."[5] Of course, he kept the high scores as evidence of ESP. He used purely random variations (and other worthless
information) as "proof" of ESP.

Because the scientific community attacked his work, he slowly
and very reluctantly added controls. When the controls finally became adequate, ESP disappeared completely. He did not produce *any*
scientifically acceptable evidence that ESP exists.

In the fifty odd years since then, nobody else has done so either.
To be accepted, research must be repeatable. If someone repeats your
research, using proper procedures, but does not get the same results,
no competent scientist will accept your findings. The reason is obvious: researchers' biases have caused innumerable mistakes.

Not one single research finding of ESP has ever been repeated
under properly controlled conditions. Many investigators have
claimed to prove its existence, but others can never repeat their results. As one critic put it, positive ESP results mean "Error Some
Place." When you take away the researchers' biases and the sloppy
procedures, ESP always disappears.

The same principle applies to the so-called research on luck. An excellent poker player encouraged me to read Dr. Wiseman's *The Luck*

5. Robert L. Park, *Voodoo Science: The Road from Foolishness to Fraud* (New York:
   Oxford University Press, 2000), 42. This book described many other cases of ir-
   responsible reporting by the media. The principle is clear, *don't* automatically
   believe what you read in the papers and see on TV. Check the evidence.

Factor.[6] He believed that he was a lucky player, and he cited various poker champions' statements about the importance of believing that you're lucky. He loved this book because it supported his own beliefs.

Dr. Wiseman's research was even sloppier than Dr. Rhine's, despite being conducted fifty years later. For example, he had no serious controls, nor did he do much statistical analysis. He just asked people, "Are you lucky or unlucky?" Then he uncritically repeated their anecdotes of wonderful or bad things happening as proof of the power of luck. Anecdotal evidence is utterly unacceptable because you can easily find anecdotes to support almost any belief.

Dr Wiseman went beyond silly claims based on anecdotes. He actually reported data that directly conflicted with his central claim: lucky people are ones for whom seemingly chance events tend to work out consistently in their favor; for example, they win more than their fair share of raffles and lotteries.

His volunteers bought an average of three tickets each in England's National Lottery. Nobody won more than £56 (about $85). Two volunteers, one "lucky," one "unlucky" won that amount. On average both lucky and unlucky participants lost about £2.50. One critic stated: "The description of 'lucky' specifically talks about winning lotteries. Yet people who classified themselves as 'lucky' . . . didn't do any better at the lottery than those who classified themselves as 'unlucky' (though 'lucky' people's expectations of winning were more than twice as high as those of 'unlucky' people). This would seem to indicate that the 'lucky' people who participated in this experiment were anything but. They may have been more optimistic, unrealistic, or self-deluding, but they weren't luckier."[7] I must say that his de-

6. Dr. Richard Wiseman, *The Luck Factor: Changing Your Luck, Changing Your Life: The Four Essential Principles* (New York: Hyperion, 2003).

7. Arlea Hunt-Anschutz, "Maybe Change Your Life, Forget About Changing Your Luck!" Review of *The Luck Factor: Changing Your Luck, Changing Your Life: The Four Essential Principles*, by Dr. Richard Wiseman. www.amazon.com (April 28, 2003).

scription of so-called lucky people as optimistic, unrealistic, and self-deluding fits *many* poker players.

Dr. Wiseman replied: "When it comes to random events like the lottery, such expectations count for little. Someone with a high expectation of winning will do as well as someone with a low expectation. However, life is not like a lottery. Often our expectations make a difference. They make a difference to whether we try something, how hard we persist in the face of failure, how we interact with others and how others interact with us."[8]

His reply deals with the positive effects of believing that you're lucky, a subject I'll discuss later. However, his results—and his own words—clearly indicate that this belief has no effect at all on random events, and the cards in poker are random. Therefore, his research—despite its sloppy procedures—is evidence *against* the belief that you have to think lucky to get good cards.

Why Do So Many People Believe This Nonsense?

The simple answer is that they want to believe it, and it is extremely easy to convince people of something they want to believe. *We have a natural desire to assign reason to randomness,* to believe in some sort of order, to deny that events occur just by chance.

"Some players . . . have a hard time accepting the fact that the cards come off randomly. . . . The human mind has a hard time understanding the concept of *randomness*. The need to seek patterns is a central element of the brain. . . . Unfortunately, poker features a huge amount of randomness; the patterns that we think we see simply confuse us and cause us to play (or think) badly."[9]

This confusion is particularly strong in people who don't understand statistics and probability. However, some other factors are also involved:

8. Ibid.

9. Barry Tanenbaum, "iPods and Poker," *Card Player*, April 5, 2005.

Factor No. 1: Selective attention and remembering cause numerous errors.

People pay much more attention to, and are more likely to remember, the times they *predicted* or *controlled* the cards, but ignore or forget the hundreds of times they failed. You remember having a hunch that the next card would be a club, and a club hits, but forget the times it doesn't. You remember when your lucky cards won a huge pot, but ignore the dozens of times they lost. You remember changing decks and getting hot, but forget the times you changed decks and went broke.

Factor No. 2: Low-probability events do occur, and they have immense impact.

When we have runs of good and bad cards, we naturally think that we're hot or cold and that our good or bad luck will continue. But these streaks are the normal result of randomness, and they have no predictive value. Your chances of having the best cards in the next hand are the same whether you're *hot* or *cold.*

We can see the belief in streaks most clearly in craps. Many people insist that you should press when the dice are hot, and they can remember the times they won a bundle by doing it. But the chances of making a pass are the same regardless of what has just happened. The dice, cards, and roulette wheels have no memories. Casino managers know that "hot dice" *add* to their profits. People get excited, bet more, and—thanks to the laws of probability and the house's edge—they lose more.

Factor No. 3: Confirmation bias makes us seek positive information and minimize contrary facts.

If you believe in ESP, luck, and so on, you may actively seek evidence that supports your beliefs and dismiss criticisms as irrelevant. That's one reason books and articles are still published about the Duke University research long after it was discredited. Reporters and readers want to believe in ESP, and they seek, find, and overestimate the value of sloppy research while dismissing the critics as uninformed or biased.

Factor No. 4. Some people willingly suspend their disbelief.

Many people go further than just ignoring contrary evidence. They have such a strong need to believe in nonsense that they deliberately suspend their critical-thinking abilities. They dismiss contrary evidence and ignore the supporting evidence's inconsistencies and weaknesses.

These points are not sophisticated. In fact, most of them come from Professor Karen Huffman's *Psychology in Action,* the textbook I used to teach college freshmen. Yet some educated, intelligent people, including world-famous players, believe they can predict or influence the cards they catch. When confronted by such a paradox, a psychologist must conclude that some important and unconscious drives make people deny or ignore the evidence.

In simplest terms, people believe in ESP, lucky charms, and other superstitions because they desperately want to deny reality. The fact that the cards are random, unpredictable, and uncontrollable is so frightening that they wish it away. They simply cannot accept that absolutely nothing they do will allow them to predict or control their cards, and that fear costs them an enormous amount of money.

The Positive Effects of Believing That You Are Lucky

Although lucky people don't get better cards than others do, believing that you're lucky can create a positive attitude, and this attitude can provide several major benefits to poker players, especially no-limit tournament players.

- You may become more confident and decisive.
- That confidence may make you more alert to opportunities and more able to exploit them.

- You may accept responsibility for your results instead of blaming them on bad luck.
- You may gain a positive attitude that will help you cope with the inevitable bad beats, losing streaks, and other adversities of poker. Instead of feeling that you can't cope, you will fight back.
- You may intimidate other players; they may not want to confront a fearless and apparently lucky player. Your bluffs will work more often, and you can make other moves.

Mike Caro has said many times that he teaches his students to feel lucky, but he does not let them believe in luck. He wants them to have a positive, "I can do it" attitude, without believing in and becoming dependent on luck.

I discuss some of these psychological effects in the chapters in this book about rushes, losing streaks, and "running bad." Dr. Wiseman makes similar points, and his work would be much more valuable if he had focused on these benefits, rather than conducting and promoting sloppy research.

What Should You Do?

There is a very thin line between having a positive, confident attitude and being arrogant. It pays to think "I'm lucky," but don't ever believe "I'm so lucky that I can buck the odds." They keep building billion-dollar casinos to exploit that belief. If you make enough negative EV bets, you *must* lose.

You must also resist the belief that luck will overcome skill. As I stated in several places, especially in part two, the most important decision in poker is selecting games and situations in which you have an edge. If you let your belief in your own luck make you repeatedly challenge superior players, you *must* lose.

Strive for the positive benefits of believing "I'm lucky" without denying the reality that cards are random:

- Have confidence in yourself.
- Look constantly for opportunities.
- Exploit these opportunities decisively.
- Keep fighting when things are going badly.
- Keep trying to intimidate the opposition.
- But don't overdo it. If you believe that your luck will over-come the odds or superior skill, you are doomed, maybe not today, but certainly over the long term.

Our game is ruthlessly fact-oriented. If you have pocket kings and another player has aces, you will lose four fifths of the time no matter what you believe. If you call huge bets with weak cards, you will win a few times, but you must ultimately lose heavily. The same result is inevitable if you play against better players.

The laws of randomness and probability apply to you, to me, and to everyone else. If Mother Teresa were alive and played poker, they would apply to her too. So throw away your lucky hat, ignore your hunches about what cards are coming, stop asking for new decks, and so on. Instead of trying to control or predict your cards, concentrate on picking games you can beat and improving your play of the cards you're dealt.

We Need a Miranda Warning

Every poker room should have a sign saying: "Warning, anything you say can be used against you." Since poker is a game of information management, your goal should be to get as much information as possible while giving away almost no information. Every time you *give away information*, you are essentially *giving away chips*.

Yet people do it all the time. They tell bad beat stories, show their hands, discuss their strategy, criticize and lecture other players, and give away lots of other information.

Why Are Players So Foolish?

Players are foolish because they care more about their own feelings than they do about winning. They may claim to play to win, but they hurt their results by trying to satisfy other needs.

Ego-building is usually the most important need. Many players care more about *looking* like good players than they do about *being* good players. Poker is a very bottom line game, and the bottom line is extremely simple: the more chips you win, the better player you are.

Even though there are no points for style, many people emphasize it. Instead of focusing on results—the only thing that counts—they try to impress other people about how well they play. Because some damned fool wants to show how smart he is, he tells others how they misplayed hands, or he describes his own brilliant plays. He is too stupid to realize that telling people about their mistakes will either drive them away or help them play better, and telling them how he plays will help others beat him.

177

Ego-building combines with a need for sympathy to cause poker's greatest plagues: bad beat stories and endless complaints about bad luck. The storytellers want sympathy and reassurance, but all they do is irritate people, create an "I'm a loser" image (which undermines their entire game), and tell others how to beat them.

If you doubt me, just remember the last time somebody described his bad beat or unlucky night. Did you listen sympathetically? Did you really care? Or did you just wait for an opportunity to tell your own story?

What you should have done was listen carefully and make a mental note about how you could use this information against the storyteller.

Giving Away a Knife to Slit Their Own Throats

If you listen, a few dummies will tell you *exactly* how to beat them. They may as well be giving away a knife to slit their own throats. I will give you a few examples; you will frequently hear similar stories. Many people have an extreme need to tell stories, give lectures, and complain.

You may be one of those people, or you may avoid them or "tune out" when they talk. These reactions are understandable, but incorrect. Instead, remember that information equals chips: give away as little as possible, and constantly try to get more of it.

All the following statements were confirmed by later observations. The comments after the word "Thanks" tell how you can use that information against them.

- "I'm not aggressive. I won't raise unless I'm almost certain I've got the winner." *Thanks*. The next time you raise, I'm outta here.

- "I'll always bet on the flop if I'm last and nobody has bet." *Thanks*. The next time I have a good hand and you're last, I'll go for a check-raise.

- "I'll call all the way with anything, if a pot is big enough, but I'm not willing to make loose calls for small pots." *Thanks.* Now I know when to value bet and bluff you.

- "I never check-raise because I believe in betting my own hands." *Thanks.* The next time you check, I'll *know* you have a weak hand. I can bluff with garbage or value bet a marginal hand without fear of a raise.

You may be thinking, "Nobody in my game would make such stupid remarks," but even players in major tournaments do it. For example, *Poker Digest's* interview with Matt Lessinger[1] told how a player's foolish remark gave away his hand, allowing Lessinger to knock him out of the Carnivale of Poker Pot Limit Championship (with a prize pool of over $150,000). Lessinger won that tournament, and this hand helped him do it.

The next time you're tempted to talk, show your cards, or give away any other information remember the Miranda Warning: *Anything you say can be used against you.*

Sam Rayburn, former Speaker of the U.S. House of Representatives, knew how important it was to get information instead of giving it away. He had a sign in his office: "You ain't learning nothing when you're talking."

To improve your bottom line, talk less and listen more.

1. Matt Lessinger, "Meet Our Matt", interview by Lee Munzer, *Poker Digest*, September 21, 2000, 33.

Paranoia at the Poker Table

If someone told us that the Martians were conspiring against us, we would know he's nuts. But at poker tables, we sometimes ignore or accept essentially paranoid delusions. *The Synopsis of Psychiatry* defines paranoia as "extreme suspiciousness, usually not based on a realistic assessment of the situation . . . [including] a perceived community of plotters."[1] Some paranoids suffer from delusions of grandeur: the conspirators are after him because he is so special. We see paranoia frequently, but may not recognize it or realize how crazy it is.

Some Examples

Countless people have said, "I've been cheated online." Of course, there is some cheating online, but it also happens in live games. Gambling has always attracted cheaters. That's why casinos have professional dealers, floor people, and video cameras. Rational suspiciousness is not paranoia, nor is protecting yourself against significant dangers. But insisting that you've been cheated without evidence is paranoid.

Complaints fall into two categories:

1. Cheating by other players
2. Cheating by the websites

1. Harold Kaplan and Benjamin J. Sadock, *Synopsis of Psychiatry: Behavioral Sciences/Clinical Psychiatry*, 8th ed. (Baltimore: Williams & Wilkins, 1998).

Is it easier for players to cheat online? Of course it is, and there is no question that collusion and other forms of cheating are serious problems. However, it is also much easier to catch cheaters. Every hand is completely recorded, but in live games, the house sees very few hands, and it usually cannot thoroughly review hands after they are over. Because they know that cheaters can destroy their business, poker websites work very hard to catch cheaters. They have programs that will automatically identify patterns that suggest collusion;[2] when a pattern is found, they investigate carefully.

If they receive a complaint, they will analyze every bet made during the hand, plus lots of other evidence (such as whether certain people have played together frequently and how they have played at other times). If they decide that people are cheating, their accounts will be debited or frozen, and funds will be transferred to the victims. Russ Hamilton, 1994 WSOP champion, told our discussion group: "Online games are safer than live games."

Cheating by the websites occasionally occurs. There is a lot of money involved, and the websites are not tightly regulated. However, it would be insane for a large website's owners to cheat customers. Online games are spectacularly profitable. They have much lower expenses, but deal far more hands per hour than live cardrooms. Some cheating is almost inevitable, but it is the exception, not the norm. The website owners are not going to kill the goose that is laying so many golden eggs.

After taking their company public, the owners of PartyPoker.com became *billionaires*. The owners of many other websites are making many millions of dollars a year, and some of them will soon go public. Do you seriously believe that any rational business owner would risk destroying such a gold mine to make a few dollars by cheating you?

Despite these obvious facts, some people insist that cheating is all

---

2. I have discussed this issue with Avner Mart, a software engineer who developed anticollusion software for a major poker website.

over the Internet, and there are dozens of complaints about online cheating for every one in live games. Many complainers offer ridiculous "evidence," and some offer absolutely none. For example, I've read posts on Internet forums that say, "I won when I first started, but now I'm behind. They let newcomers win to get them hooked, then fleece them."

But exactly the same pattern occurs all the time in live games. You win, then you lose; what's so unusual about that? A few beginners win their first time in a cardroom and then lose ten times in a row. Were they cheated? Obviously not. They got lucky, and then their bad play caught up to them.

In a comment posted to twoplustwo.com's Internet Magazine Forum, a player insisted that the "online poker is rigged 100% & if you continue to play you will lose all of your money." Thousands of people read that series of posts, and dozens of people agreed. I replied, "Since several of my friends make a nice living playing online, I have extreme doubts about your conclusion. . . . The conclusion that online is 100% rigged is not justified without *very solid* evidence, and you have not presented *any* evidence." Since he knew of the *Poker Digest* version of this chapter, he requested that I send it to him.

After reading it and a personal message that said his suspicions were not justified, he became enraged. He insisted that he had beaten the pros at one site, "before they rigged my account." He then lost his entire bankroll playing $25–$50 blinds, no-limit hold'em against John Juanda. He offered no evidence other than the fact that he had won and then lost. When I made the obvious point that John is one of the world's best players, he got even angrier and accused me of being ignorant or part of a conspiracy against other players and him. He insisted, "I know I can play with anyone in the world."

He is an unusually obvious case of paranoia:

- He offers no evidence that he had been cheated.
- He states that cheating is the only possible cause for his losses, despite losing to a great player.

- He states that those (including me) who disagreed must be ignorant or part of the conspiracy.
- He has obvious delusions of grandeur ("I can play with anyone in the world").

But what about less delusional players who have beaten live games, then lost online against players at the same limits that they beat live? Some people insist they must have been cheated because they have always been winners. That position violates one of science's most important rules: Before deciding on a cause, you must reject all other likely explanations.

A winning live-game player may lose online for many reasons, including:

- He is dependent on tells and a feel for players.
- He is uncomfortable playing on a computer.
- He can't adjust to the games' higher speeds
- He is up against online players who are either better or the wrong style for his type of play.

In fact, many *losers* believe they beat live games just because they keep bad records. They forget how many chips they buy or how often and how much they lose, but exaggerate their good nights. Their results online are the same as in live games, but the websites keep accurate records. Selective forgetting is a major cause for the online losses of many self-proclaimed winners.

Most of the "I've been cheated!" complainers never seriously consider these other possibilities, especially the one about bad records. They insist: "I'm a good player. I have always won before, and cheating is the only possible explanation for my online losses." Nonsense! Until you can clearly reject all other possibilities, you have no right to claim that your losses were caused by cheating.

Let's look at a much more common form of paranoia: At times

many people have asked themselves: "Why am I being punished with such terrible luck?" Even if they don't express it so directly, they may try to manipulate the poker gods by changing seats or tables, demanding a new deck of cards, or promising to be nicer to their families if their luck will just change. Being unhappy about bad luck is normal, but believing that it's some sort of punishment or trying to manipulate the poker gods is a form of paranoia.

What Causes Poker Paranoia?

Poker players aren't any crazier than other people, but paranoia occurs fairly frequently. Why? I can think of two main reasons (and there may be others):

1. Paranoia protects egos.
2. Randomness is profoundly frightening.

Cause No. 1: Ego Protection

Blaming cheaters makes people feel better than admitting that they don't play well enough to win. Instead of looking critically at the way they play, they avoid responsibility by blaming others. Losing can't be their fault because they play well; they lose because of those crooked websites or dealers, cheating players, and spiteful poker gods.

Cause No. 2: Fear of Randomness

This fear is part of nearly everyone's psychology, and it is the primary cause for religions, superstitions, and silly betting systems.[3] Deep down we don't want to believe that nobody is in charge, that cards, coin flips, dice, roulette wheels, and so on, are absolutely ran-

---

3. For more discussion on this subject, see the chapter called "Luck, ESP, and Superstitions," p. 167 in this book.

dom. We desperately want to believe that *something* is in control. Then, if we could figure out a way to understand or manipulate it, we could have power over our destinies. We blame cheaters and change decks, dealers, tables, seats, and casinos because we can't accept that we can do absolutely nothing in the short term to influence or predict random variables.

This fear is increased by the fact that most people don't understand how randomness operates. Authorities have written that a few people will win two tournaments purely by chance, but most people will conclude they must be extremely skilled. Malmuth and others have written about how large a bankroll one needs to avoid going broke, and many people think they are exaggerating. If you don't understand the laws of probability, you can easily conclude that some *purely random* events are proof that something mysterious is happening.

Recommendations

Five actions can reduce the effects of paranoia, but you can't stop it completely:

1. Monitor yourself.

Keep asking yourself: "Is this idea based on reality or paranoia?" Remember that you *want* to believe that you're a good player, and this desire can distort your thinking. If you are not sure, ask someone you trust. You may be surprised—and dismayed—by the answer.

2. Accept responsibility.

If you are losing for more than a short time, it's probably *your* fault. Of course, several authorities have written that you can lose for a long period just on bad luck, but the odds are against it. It's *much* more likely that you're doing something wrong, and you won't win until you accept the responsibility for your results and work on your game.

3. Accept randomness.

It is a fact, just as concrete a fact as the page you are reading or the chair you are sitting on. Since there is absolutely nothing you can do to control random events, you *must* learn to live with that reality.

4. Learn the laws of probability.

I do *not* mean just memorizing the odds of making a straight or a flush. I mean the underlying laws and their logic. If you do not understand them, you will draw many foolish conclusions. The "long run" is much, much longer than most people believe.

5. Focus on things you can control.

In poker you have more control than in other casino games. You can control the way you play your cards, the games you select, and the seats you choose. These decisions should all be made—not in the hope of getting lucky—but for strategic reasons. If you play your cards well, choose the right games, and take seats that give you good position, you will win, perhaps not tonight, but certainly over the long term. If you do not make good decisions, you will lose over the long term, and it will be *entirely* your own fault.

Machismo

Although men have a natural edge at poker,[1] machismo—which is exaggerated masculinity—can be extremely destructive. Poker looks like a macho game, and some men (and a few women) try to prove their machismo by being too aggressive. Usually, they just prove that they are foolish. Poker is actually a predatory game, and *machismo violates the fundamental law of all predators: Attack the weakest prey.*

Definitions

The word comes from the same Latin root as "masculine," and men are much more likely than women to be foolishly macho. *Webster's* dictionary contained two definitions:

1. "A strong sense of masculine pride: an exaggerated masculinity"
2. "An exaggerated or exhilarating sense of power or strength"

Note that both definitions include "exaggerated," and this exaggeration causes the problems.

Machismo's Positive Elements

Poker is not a game for timid people. Unless you have some self-confidence, "heart," and aggression, you don't stand a chance.

1. See "Male and Female Advantages," p. 86 in this book.

1. You must have enough confidence in your judgment to act decisively.
2. You must take stands to prevent aggressive players from running over you.
3. You must bet and raise to protect your hands and get the full value from them.
4. You need enough cockiness to create a strong image.

That's the good news, but there's lots of bad news.

Machismo's Dangers

Many men and a few women are *too* macho. By definition, machismo is *exaggerated*, and poker is a brutally realistic game. If you don't understand, accept, and work within your limitations, you are going to pay for it. Let's look at some of the mistakes or dangers machismo can cause.

Playing Above Your Financial or Psychological Bankroll

You may play in games you can't afford. You either don't have enough money or can't psychologically handle the swings. Instead of admitting and working within your limitations, if you play above them, you will get clobbered.

Playing Against Superior Competition

Many experts have stated that game selection is extremely important, and we have two wonderful aphorisms:

1. Already mentioned, but worth repeating, "It's no good to be the tenth best player in the world if the other nine are at your table."
2. "If you look around the table and don't see the sucker, you're it."

Unfortunately, if you are really macho, you may not accept that others are better than you are. You may try to prove your toughness by playing against people you should avoid. Some excellent players are huge losers because they cannot resist the temptation to play against better players.[2] They deliberately seek tough games. If they are at a table with many weak players and a few strong ones, they deliberately attack the strong ones. It is more fun to beat a good player than a bad one, but it is immeasurably more profitable to focus on the weak ones.

Playing Inferior Cards

We all know that tight play is essential, but waiting for premium cards is boring and—to some people—a sign of weakness. They say, in effect, "*You* have to wait for premium cards, but you're a wimp. *I* have the courage and skill to play weaker cards." Of course, playing weak cards is a prescription for disaster, especially against strong players, but some people can't restrain themselves. If you find yourself playing weak cards, look hard at yourself. Machismo may be a cause for your foolishness.

Playing Too Aggressively

A few people go beyond just playing inferior cards; they *over*play them (and their other hands) to prove that "I'm a real gambler." This form of silliness is especially common when a man is trying to impress a woman. Of course, many women think he is childish, and the good players exploit his stupidity.

Overprotecting Their Blinds

Some macho fools regard attacks on their blinds as personal challenges, almost insults. They say, in effect, "Don't you know who I

---

2. See the discussion of Andy Beal's loss of $50,000,000 in the chapter called "Arrogance," p. 161, in this book. Arrogance and machismo are very closely related.

am?" They lose lots of bets with weak hands from a terrible position just to prove that "nobody runs over me."

Challenging Someone to Heads-Up Matches

These challenges are the poker equivalent of "You wanna step outside?" They rarely result in actual heads-up games, but the individuals involved may play as if beating each other was their primary objective. They focus too much on each other, ignore the rest of the table, try too many fancy plays, and give their money to the by-standers.

Seeking Revenge

This mistake is extremely common, and it's a factor in some of the other situations I've described. Anytime you wage war on a specific player, you'll probably hurt your bottom line. First, you give your enemy an advantage because your emotions affect your judgment. Second, while you are taking foolish chances to beat him up, the other players can clobber both of you.

Criticizing or Lecturing Other Players

Countless authorities have stated that criticizing or lecturing reduces your profits by driving away weaker players or teaching them (and others) how to play better. Yet many people do it. Why? Because putting down other players makes macho fools feel superior.

Lying About Results

These lies are extremely common. In fact, if you believed what people say about their results, you may wonder who loses all the money that so many people claim to win. Lying protects egos, but prevents people from recognizing their limitations and taking steps to overcome them.

Why Are Macho People So Foolish?

Every one of those mistakes will obviously cost you money. But you have probably made a few of them, *even though you knew better.* You made them because—at least for the moment—proving your machismo became more important to you than your bottom line.

Recommendations

A few simple recommendations will reduce the dangers.

Don't try to prove ANYTHING about yourself.

If you try to prove your machismo, skill or anything else, it's going to cost you. At the end of the year, the only thing that matters is how much you win or lose. Roy Cooke said it best: poker is "not about winning respect. It's about winning chips."[3]

Monitor your motives.

Constantly ask yourself, "*Why* did I do that?" If you did it to increase your EV, it will probably improve your results. If you did it for any other reason—especially trying to impress people—it will probably cost you money.

Understand and work within your limitations.

Many of these errors violate this principle, and they are caused by a misunderstanding of poker's essential nature. It *looks* like a macho game, but it is really a predatory one. Successful predators attack *only* when they have an edge, and their first rule is *attack the weak.*

If lions were macho, they would attack adult elephants; one would feed them for months. But lions are smarter than macho poker players. They and all other predators avoid strong prey and go after the

3. Roy Cooke, "Perception, Deception, Respect, and Results," *Card Player,* January 23, 1998, 13.

weakest, most vulnerable animals, such as the aged, the feeble, babies, and pregnant females. It isn't macho, but it keeps them alive.

The same rule applies to poker winners: they attack *only* when they have an edge, and they don't care whether it comes from being a stronger player, having better cards, being in a better position, or any other factor.

Doing so is the exact opposite of machismo. It requires brutal honesty about yourself, other players, and the essential nature of our game. It demands sacrificing the temporary pleasures of building your ego and putting down others for the much longer and more important pleasure of improving your bottom line. But winning money is what poker is all about.

Preventing and Handling Tilt

If you go on tilt, you can quickly lose your entire stack. If you stay on extreme tilt long enough, you can lose everything you own: your bankroll, your savings, your business, and even your home and family. It has happened repeatedly. Someone on tilt is out of control, and severely uncontrolled people can easily destroy themselves.

Because luck has such huge short-term effects, you can occasionally go on tilt without losing any money or even realizing that you're off balance. However, since the dangers are so great, you should constantly watch out for it.

Definition

Tilt is often defined too narrowly. Many people use the term only for playing too many hands too aggressively. It is the most visible and destructive type of tilt, but there is another form. After losing too much money or having some bad beats, you may become so upset, frightened, or convinced you cannot win that you "play scared."

Your play can deteriorate so much that the "I can't win" belief becomes a self-fulfilling prophecy. Because you think you can't win, you play in ways that cause you to lose. You may check when you should bet and call or even fold when you should raise. This form of tilt is less dramatic and noticeable than wild aggression, but it can be very destructive. Perhaps you won't take such large short-term losses, but—because it's harder to recognize—this form of tilt can last much longer.

This point relates to tilt's second dimension: time. Tilt can be quite brief or last for a long time. Very short-term tilt is yielding to an impulse, while long-term tilt is continuing to act foolishly for emotional reasons.

A steam raise is an example of very brief tilt; a player may be so upset by previous hands that he raises this one on nothing more than his anger. Conversely, a few players have gone on tilt and stayed there for days, weeks, or even longer, getting deeper and deeper into trouble. A common, but incorrect, term for long-term tilt is "nervous breakdown." Some people *never* recover from various traumatic events.[1] Poker rarely causes such a breakdown, but it can happen.

Some people have even called a very brief period of tilt "alien-hand syndrome." They feel that their brains have lost control over their hands. They watch, almost helplessly, while their hand does something stupid with their chips or cards. For example, Jan Fisher wrote: "What was I supposed to do, and what did I do? Well, the answers are as different as night and day. With my arm in 'alien-hand syndrome' mode, I mucked the two eights without a thought."[2]

The critical words are "without a thought." Poker is a thinking game, and Jan ruefully admitted that she didn't think. She just acted. Note that her tilt lasted only a moment, that it was the playing scared type, and that—as she admitted in that article—it cost her a chance to get some desperately needed chips. Also, note that she learned from the experience.

Because they are out of control, some people shift erratically from one type of tilt to another. For example, after losing a bad beat because he timidly gave away a free card, a scared player may overreact: "I'm not going to let anybody draw out on me again, I'm raising all-in!" A wildly aggressive player may suddenly realize how much

1. The psychiatrists call it Post-Traumatic Stress Disorder, and it can last forever.

2. Jan Fisher, "My No-Limit Hold'em Learning Curve Lesson," *Card Player,* May 23, 2003.

money his craziness has cost him, but will be unwilling to quit playing. He may think, "I can't keep playing like this, but I've got to get even. I'm going to play super-tight to build up my stack."

People who shift from one extreme to another may think they are doing it for rational reasons. "I'm switching gears to keep the other players off balance." Sometimes, of course, people change styles for exactly that reason. The important issue is their motives. If they are doing it to confuse people and they pick their spots well, shifting gears is probably a good move. If they are doing it for emotional reasons or they do not know why they are doing it, it may be a complicated form of tilt.

If you're always timid or wildly aggressive, you're not on tilt; you're just playing in your usual foolish and emotionally based way. I'll use a broad definition: "tilt" means that you are making bad plays—ones you wouldn't usually make—for emotional or unknown reasons. There are three important points:

- Tilt is a much broader concept than many people believe.
- People on tilt often do not recognize why they are acting out of character.
- Tilt is *extremely* dangerous.

Preventing Tilt

Since you can go on tilt, you should learn how to handle it, but it is much better to prevent it. There is an old saying, "An ounce of prevention is worth a pound of cure." It applies to many kinds of disasters. For example, it is immeasurably easier to prevent a heart attack or a fire than it is to fix one.

Good professionals emphasize preventing problems more than solving them. Insurance companies tell clients how to lower the chances of accidental fires. Good doctors recommend diet and exercise to avoid heart attacks.

Exactly the same principle applies to tilt. Once you have gone on tilt, you may be unable to regain control. You are on a slippery slope toward trouble, and you often slide faster and faster. For example, a poster on an online forum said that he lost a trivial amount: $100 in a $2–$4 game. Instead of shrugging it off, he became so obsessed with getting even that he kept moving to larger games and lost several thousand dollars that night.

A few people *never* regain control. They keep getting crazier and crazier until their ATM and credit cards are maxed out. So they borrow every cent they can get. Then they may become so desperate that they commit crimes. You probably are too sensible to act so foolishly, but don't be too sure. Some of the people who destroyed themselves once had tight control of themselves.

The principle is clear: If you wait until you're on tilt before taking corrective action, some of the damage has already been done, and your problems will be *much* harder to solve. So stop tilt *before* it starts with the following steps:

Step No. 1: Master poker theory and odds.

The more thoroughly you understand these subjects, the less likely you are to lose control. Malmuth once wrote: "Emotional control is . . . aided by a thorough understanding of how the game should be played." Without that understanding, you may overreact to events that would not severely upset a more informed player.

For example, many bad beat stories show that the storyteller doesn't understand the most basic fact of poker, the odds. People whine that they raised with ace-queen suited and were called and beaten by someone with king-deuce offsuit. They seem to believe that their hand should never lose, but it was really only about a 2-to-1 favorite, meaning it will lose about one third of the time. Or take ace-king versus a pair of deuces. Some people think that ace-king is a huge favorite, but every knowledgeable player knows that it is a small underdog. If you don't understand the odds and theory, you can easily overreact to predictable losses.

Step No. 2: Keep good records.

As I mentioned earlier, if you know how much you have won or lost this year, the bad beat you just took or tonight's loss will become less important. One pot or one bad night doesn't have that much effect on your long-term results. That's why so many experts recommend treating all sessions as parts of one continuous poker game. When you put a bad beat or a session's loss into a larger context, you're much less likely to overreact.

Step No. 3: Identify your triggers and warning signals.

You can't prevent tilt without knowing the triggers that cause it and the signals that suggest you're in danger. You should carefully review the times you have gone on tilt and recognize the factors that preceded it. Then when you see them recurring, you can protect yourself. Don't restrict yourself to obvious causes such as having a bad beat, taking a huge loss, or drinking too much. They are certainly important, but you should consider four types of warnings.

- Type No. 1: Events at the poker table. Do you overreact to having bad beats, being card dead, losing too much money, playing with weak or excellent players, sitting with obnoxious loudmouths, or even having an incompetent or irritating dealer?

- Type No. 2: Distant events. Have you played poorly after problems at work or home or with your health or with impersonal events such as a nasty driver or heavy traffic? Have you taken prescription or street drugs? Have you had too much to drink?[3]

---

3. Drinking is particularly dangerous because it causes both poor judgment and blindness to its effects. Countless drunks have played terribly while insisting that they are in complete control of themselves. Once you pass a certain point, it may be very difficult to stop. The only sensible thing is *to completely avoid alcohol while playing.*

- Type No. 3: Signs of thinking badly. You should frequently compare the way you are thinking now and your usual pattern. For example, you may usually remember your cards and the board but find that you have to keep checking them. Or a player you know sits down, and you cannot remember how he plays. You clearly are not thinking as well as you usually do.

- Type No. 4: Signs of harmful moods or emotions. If you find yourself getting irritated by trivial things that would not normally bother you, you may be in danger. For example, if you overreact to a slow or chatty dealer or a loud, obnoxious player, you may be at risk, even if your play has not changed.

Note that type numbers 3 and 4 require you to monitor yourself, not just your environment. A part of you has to be a detached observer, telling you that you're not thinking and acting as well as usual.

Your goal should be to become much more conscious of the factors that signal that you are in danger.[4] These factors are individualistic. You may not even notice things that really bother me, and vice versa. Remember what caused or preceded past tilts; then avoid as many of them as possible. Of course, you can't avoid all triggers, but you can avoid alcohol, nasty people, and many others.

Step No. 4: Question your motives.

You should always be aware of what is happening around you and also what is going on inside your head and body. The poker literature emphasizes observing others, and doing so is extremely impor-

---

4. This approach is essentially the same as the ones doctors use to prevent heart attacks. You may have taken tests in which you give yourself points for your weight, blood pressure, cholesterol, exercise, and other coronary risk factors. If your score is too high, you're in danger, even if you have never had a heart attack.

tant. But you should watch yourself even more closely. If you miss a signal from another player, it will cost you a few bets or a pot. If you miss a signal that you're going on tilt, it may cost you your bankroll or more.

Constantly scrutinize both your play and your emotional state. Ask yourself again and again:

- Am I playing well?
- What was my reason for making that play?
- Am I angry, confused, sleepy, or eager for revenge?
- Am I feeling the effects of alcohol?

If you don't recognize how off balance you are, you can take huge losses.

There are many similar questions, but people rarely ask or answer them. The poker culture is extremely anti-introspection. We would rather focus on how other people think, feel, and act than seriously analyze ourselves. In fact, your opponents will often see that you are on tilt or approaching it long before you do.

Step No. 5: Explain your decisions.

Imagine that an expert is looking at your cards and watching how you play them. He is essentially acting as your "conscience," checking everything you do. Can you give him a clear, logical explanation for every move you made? If not, your emotions (or some other factor such as being distracted) are probably affecting your decisions. You should always know why you have made a significant decision.

Would you be embarrassed by anything you've done? If you can't give a good explanation for an embarrassing decision, you may be on tilt or heading in that direction. Regard your confusion and embarrassment as warnings. Either get back into control or get out.

Step No. 6: Don't try to get even.

Perhaps the stupidest words in poker are "I've got to get even," and countless people have said them. When you feel that way, you are in danger of turning an unpleasant loss into a catastrophe. You can get further off balance, play more poorly or perhaps go to a larger game or the craps table, desperately trying to get even.

The money you have lost is gone, and you should try to ignore it. Sklansky wrote: "So many otherwise good players ... play badly when they are losing. The basic problem is that they can't be content with getting back just a portion of their losses for that session.... They want to go to sleep a winner, and if they don't, how much they lose doesn't matter."[5]

Instead of worrying about how much you have lost, concentrate on your current prospects. If you have a *realistic* chance to win, stay. And remember that you are likely to overestimate your chances of winning. If you are not confident about your chances of winning, quit. Keep in mind that tonight's results don't matter that much; only the long term really counts.

Step No. 7: Go home or log off if you think you are in danger.

Although I'll discuss ways to handle tilt, *don't wait until you're sure you're on tilt.* If your play is deteriorating or you see that you're getting upset, *stop playing.* That advice is often ignored. You may recognize the signs, but keep playing because you won't admit that you're off balance. Or you may think, "Perhaps I'm not playing my best, but this game is too good to leave." You may say it even when the game is too tough for you.

You may think I'm being too conservative, but if you go on tilt, you can lose your bankroll or take even worse losses. There will always be another poker game, but—if you go on tilt long enough—you may not be able to play in it. Since you may be unable to assess

---

5. David Sklansky, *Poker, Gaming & Life* (Henderson, NV: Two Plus Two, 2000) 20.

yourself or the competition objectively, do the smart thing: *stop playing.*

Handling Tilt

Eventually, almost everybody finds himself on tilt, at least for a few minutes. It doesn't matter why or when it happens; the important point is that you're responding to your emotions, not your intellect.

If you can recognize it, you are *way* ahead of many players. They can be completely off balance, but not know it. Even if you recognize your condition, you may not fully accept its implications. You may not realize how badly you're playing, or you may underestimate your competition. You may know that you're not playing your best, but think that you can still beat this game. Of course, if your play has really deteriorated or if the competition is tough, you can take a real bath. If you won't go home, at least take some steps to minimize tilt's destructive effects.

Step No. 1: Keep quiet.

When you are hurting, you may want to tell everyone how you feel, but it's exactly the wrong thing to do. You may hope for sympathy, but give away information that comes back to haunt you. You may whine about bad beats, say that you're playing scared, or growl, "Since they beat my good hands, I'll play trash." The effect is obvious and extremely destructive: you tell opponents how to adjust to you.

You have seen criminals get Miranda warnings on many television shows, and, as I said in the chapter called "We Need a Miranda Warning" (see p. 177), the same principle applies to poker: anything you say can be used against you. You don't want people to know how badly you're hurting or how it's affected your play.

Step No. 2: Don't pray to the poker gods.

They aren't listening; in fact, they don't even exist. As I mentioned earlier, your cards are always random, and praying or any other ritual such as squeezing your cards or changing seats or decks will accomplish absolutely nothing. If you find yourself taking silly actions, hoping to change your luck, *stop!*

Recognize that you are being irrational, and push those thoughts from your mind. Focus on the only thing you can control: your own decisions, especially, how can I regain my *psychological balance?*

Step No. 3: Use the buddy system.

Since it is usually easier to see that someone else is on tilt than to recognize it in yourself, agree with one or more friends that you will help each other. If one of you is on tilt or in danger of getting there, you should very quietly tell him. For example, your friend may pull you aside and say, "You would not usually three-bet a solid player with king-jack offsuit. Why did you do it?" or "I noticed that you did not value bet on the river, and I wonder whether you are playing scared."[6]

Step No. 4: Take a break.

Get away from the table and think about something besides poker, especially the things that upset you such as bad beats and tonight's losses. Enhance the break by taking a walk, watching television, telephoning someone, or doing whatever shifts your attention from poker.

If you can't help thinking about poker, *don't* focus on bad beats or losses. It will just make you more upset. Analyze everybody's play, including your own. What are you doing right and wrong? How are the others playing? How should you change your strategy?

---

6. A good friend told me that my frequent suggestions to trade help with others are unrealistic because poker players are too competitive to help each other. I agree that most people won't do it, but most people lose. To be a winner, you have to take many unnatural, but useful actions.

Step No. 5: Put yourself into your opponents' shoes.

What do they probably think about the way you have played recently? How will they adjust to you? Since the wildly aggressive form of tilt is so visible, the better players will see it and adjust their strategies. However, the oblivious ones may not have noticed anything, or they may not understand what your play meant. Focus primarily on the better, more observant players.

The passive, timid form of tilt is much less obvious, and many people may not have noticed it. They don't know what is happening inside you. All they know is what they saw you do, and passive play isn't very visible. In addition, some people are much less aware than you may think they are.

You must counter any adjustments that your opponents are making. If you have been too aggressive, your bets and raises will not be respected. If they have recognized that you have been playing scared, they will try to run over you. Recognize what they are doing and adjust your strategy.

Step No. 6: Consider changing tables.

The players at the new table won't know that you've been on tilt. Moving will also get you away from the people who gave you bad beats or otherwise upset you. If you don't want to move because you want "revenge" or to express other feelings toward someone, then you are *certainly* on tilt. Your emotions are affecting your thoughts and actions. Recognize how vulnerable you are, and *get away from that table!*

Step No. 7: Avoid fancy plays.

If you're playing your best, you may be able to make moves on these players. Since you're off balance and don't have either your usual judgment or the right table image, stay close to the formulas. If "the book" says fold, call, or raise, do it. To adjust to your table image, overcorrect a *little* from your previous play. If you were playing scared, be a *bit* more aggressive than the book recommends. If you've been too aggressive, be *slightly* too conservative. But don't overdo it.

Step 9: Keep monitoring yourself.

From a psychologist's perspective, the central gambling problem is denial of reality. It's strongest and most dangerous when you're on tilt or any other form of emotional disturbance. Every mental health professional knows that many disturbed people don't know that they are unbalanced, and that they often won't take their medication because they think they don't need it. The same process occurs with tilt.

The more off balance you are, the less likely you are to realize it. For example, I have tried to warn friends that they were on tilt. Even if the signs were obvious, they usually rejected my comments. A few of them became quite hostile. "I'm fine. I can beat these jerks. Mind your own business." This reaction is most common when someone has been drinking. Their defensiveness showed how tilted they were, but they didn't want to hear it.

You may not want to believe that you're playing badly for emotional reasons, but you can't afford to deny that reality. Accept that almost everyone occasionally gets off balance and that admitting it is both intelligent and mentally healthy. If your attempts to regain your balance aren't successful *quickly*, accept that it's not your night, shrug your shoulders, and do the only intelligent thing: *go home or log off!*

Afterthought

We have seen that unconscious and emotional factors are *much* more important than many poker players and nearly all poker writers believe.[1] They emphasize the rational, thinking side of poker, even though emotions and unconscious factors affect everything we do, at the poker table and everywhere else.

Economists made the same mistake, plus two others, for over a century. Until fairly recently most economic books were based on three absurd assumptions:[2]

1. People's primary (or only) motive is to maximize their profits.
2. People consider all their alternatives and then make rational (i.e., profit-maximizing) choices.
3. People work in perfect markets.

Economists weren't blind or stupid. They could see that everyone had many other motives—including quite irrational ones—and that these motives were often much stronger than the desire for maximum profits. They knew that people did not even look at many of their alternatives and that they made irrational choices for many rea-

---

1. Perhaps they don't really believe that unconscious and emotional factors can be ignored, but their published works clearly give that impression.
2. You will occasionally see these assumptions in somewhat modified form in books published recently. However, most modern economists are much less simplistic.

sons. They could not help noticing that monopolies, cartels, governments, and other factors interfered with markets. Yet several generations of economists clung to these absurd assumptions.

Why did they act so foolishly? Because it was easier to work with that simple, but fatally flawed, model of people and markets than to deal with the more complicated realities of the world they lived in.

Poker players and writers cling to their delusion of rationality because it seems to make their life simpler. Instead of having to consider the effects of emotions and unconscious factors, they just pretend they don't exist or matter that much. When they do mention them at all, they usually insist that people should ignore or control irrational thoughts, feelings, and actions.

But ignoring or minimizing them is supremely irrational, a form of denial which actually increases their destructive effects. The absolutely indispensable first step toward becoming a more rational player is to recognize the irrational forces that affect you, me, and everyone else. Only then can you take steps to reduce their destructiveness. However, absolutely nothing will completely eliminate either the forces or their effects. All you can do is to reduce their effects by understanding them and taking the right countermeasures.

Parts one, two, and three have focused primarily on understanding ourselves because self-understanding is both critically important and extremely neglected. Because the poker culture is so anti-introspection, many players don't seriously try to:

- Think about whether they should emphasize logic or intuition
- Evaluate themselves and the competition objectively
- Consider the ways that unconscious and emotional factors affect them

These first three parts lay the foundation for the remainder of the book. Now we will examine ways to use this knowledge to adjust to change, handle stress, and take other actions to improve your results.

PART FOUR

Adjusting to Changes

Introduction

In poker, changes occur so rapidly and frequently that you cannot possibly win without adjusting quickly and effectively:

1. You must adjust your play because every new card can change the situation, sometimes completely. A fifth spade makes a worthless hand unbeatable, and the formerly unbeatable top set becomes valueless. The players holding both hands must quickly adjust to the new situation. In just a few seconds, the lucky player must decide how to maximize his profits, while the unlucky one has to minimize his losses.

2. You must change your center of attention when a hand is over and a new one is dealt. Many players don't do this well; they worry about past beats or enjoy replaying their winning hands, which prevents them from playing this one well.

3. You must be aware that position, a major source of power, can change with every card in stud, and everyone must immediately adjust to a stronger or weaker position. It changes more slowly in hold'em and other flop games, but the adjustments are even larger because they affect every street. One hand after being in the weakest position, the small blind, you're the button, the strongest position.

4. You must be mindful that the number of players changes constantly as people take breaks, change tables, or go home. Everyone must adjust to the number of players involved in the current hand. Tightness gives you an edge at a full table, but it can be a liability in a shorthanded game, especially against aggressive players. A loose-aggressive style is a liability at a full table, but it becomes an asset when the game becomes shorthanded.

5. You may have to make huge strategic changes if one or two players leave and are replaced by very different ones. For example, if two rocks leave and are replaced by maniacs, the game will be turned upside down. The strategy that worked well just a few minutes ago will become utterly inappropriate.

6. You have to be conscious that your opponents have a customary style, but occasionally act out of character. The tight-passive rock may bluff because he thinks he can get away with it, is angry with someone, gets a wild impulse, or goes on tilt. The loose-aggressive maniac may suddenly become tight-passive because he is short of money, is distracted and thinking about something else, or is just tired of throwing his money away. Every good player repeatedly asks himself, "How is everyone playing *now*?"

Longer-term changes are even more important, and they will be our primary focus. In the past few years, poker has changed immensely:

1. Poker was once legal in only a few states but can now be played in many of them.

2. Television has made no-limit hold'em an extremely popular game. Because many of the newest, weakest players prefer

no limit, these games have become very soft, but seven-card stud games are hard to find, and many of them have become much tougher.

3. The Internet allows millions of people to play regularly, something that the old-timers never even imagined. Many Internet players try their luck in cardrooms, and they bring their Internet habits with them.

4. New, weak players are participating more than ever, and the games are so soft that mediocre players are winning, and some of them are turning pro.

5. Online games enable players to play on six or more tables at a time. Because they use new teaching resources, some Internet players have extraordinarily steep learning curves. Some of them have become successful pros in their early twenties, and a few Internet pros are not old enough to play in cardrooms.

6. Tournaments were once rare, but now they are everywhere. The top players can't make all the major events, and there are thousands of smaller ones every month. Entry lists have skyrocketed, and nobody knows how much higher they will go.

7. Televised tournaments are being watched by millions of people regularly, and the top players have agents and endorsement contracts that would have been unthinkable just a few years ago.

8. Blue chip corporations are even hiring poker players and tournament directors to spice up their conferences.

As mentioned early in the book, there has always been a "Darwinian" evolution in poker. His most important principle is "survival of the fittest," and it certainly applies to our game. The ones who adapt well to changing conditions will do the best. The others will probably get left behind. Because poker has never changed so rapidly, this evolution is occurring much more rapidly now, but the process is often obscured by the massive influx of weak players.

You must continue to adjust to the current reality and prepare for future changes. If you keep playing the same old way, your results will slowly deteriorate. Because the supply of fish has continued to grow, most people can't see the danger. But that supply of fish MUST ultimately dry up. They may not realize that their world is changing until it's too late. Don't let it happen to you.[1]

1. After I submitted this book to Kensington, Congress passed and President Bush signed a law that caused many huge poker websites—including Party Poker.com—to withdraw from the U.S. At this moment, nobody knows this law's effects, but it will almost certainly slow down poker's expansion and lead to fewer weak players.

Darwin: The Struggle to Survive

Charles Darwin never played poker, but his principles fit our game. He argued that life is always competitive and that the competition gets continuously tougher. Because conditions change, only the organisms that adapt well can survive, and the survivors become stronger competitors for food, mates, and everything else.

The same sort of evolution has occurred and will continue to occur in poker, but it's happening much faster. Darwinian evolution occurred slowly over millions of years, while our game changes very rapidly. The losers go broke, get discouraged, or quit playing for other reasons. Some new players come along to replace them, and the rapid expansion of poker multiplies the influx of new and vulnerable players. However—because it's easier than ever to learn how to play— many of them quickly shift from clueless to not bad to competent, and a few become excellent. Because the weakest players leave and the survivors improve, the competition will usually intensify, and only players who adapt well can survive. Again, as Darwin noted, it is survival of the fittest.

Because the Internet and television have caused a poker explosion, the games today are softer than they've ever been. Former losers are now breaking even or winning. Former small winners are doing so well that some of them have become pros or semipros. Some people therefore believe that Darwin's evolutionary principles don't apply to poker today and won't apply tomorrow. They are flat wrong. Evolution never stops; it just changes the way it operates, a subject I'll discuss in the next chapter.

The End of the "Seat of the Pants" Players

When I started playing in the 1950s, there were hardly any poker books, nor were there any good poker magazines. The available information and advice were simplistic. Just read some of the classics such as *The Education of a Poker Player, Oswald Jacoby on Poker,* and *Scarne's Guide to Modern Poker.* By today's standards, their "expert advice" is primitive.

Those books were among the best of their time, and they certainly helped me. But poker has progressed so far that they are obsolete. Anyone who blindly followed their recommendations today could beat only very soft games. And most players did not even read them! Their primary school was the one of "hard knocks," and it has always charged high tuition and taken a long time to graduate. You had to lose a lot of money and play for a long time to learn how to play well.

Today you can read dozens of books, watch many DVDs, attend seminars, subscribe to several magazines, and debate strategy on Internet forums and at poker discussion groups. Instead of relying on dubious information and learning through experience, you can get excellent advice, and much of it is based on data—such as computer simulations and the pools of actual online hands—that did not even exist until recently. This new information greatly reduces the time and expense of learning how to play well, steepening the learning curve, and strengthening the competition.

Perhaps the clearest evidence of the learning curves' steepness is the number of *extremely* young players who are winning major tournaments, making big money in cash games, or both. It used to take many years to become a top player, but now people who are barely old enough to play legally (and a few who are still in their teens) are winning big. As I just noted, some people in their early twenties have won major tournaments, and they are writing books and magazine columns.

Some Examples of Evolution in Action

Some other betting games show evolution in action. Betting on horse races resembles playing poker. Since you bet against the other people, not against the house (which takes a cut), the difference between your own and their skill is the critical factor. If the weak bettors go away, the good ones can't make a profit. Professor Arthur Reber, author or co-author of *The New Gambler's Bible, Gambling for Dummies, The Penguin Dictionary of Psychology*, and other books, e-mailed me: "The folks who were terrible handicappers because they were gambling and not handicapping were providing the stupid money that the wise guys were taking. Now, with these folks buying lottery tickets and dumping quarters into the slots, we've got a problem. The only people left are the skilled. Because the odds are set by a pari-mutuel system, the big overlays aren't there anymore."

A similar process occurred in California's cardrooms. Just twenty years ago, many pros made a good living at draw and lowball, but they can't do it today. When stud and hold'em became legal, the gamblers stopped playing those games. It's hard to find a game today, and the few that do occur may be unbeatable because almost everyone knows how to play.

In the past few years, the same thing has happened to seven-card stud pros in Las Vegas and many other places. The weakest players want to play hold'em because they see it on television, and many mediocre stud players have switched to hold'em to exploit them. In Las Vegas there are hardly any soft seven-card stud games.

In 2002 (when I published an earlier version of this chapter in *Poker Digest*) a Las Vegas-based professional e-mailed me: Your comments about "games getting tougher and the weaker players getting eliminated over time is a phenomenon that I have observed in my travels around the country. The Tunica $20–$40 game is a tougher game now than it was 3 years ago. . . . The Bellagio's $30–$60 game has had an incredible turnover since it began over 3 years ago. Many of the $30–$60 pros are now either playing in the . . . $20–$40 game at the Mirage, the $15–$30 game at the Bellagio or have moved out of town to play elsewhere."[1]

Keep Ahead of the Learning Curve

Since the competition will eventually get tougher, you must continue to learn to keep ahead of the learning curve. If you play the same way tomorrow that you do today, your results will slowly deteriorate. Once the influx of new players subsides, the games will get tougher. If you win, say, one big bet per hour, your win rate may gradually drop to one small bet, to break even, and you may become a loser. It has happened many times. Many cardrooms have former winners in the larger games who now struggle to survive in the smaller ones. They may reject responsibility and blame other factors, but it is probably their fault for not developing their games.

Many licensed professions require continuous education. For example, in many states doctors, lawyers, psychologists, and other professionals cannot renew their licenses without taking formal courses, and a few states require periodic exams. You do not have to take a formal exam about poker, but your opponents will put you to a more demanding test every night.

Some professions provide continuing help to their members. In addition to formal courses, there are peer reviews, evaluations, and coaching. We don't have a large organization to provide that sort of help, but it's not hard to find. Serious players look for help because they know that they cannot accurately assess our own skills and developmental needs. Macho fools deny their need for help, keep playing the same old way, and fall behind.

You need outsiders' opinions to develop yourself. I have repeatedly mentioned coaching and my poker discussion groups because they have been so valuable to me. They provide new information, tell

---

1. The very next year the poker boom began, and the games became astonishingly soft. However, as I'll discuss later, this softness will be quite temporary.

me how I have misplayed hands, criticize my thinking, and help me keep learning. Because I live in Las Vegas and write about poker, it is easy for me to get good advice, but you can start a poker discussion group any place with enough players.

If you can't find or start one, visit the online forums. They're just one way that technology is creating opportunities to play and learn faster. Some players in their early twenties (or younger) have played hundreds of thousands of hands, and they're willing and able to learn from totally new analytic tools that some old-timers don't understand and won't use.

Darwin: The Poker Explosion

We're having a great party because so many new players are throwing away their money. Alas, sooner or later all parties end. The poker economy requires a constant influx of new players, and—thanks to television and the Internet—that influx has been incredible. The number of people playing online more than doubles every six months or so, and millions of players now play online and in cardrooms.

Nobody knows how many more new players we will get, but eventually, the supply of new fish will disappear. Poker is very "fashionable" now, causing many faddish people to start playing. When it goes out of fashion—as it *certainly* will—the number of beginners will shrink drastically.[1]

The house takes so much money out of the game that the new players are absolutely essential. Without their contributions, the good players won't make a profit, and the games will dry up. In fact, just a few years ago many casinos *closed* their poker rooms.

Accept that this party will end and start preparing now for the future. If you just act like a drunken reveler, blithely enjoying the party and ignoring reality, you may end up with a painful hangover.

---

1. Many people have insisted that this boom will go on forever. They give apparently plausible reasons, but similar arguments have been made for every boom in history (real estate, stock market, tulips, and so on). Any serious student of history knows that *all* booms end. Only shortsighted fools deny history's lessons.

Television and the Internet

As a result of television and the Internet, the pace of change and evolutionary pressure have dramatically escalated:

- The games are much softer.
- The Internet allows you to play far more hands per hour online than in live games.
- The learning curve is much steeper.

Change No. 1: The games are much softer.

Because so many terrible players are giving away their money, you may think that evolutionary pressures have disappeared, but the softer games just change the way evolution operates. For example, because business is so good, many places have greatly increased their charges. In Las Vegas the maximum rake in many rooms has been increased from $3 to $4 per hand, and the increase in the charges for small tournaments has been even larger. Despite these increases, mediocre players are winning because the games are so soft. However, when the games get tougher, those higher charges will make it much harder to win.

Change No. 2: The number of hands you can play per hour online is far higher than in live games.

The games are much faster, and many people multi-table. Some young people have played more hands in a few years than the old-timers played in their entire lives.

Change No. 3: The learning curve is much steeper.

Just playing more hands will steepen the learning curve, and today's players have immeasurably more information and advice than poker players have ever had. Some new players are also much more open-minded and willing to use these resources. For example, many old-timers brag that they never read a book, which is an astonishingly stupid position. Even though some information sources have been mentioned earlier, we should take another brief look at them:

1. An unprecedented supply of new books, DVDs, and videos are available.
2. Seminars are held every month.
3. More people are paying for coaching, which hardly ever occurred until recently.
4. An ever-expanding number of online forums and poker discussion groups provide a wide variety of information and advice.
5. Computer programs supply online players with information that never previously existed.
6. Pools of millions of online hands have been created, and some people are "mining" the data, learning what works and doesn't work in real money hands. Their research will add to poker theory. For the first time in history, some people will know the answers to many contentious questions.

Because of these and other factors, some players—especially very young ones—are developing their knowledge and skills extremely rapidly. A few of them have moved into the top ranks of professionals at an age that was almost unthinkable just a few years ago.

Evolution During Good Times

Many people are winning now *only* because the games are so soft, but they don't know it. They think they play well and expect to keep winning forever. They are dead wrong. Our current situation resembles one that has occurred thousands of times in nature. Instead of getting tougher, our situation has gotten much easier, but evolution never stops, even during good times. Ask a biologist, "What happens when an animal's living conditions suddenly improve?"

He will tell you that the population will increase enormously. For example, if an animal is introduced into a new environment without its natural enemies, it will flourish. Life will be so easy that later generations won't develop necessary survival qualities, including the ability to resist certain diseases. In hard times the weakest creatures will die before they breed, but when life gets easy, the weak ones will multiply, and their genetic defects will become widely distributed. Then overpopulation will create its own problems such as a lack of food, and the weaker ones will starve or die from diseases caused by overpopulation. It takes a demanding environment to create tough animals.

The same pattern has occurred recently in poker. Because the games are so easy, the number of winners has increased enormously, and many of them don't play that well. They have huge holes in their games, the crude equivalent of an animal's genetic defects. Despite these defects, they have won because the games were so soft. Severely flawed players can beat soft games, as I learned when I moved to Las Vegas shortly before the poker explosion.

Some winning players in Las Vegas were weak-tight, but they couldn't play that way in Atlantic City and be winners. Many Atlantic City tourists had developed their games from ten or more previous visits, but many Las Vegas tourists had little or no casino experience. In addition, if they had a "gambling budget" for their trip, they might not care whether they lost it at poker, craps, roulette, or slots. Since they played abysmally, even weak-tight players could win, and some Las Vegas regulars never developed other skills.

The same general process has occurred in many industries, especially on Wall Street. Whenever the market booms, some people get rich, complacent, and sloppy. They spend money too freely, and they don't work hard enough. Why economize or work hard when money seems to be falling from the sky?

Then the market drops, and the sloppiest, most extravagant people go broke. It has happened again and again, but many people don't learn. The next time the market goes through its cycle, you'll see the same foolish reactions.

Every Wall Street boom also produced a few young people who violated the old rules and did spectacularly well. Perhaps they were brilliant; perhaps they were just lucky, but they claimed to have a new system for beating the market. The dot.com craze was an extreme example: some people, especially young ones, made huge fortunes by buying stocks with no assets or earnings.

These hotshots insisted that assets, earnings, and other normal investment criteria were irrelevant; all you needed was a great concept and a lot of hype. Because they believed that nonsense, some people—including ones who had made fortunes in the early stages of the dot.com boom—took serious losses.

We're seeing similar drivel in poker. Some people are learning absurd strategies from heavily edited television shows. A few tournament stars are very young and have extremely unorthodox styles. Some of them are very, very good, but I believe that others will end up just like the hotshot portfolio managers who insisted that the time-tested investment strategies were obsolete. Ten years from now people will ask, "Whatever happened to whatshisname?"

Don't get confused by those television shows and a few young players' successes. Keep working on your game and take advantage of the new information, but don't forget the fundamental strategic principles.

Did the Poker Explosion Invalidate My Darwinian Position?

The party is so great that you may think that Darwin's principles no longer apply. Former losers are winning a little, former small winners are cleaning up, and some very young people are successful pros. Has the explosion relieved you of the obligation to keep working on your game?

Not for a heartbeat! If you stand still, the competition will blow right past you, perhaps not today, tomorrow, or next month, but eventually, you will be in big trouble. The forces I've described will continue to operate, and some players will keep developing their games. When the weakest players stop playing, the remainder will probably be tougher than the opposition you faced a year or two ago.

More species have become extinct than now exist, and evolution has made the survivors much tougher than their ancestors. The evolutionary process is a fact in Mother Nature's world and in ours. The weak disappear, and the competition gets tougher. The only question for a serious player is, Will you be foolishly complacent today and be forced to struggle tomorrow, or will you prepare in advance for tomorrow's challenges?

If you let today's soft games lull you into complacency, you can easily be wiped out when conditions get tougher, as they *certainly* will.

Darwin: The Technological Revolution

Technology is now the dominant force for change. Because of computers, jumbo jets, organ transplants, miracle drugs, and countless other technological miracles, we live in a world our grandparents could not even imagine. Technology has already had significant effects on poker, and it will soon have even greater ones. We have a simple choice: we can *understand and adapt* to these changes or *lose* our competitive edge to those who do.

Technology and Information Management

Poker is a game of incomplete information, and the critical tasks require information management. If you know more than I do—about the odds, strategy, psychology, or the cards in each other's hands—you'll beat me, and vice versa. Technology has dramatically changed the way information is managed, and future changes may be even greater.

It once took a large investment of time and money to produce and distribute information, but computers and the Internet have drastically cut this investment. You and your competition have easy access to an unprecedented amount of information. If your competitors use this access more effectively than you do, you will slowly be left behind.

Every month new books are published, and another website offers readings, lessons, or forums. In addition to providing new insights, they can use tools that did not exist until recently. Three of the most promising are Internet forums, computer simulations, and data pools of actual hands played online.

Internet Forums

Several websites have forums, and twoplustwo.com and card player.com are the largest and best known. They get hundreds of thousands of hits every month, and tens of thousands of posts (written comments). Most series of posts (threads) include feedback. Someone will describe a hand he played and ask for comments. Another thread may discuss a more general problem such as going on tilt or playing against a certain type of opponent. This feedback—which often combines theory and personal analysis—greatly improves everyone's game.

Many people have said that these discussions have been extremely helpful. They sharpen your understanding of theory, help you apply it, and teach you invaluable lessons about yourself and other people. On a twoplustwo.com forum, Greg "Fossilman" Raymer, after making thousands of posts, said, "I can say with full confidence that if it were not for Two Plus Two Publishing and their website, I would not have the 2004 World Championship bracelet on my wrist."

Computer Simulations

Several years ago I encountered my first computer simulation in Kanstantin Othmer's *Elements of Seven Card Stud*. I had thought I really understood poker. I had read a number of books and won consistently. After reading it, I realized how primitive my understanding was. I wasn't a "seat of the pants" player, but I had some rigid and foolish ideas.

I learned just how large an edge aces had heads-up against kings, the exact value of an overcard kicker, and other information that greatly improved my game. Many players have forcefully debated the value and limitations of simulations, and I won't take a position. The debaters know much more than I do. However, simulations have already provided insights that could not be developed in any other way, and they will become more useful as artificial intelligence and other techniques are developed.

I agree with the critics that the assumption of random cards severely limits their value, but not all simulations are based on that assumption. For example, Dr. Daniel Kimberg has performed simulations of hands such as pocket jacks against specific cards that people are likely to play.[1] In addition, the computer gurus are constantly finding new ways to make simulations more realistic.

Because of their limitations, don't take simulations too seriously or apply their lessons too rigidly. But rigidity is wrong for virtually everything in poker. Regard simulations as a source of insights and hypotheses that have to be checked by other means. Use them to get new ideas, but don't let them (or anything else) displace your judgment.

Data from Online Games

Some websites have analyzed the records of millions of actual hands, and some groups of players are sharing their data from programs such as Poker Tracker. When I wrote this chapter in 2002, the study of these data was just beginning, but I was sure that it could revolutionize our thinking. For the first time we could make profitability calculations based, not on theories, mathematics, or simulations against random hands, but on games with real people playing for real money.[2]

---

1. You can read about his own work and get links to similar research at www. seriouspoker.com.

2. The next two chapters will discuss the way this research has progressed since an earlier version of this one was published in 2002.

After discussing this issue, several friends have become excited about their potential, but we emphasize different opportunities. As a psychologist, I am naturally interested in what they can teach me about people, but my friends care much more about strategic questions. Barry Tanenbaum, a successful pro who later became a *Card Player* columnist, e-mailed this information to me:

> The idea behind mining the wealth of data generated by online poker games is to prove or disprove theories of betting and playing. . . . For example, is KJs profitable UTG? . . . Let us look and see how many times it was played, and did it in fact have a positive expectation? Did it matter if the KJs was raising or calling?
>
> I do not want to analyze one person or even a style. I want definitive in-practice answers to real questions by GROUPS. . . . For example, let us plot the profit/loss of players who have played more than 2,000 hands, then re-sort them by average number of hands played pre-flop, or by average number of raises pre-flop . . . [so we can determine] the winning potential of each playing style.
>
> I want to see some theories proved. Can anyone beat the rake in a 1–2 game? What is the real-life profit or loss in playing 54s? Early? Late? What hands make money in the blinds? Let's sort total winnings by position and see exactly how much the button is worth. In baseball, I can obtain the ERA of all pitchers with 3–1 counts vs. 1–2 counts. Poker should yield the same things.

Although we have different research objectives, Tanenbaum and I agree that these data offer an unprecedented opportunity. He urged me to write about this opportunity in a way that would "capture the imagination of the playing community and fire them up to demand some of these answers. I want them to get excited by the prospect of data mining." I already have that excitement, and I hope you share it. I also hope that you keep your mind open to the new and surprising lessons from these data. You will need an open mind because you may find that some of your cherished ideas are just plain wrong.

A later chapter called "Darwin: The Computer as Poker Psychologist," (see p. 244) discusses some of the lessons these data can teach us about poker psychology. These data will probably prove that some of my positions are wrong, and that's fine with me. It may embarrass me, but it will also make me a better psychologist, and, I hope, a better player.

Darwin: Quantifying "It Depends"

The standard answer to most poker questions is, "It depends on the situation." When you ask for more specific guidance, the answer is often a long list of factors: your hand, the board cards, your position, the previous and current betting action, the number of opponents, the pot size, the current odds, the implied odds, your image, the way you are playing, the skill of your opponents, the opponents' state of mind, and so forth.

If you ask, "How much weight should I assign to each factor?" the usual response is a vague platitude such as "You need to develop judgment through experience." Those answers don't work for me. I want to know how much weight to give to my position, the table image, the other players' skills, and so on.

If I keep asking for weights, I'm usually told—directly or indirectly—"You're too simplistic." You're looking for a formula, but there are no formulas. Everything—even the weights you assign to factors—depends on the situation, and every situation is unique. In some situations position is most important. In others it is your skill or table image. In others it is other players' skill, style, or state of mind. And the way you determine the relative weights depends on those old standbys: judgment and experience.

The data from online games and computer simulations will help us quantify some of those factors, but many people won't take advantage of this information. The open-minded people will learn how to assign increasingly precise weights to position, table image, the type of game, and so on. We will also be able to measure—crudely at first, but with ever-increasing accuracy—the interactions between factors.

For example, many experts agree that position's importance depends on the type of game, but they have extreme disagreements about that relationship. We'll learn, for example, how much more or less weight to assign to position in loose-passive versus tight-aggressive games.

A Little History Lesson

Sklansky took one of the first and most important steps toward quantifying "it depends" for hold'em. Until he wrote *Hold'em Poker*, nearly everyone relied on seat of the pants thinking to decide which hands to play in various positions and types of games.

He ranked starting hands from best to worst and put them into eight numbered groups and a larger bunch that were too weak to be rated. He stated that hands in the same group could often be played about the same way before the flop. He then used the hand groups as a communication tool for discussing pre-flop play by position and type of game. In a normal game, you should play Groups 1–4 in early position, Group 5 in middle position, and so on. However, if a game was loose and passive, you could call in unraised pots with weaker hands, say Group 6 in middle position. If the game was tight-aggressive, you should call with only lower grouped hands in each position. That is, instead of having to consider all the factors that make each situation unique, players could apply some consistent decision rules to types of hands and situations.

As hold'em evolved over the next thirty years, reactions have varied significantly. Many players are delighted to have some definitive guidance. However, a few writers have argued that the hand groups were too simplistic, perhaps even silly or destructive. They insisted that there can't be any "formulas" because every situation is unique.

Some critics even claim that relying too heavily on hand groups and formulas prevents the development of judgment, and Sklansky has told me, "I have sympathy with those who believe that too much reliance is put on those rankings." However, some writers have misstated his (and Malmuth's) position. Instead of urging people to apply their guidelines rigidly, they wrote: "In fact, the starting hands actually move up and down the hand rankings depending on the circumstances. Because of that it can be a mistake to rigidly adhere to the hand rankings."[1]

The Benefits of Quantifying Factors

Numbered hand groups and other quantifying steps are good tools, but they are only tools, and they should not replace judgment. They should routinize parts of the decision-making process so that you can use your limited memory and data-processing capacity for other tasks. If you have to consider each hand as unique, then relate it to a dozen factors, such as your position, skill, and table image, and the opponents' personalities and state of mind, you will overwhelm your data-processing capacity. You will be so busy doing the little things that you can't do the big ones.

Let's digress and relate this point to computers and our everyday life. Computers are just tools, but they are extraordinarily useful ones. By saving the time we once spent on routine tasks such as keeping track of our bills, writing letters by hand, and buying stamps, computers let us use our limited time, memory, and decision-making skills on more important tasks. The same thing happens when we quantify part of "it depends." It lets us use some of our brainpower for other purposes.

Sklansky (and Malmuth in later books) made that first decision— should I fold, call, or raise?—much simpler, but mere simplicity was not the only or even the primary benefit. Quantifying part of the decision lets us focus more attention on highly specific questions such as:

1. David Sklansky and Mason Malmuth, *Hold'em Poker for Advanced Players, 21st Century Edition* (Henderson, NV: Two Plus Two, 1999), 14.

- What does it mean that Joe, a tight-passive rock, called under the gun?
- What should I do? Helen is steaming, and she's short-stacked; will she raise behind me?
- How should I adjust to Tom's tell that he will fold?

If we had to regard our own cards as unique and then tried to evaluate them in terms of all the factors that made this situation unique, we could not consider these other questions. In fact, we might be so busy trying to evaluate our own cards that we might not even notice that a rock has called under the gun or that Helen is steaming and short-stacked or that Tom is ready to fold. And we could not devote as much attention to the information's implications.

The simple, inescapable fact is that all of us have limitations. If hand groupings or any other quantifying tool can simplify parts of the decision-making process, we can use our limited abilities more effectively, giving us an edge over anyone who does not have that tool. The data from online hands and computer simulations will allow some people to quantify an every-increasing part of "it depends," giving them and anyone who knows how to use these data a slowly increasing edge over the competition.

Darwin: Then and Now

This series of chapters was originally published in *Poker Digest* in 2002. At that time hardly any research had been done using the data from online games. Now data pools have been formed, analytic tools have become available, and some research has been conducted. Soon this research may change some of our strategic conceptions.

Many poker players love to argue about how to play various hands, and these arguments occasionally become quite heated:

- Player A insists, "You should raise."
- Player B says, "No! Just call."
- Player C says, "You're both wrong. You've got to fold."

They can usually make plausible arguments, but nobody has solid evidence. They may cite excellent poker logic and theory, but logic and theory are not satisfactory substitutes for evidence. They almost never have good statistical evidence to support their positions.

Of course, they can tell anecdotes about pots they have won or lost, but anecdotes have no evidential value. They may also have records that show that they have won or lost a certain amount playing this way or that, but their samples are too small and their results depend (at least partly) on their own skill, style, image, and other factors. The fact that a certain strategy has worked for them does not mean that it will work for other players.

In fact, there are no solid data about nearly everything in poker. The math is solid, but mathematicians don't collect data. They work deductively, applying general principles to specific situations, while researchers work in the opposite direction: they use statistical data to derive general principles. Until recently, not enough solid data were available to conduct serious research.

Because of online poker, we now have an enormous amount of data and the tools to analyze them. Researchers will find that some of the most emphatically presented positions are just plain wrong. Some of them must be wrong because there are such extreme disagreements. This research will allow us to answer some strategic questions with solid, factual evidence.

The Data Are Readily Available

You can buy readily available programs that record the data from all the hands you and many others have played. They provide a wide range of statistics such as:

- The percentage of hands you play in each position
- The percentage of hands every opponent plays in each position
- The number of times you and they raise
- The number of times you and they defend the blinds
- The amount you win or lose in various positions with every type of hand such as ace-king suited, eight-nine offsuit, and pocket aces.

Some players multi-table and play hundreds of thousands of hands per year. Some of them have formed data pools, sharing their data to draw more general conclusions. A few commercially available programs provide data from many different players. No matter how they are formed, these pools can contain millions of hands.

Some people have stated these data pools are not much better than computer simulations of random hands. Nonsense! They are real hands played for real money.

The Analytic Tools Are Readily Available

With these huge pools of data competent researchers can easily evaluate various strategic decisions. The first step is to follow the usual scientific practice of defining everything *operationally*. People can argue endlessly about the meaning of terms such as "expert," "fish," or "maniac," but the meaning of an operational definition is the same for everyone. For example, a researcher can use the win rate per one hundred hands[1] to define various skill levels:

- An "expert" wins more than three big bets (BB).
- A "good player" wins between two and three BB.
- An "okay player" wins between one and two BB.
- A "breakeven player" wins or loses less than one BB.
- A "weak player" loses between one and three BB.
- A "fish" loses more than three BB.

Operational definitions can also be used for types of players and games:

- A "maniac" sees over 75 percent of the flops when he is not a blind and raises pre-flop over 50 percent of the time.
- A "rock" sees fewer than 10 percent of the flops when he is not a blind and raises pre-flop less than 3 percent of the time.
- A "tight-aggressive game" has three or less people see the flop, and over 70 percent of the hands are raised pre-flop.
- A "loose-passive game" has six or more people see the flop, and less than 15 percent of the hands are raised pre-flop.

1. Live game results are usually expressed in big bets per hour, but—because on-line games are faster and some players multi-table—results are usually expressed in big bets per hundred hands. One hundred hands would take about three hours in a live game. Therefore, a win rate of three big bets per hundred hands is approximately equal to one big bet per hour of live play.

These definitions are for illustration purposes only, and I do not claim they are accurate. Other people would make different ones. But they would all have the immense value of being the same for everyone. Once you operationally define "expert," and so on, you can manipulate the data to determine the most profitable way for players with different skills to play hands in various positions and types of games.

Let's say you want to learn how KJ offsuit should be played in a limit hold'em game:

- In various positions (small blind, big blind, early, middle, and late)
- In different-sized games (6, 7, 8, 9, and 10 players)
- In different-type games (loose-passive, loose-aggressive, tight-passive, and tight-aggressive)
- By people of different skill levels (expert, good, okay, breakeven, weak, and fish).

Until very recently it was impossible to conduct such research, but data pools with millions of hands are currently available. These data are potentially available to researchers, and some of this research has already been conducted. For example, Party Poker has compared the expected value of various hands in different positions.[2] Researchers could add other factors such as skill level, number of players, and type of game.

With a large enough database, you could determine the best way for various levels of players to play specific hands in different position in certain types of games. The data may show that in a ten-handed, tight-aggressive game, KJ offsuit under the gun is most profitable for:

2. You can find this comparison at www.tightpoker.com/hands/ev_position.html. Some people have criticized these data, and their criticisms may be correct. But they are certainly a good start. If there are errors in the data, they can be corrected. When people argue without data, corrections are almost impossible.

- An expert or good player if he raises
- An okay or breakeven player if he calls
- A weak player or fish if he folds

Although the weaker players should fold KJ offsuit in a tight-aggressive game, the data may show that they should play them if the game is loose-passive. That is, the data could clearly indicate the way your strategy should be changed to fit your skill level and type of game.

I am definitely not saying that the data would support those conclusions. I have no idea what the data will indicate, nor should I prejudge the results. Doing so is exactly the wrong thing to do. The more open-minded the researchers are, the better the research will be. Biased researchers tend to find what they are looking for.

Since conducting this research is ethical, intellectually challenging, and do-able, and the conclusions will be extremely valuable, you can be sure that somebody will do it.

The researchers will probably find some unexpected relationships. They will draw solid, data-based conclusions about the best way for different types of players to play various hands, in early, middle, and late position, against different numbers of players of specific styles and skill levels. It will give them an enormous competitive advantage.

Computers have already had dramatic effects on other games such as backgammon. Dan Harrington, primary author of the *Harrington on Hold'em* books, told me that he was once a world-class backgammon player. He stopped playing for several years and then started again. After studying the computer simulations and other materials that had come out during his absence, he realized, "I was unquestionably a much better player than I had been before, but I was no longer world class. The game had advanced more than I had."

The same process will happen in poker. Because of research using these online data pools and other resources, poker strategy will continue to advance. The last word has not been written about poker (or any other subject), and it never will be written.

Recommendations

Since you must stay ahead of the competition to survive as a winning player, you should take a few actions.

- Accept that poker strategies are like every other field of knowledge. They have always evolved, and they will continue to do so.

- Commit yourself to learning continuously; otherwise, you will fall behind your competition.

- Keep your mind open, and be ready to cast off your most cherished ideas if research indicates that they are wrong.

- Actively seek the new insights that this research will produce. They may be hard to find. To gain and preserve an edge, some researchers may try to keep their results and conclusions secret. But as the old saying goes, "Three people can keep a secret only if two of them are dead." The research findings will leak out, eventually. Make sure you're one of the people who gets to use them.

Darwin: Machismo and Complacency

An earlier chapter called "Darwin: Quantifying 'It Depends'" (see p. 229) noted that some writers objected—often heatedly—to putting the starting hold'em hands into numbered groups. Many people will make similar objections to any attempts to quantify "it depends." They will insist that judgment and experience are the critical factors and blindly reject the lessons from computer simulations, online data pools, and other new developments. You will read the same fatuous arguments:

"Every situation is unique."

"Real poker players don't need training wheels."

"You've got to rely on your judgment."

People will claim that weaklings may need these "formulas," but they can do without them because they have judgment and skill and other good, macho qualities. I've deliberately used a negative term because machismo causes objections to quantification and other changes. Complacency has similar effects. People naturally believe, "If it ain't broke, don't fix it. Since I win consistently, I don't need to change."

In a stable situation, we wouldn't have to develop new skills, but constant change is a fact of poker and life in general. I don't know what changes will occur in our game, but I'm absolutely certain they'll be very large. As I said before, many people used to make a good living playing draw, but it's essentially gone. A similar process is now destroying the incomes of seven-card stud pros. And some limit hold'em players are switching to no limit because that's where the weakest fish are. Can you seriously believe that the future won't bring equally large changes?

Machismo and complacency cause many people to insist the following:

- They have certain unique abilities that cannot be simplified or precisely defined.
- They think that nobody without their unique gifts can do what they do.
- They believe, "My skills can't become obsolete because I'm special."

My answer to those assertions is very, very simple: Nonsense! Countless people have stated that only those with special training and gifts can perform certain tasks, and they have repeatedly been proven wrong. Please forgive my making another historical digression, but I believe that treating poker as if it were unique is just plain silly. Pretending that poker is immune to the principles that apply to other competitions just proves that old saying, "Those who forget history are doomed to repeat it."

The resistance to quantifying that we see in poker mirrors earlier conflicts. For example, centuries ago the Luddites destroyed machinery that threatened their livelihood and insisted that only well-trained people could manufacture good products. Today virtually everything we buy is machine made. When my father was young, he sold adding machines, which were not widely used then. Bookkeepers would challenge him to races, and occasionally they would add numbers faster by hand than he could add them on his machine. Today everybody uses calculators.

In recent years millions of people have lost their jobs because computers or other developments made their skills obsolete. These skills include extremely complicated ones that people once thought could never be replaced, such as designing airplanes or teaching pilots how to fly them. If computers and other changes can make hundreds of complex, highly valued skills obsolete, do you seriously think they can't have an impact on your poker skills?

You may insist that these historical facts are irrelevant because poker is different. Perhaps a computer or other machine can add numbers accurately or teach pilots, but only people with judgment and experience and other good stuff can play poker well. As a friend put it, a computer can't play good poker because "poker is interactive and adjustive" and "poker is a game of incomplete information."

Clinging to the belief that poker is different may make you feel good, but it's just an illusion, albeit a common one. The most common reasons for insisting that quantitative analysis can't replace experts' judgment are:

- These variables are too numerous.
- These variables are too complicated to be quantified.
- Poker is a game of incomplete information.

None of these arguments is convincing. I've already shown how researchers can use data pools to quantify the effects of various factors while playing poker. The same principle applies to much more complicated tasks.

Computers simulate extraordinarily complicated conditions to train pilots. Flying a simulator is extremely interactive and adjustive, and the pilot's information is exceptionally incomplete. He must adjust correctly—sometimes almost instantly—to whatever conditions the simulator creates. Otherwise, he crashes. For example, he can be a few seconds from landing a 747 with two engines out, with almost no fuel, in a blizzard, when a light shifts from indicating that his landing gear is okay to warning that it's out of position. Maybe the landing gear is okay, and the light is wrong. Maybe not. Do you really believe that his decisions are less complicated, interactive, and adjustive or based on better information than deciding whether to check, bet, call, raise, or fold?

A Reader's Rebuttal

Larry Duplessis is a friend who has privately commented on some of my published articles. He disagreed with one of the chapters in this series.

The fact that there will be more information available is not really bad news for the good poker players. Why? Because . . . most players will not take any time to try to improve their games. . . . They don't want to go through the "pain" of re-reading one poker book. . . . These players simply do not have the patience and discipline to do so.

So whether or not there is only a limited amount of information out there to improve a player's game or an abundance of information doesn't matter for those who do take the time out to continue to learn the game.

While I agree that many players will not use or even learn new information, it is very risky to rely on other people's laziness. In fact, assuming that other people will not take advantage of new information is a splendid example of complacency and its dangers.

Your real competition is not the indifferent, sloppy players; you'll beat them no matter what happens. Focus on the other good players because many of them will grab every new weapon and use it against you. Poker has often been compared to war, and generals lose by following the strategy that worked in the last war, while their enemies learn from the past and develop new strategies. That's why the French relied on The Maginot Line in WWII, and we lost in Vietnam. The Germans went around the Maginot Line, and the Viet Cong wouldn't fight the massive, high-tech battles we knew how to win.

Darwin and the entire history of evolution prove that past or current success does not guarantee survival, and that your competition is not the weaklings; it's the tough guys. If you assume that you will win tomorrow's battles with today's weapons and strategies, you can easily get wiped out.

Darwin: The Computer as Poker Psychologist

An earlier chapter called "Darwin: the Technological Revolution" (see p. 224) said the data from pools of online hands "will prove that some of my positions are wrong, and that's fine with me." I'm a scientist, and all scientists know that our worst sin is to refuse to revise our thinking when the data conflict with it. The machismo and complacency I discussed recently are bad for anyone, but intolerable for scientists.

Our job is to develop theories that fit the existing data and then revise them when we get new information. Because we rely on data and let go of disproved ideas, science has progressed much further than virtually all other human endeavors.[1]

Let me go a step further. Someday (and it may be quite soon) a computer will be a better poker psychologist than I—or anyone else—can ever be. In the chapter just mentioned, Barry Tanenbaum was quoted on the types of questions the data pool should answer (see p. 226). I agree that his questions are important, but the data could also answer important questions about poker psychology.

Assessing Types of Games

How can a computer assess the type of game? Very, very easily. In fact, many sites now provide a limited, but useful statistic about

---

1. Many scientists are not exceptionally brilliant, but we all use methods that prevent or discover our mistakes. A scientist who does not use these methods and does not accept the corrections to his positions will be ignored or held in contempt by the scientific community.

looseness: the percentage of players who see the flop. It would be very easy to provide similar statistics for the turn, river, and showdown, plus how often there is a raise, reraise, or cap on each street.

Perhaps the websites won't provide these data, but a good computer analyst could determine them. As a psychologist specializing in the styles of players and games, I believe these data can provide better assessments of player psychology and its effects than *anyone* can make.

Those words were written in 2002. Since then I've learned about Poker Tracker and Poker-Spy, and there may be other programs that I've never encountered. They perform some assessments of games and people better than I can do them. Am I embarrassed to admit it? Not at all.

Most people have no idea of how much the science of psychology depends on statistics. Amateur psychologists rely on feelings and intuitions, but professionals want hard data, preferably numbers. Scientific psychology is mostly based on statistical analysis of large groups of subjects, and it focuses primarily on understanding and predicting how people will usually act, not on what one individual will do.

In a way it resembles winning at limit poker. At the end of the year, brilliant plays have a trivial impact on our results. What counts is making the best decision most of the time. Brilliant insights are exciting, but solid, databased conclusions are much more valuable.

Assessing Individuals' Playing Styles

The data from online games will allow us to draw those conclusions. For example, instead of judging people by feel, insightful observations, or theory, a computer program can perform some simple counts to assess players on the two dimensions I used in *The Psychology of Poker*: loose-tight and passive-aggressive.

For the loose-tight dimension, the computer would simply count how often each player called before the flop, on the flop, on the turn, and on the river. If you play online, you can now buy programs that do it automatically. If we wanted more detailed information, a computer could perform separate counts for various positions. How often did he call in early, middle, and late position? Then it could compare those numbers and use a formula to assign the same scores I used, from 1 (extremely tight) to 9 (extremely loose). It could even give more detailed scores, such as how often someone called on the flop, turn, and river, but didn't win the pot. Those data may indicate that someone is moderately tight before the flop, but chases too long and can't lay down losing hands.

For the passive-aggressive dimension, the computer could count the ratio of raises to calls on each betting round. People with the lowest ratio (meaning they hardly ever raised) would be rated 1 (extremely passive), and those who raised most frequently would be rated 9 (extremely aggressive).

You may think that these methods are too simplistic. You may want to see the hands on which he called or raised, but this system would give immeasurably more accurate assessments than anyone could make by judging the way he played specific hands. Why?

Because the data would be more complete and less biased. You and I cannot see other people's cards in most hands, nor can we remember every hand we see. We naturally remember the unusual ones, but a computer can easily keep track of almost everything, and it would not give extra weight to unusual events. In addition, it would not be misled by people who "advertise" by showing bluffs, folds, or other atypical actions.

Assessing Complex Qualities, Such as Judgment and Card Reading

You may agree that a computer could assess tightness or aggression, but feel that judgment and card-reading skill are too complex. But all it would take would be a good team of computer specialists and psychologists. The computer could, for example, discover that a player called about as often in early, middle, or late position, which clearly indicates that he does not understand and adjust to position. It could also see how often he raised with winning and losing hands, which tells us a lot about his judgment and card-reading skill. Players' style, judgment, and hand-reading skill are central parts of poker psychology, and a skillful analyst with enough data can assess them much better than I or any other psychologist.

Understanding Why Computers Can Be Better Poker Psychologists

There are two major reasons for computer superiority:

1. The computer will retain and use much more data.
2. The computer will be much less affected by biases than a psychologist.

If I saw someone make a few apparently terrible calls, I might conclude that he was extremely loose or could not read cards. However, the computer analysis might find something I forgot or did not notice: he made many losing calls, but he also called with several weak hands to catch bluffers.

His apparently bad calling habits actually increased his profits. What I had mistakenly seen as looseness and poor judgment was actually an ability to snap off bluffs. In scientific terms I had committed a sampling error, allowing a tiny sample to affect my overall conclusion.

For years I have studied and written about the styles of players and games. Many other writers have written on these topics, and we can all make plausible arguments. We agree on some points, disagree on others, but none of us can prove that he is right. Nobody has solid data, and they are the only acceptable scientific proof. Studies of millions of hands may prove that some of the things I've written are wrong. The researchers may not be able to explain why the data conflict with my theories, but they're not required to do so. If the data say I'm wrong, then I'm wrong. Data trump authority, credentials, logical theories, and everything else.

The worst thing I could do would be to get angry and defensive. I might be tempted to insist: "I'm a Ph.D., and my theories are based on over forty years of training and experience, while you don't even know why your data conflict with my position." If I said it, my scientific and poker friends would laugh at me—and I'd deserve it.

If the data say I'm wrong, the only intelligent thing to do is learn from them. The question then becomes, Why am I wrong? When the inevitable conflicts occur between my ideas and the data, I'll be a bit embarrassed, but I hope I'm open minded enough to learn from them. I encourage you to do the same. Set aside your machismo and complacency and keep your mind open.

Darwin: Can Computers Beat Poker Champions?

Many of my friends accept the basic Darwinian premise: to survive we must understand and adapt to poker's inevitable changes. But we disagree about which changes are most important, the effects of the changes, and the way we will adapt to them. This chapter will take a position that almost none of them will accept: within a few years, computers will beat champions in limit games.

I am confident it will happen fairly soon. This new circumstance is all part of the technological revolution, the same one that has cost millions of people their jobs. If you play online, you may already be losing money to bots (short for "robots," computers that play online). Some companies are selling them, and there are persistent rumors that some sites use them to start and keep shorthanded games going.[1] They may soon be beating almost everybody.

A group at The University of Alberta is programming computers to play poker and other games. Their interests are scientific, but you can be absolutely certain that their results (and other research I don't know about) will soon affect poker strategies, including the way bots are programmed.

---

1. There are over 200 poker websites, and there is hardly any regulation of them. Some websites—including Party Poker—have paid "props" to play in short games. Since bots are much cheaper than props, and they unquestionably exist, I suspect that the rumors are true. However I have not seen proof that bots are winning.

Avoiding Mistakes Is Almost Enough

Computers can now easily beat low-limit games because the players make so many fundamental mistakes. A well-programmed computer will hardly ever make a basic mistake such as calling before the flop with the wrong group hand or playing a draw without the proper pot odds or betting middle pair into eight players. If a computer (or you) just plays solid, "formula," nearly error-free poker, it will beat most low-limit games.

In fact, avoiding mistakes is critically important at every level. The late Andy Glazer, *Poker Digest*'s tournament editor, wrote that Phil Helmuth and T. J. Cloutier, two of the best tournament players, "make more money by taking advantage of opponents' errors than by making brilliant plays."[2] At their level the mistakes are more subtle and sophisticated, but avoiding them is still the key to winning. Computers can play nearly error-free poker.

Adding Good Psychology and Quantifying "It Depends"

Previous chapters have shown that computers can quantify "It depends" and make excellent psychological assessments. The combination of no mistakes and these qualities will beat almost anyone.

The computer would usually choose the optimal strategy for this situation with these opponents. In addition to knowing the exact size of the pot, calculating the odds, and applying the optimal strategy, it would never go on tilt, and it would know how every opponent played every hand in its memory bank. You and I forget how someone played last week or last month, but a computer doesn't forget anything. It can instantly compare this situation to every other hand these opponents have played and then make an experience-based assessment of every possibility.

2. Andy Glazer, *Poker Digest*, May 2, 2002.

For example, what is the probability that he is bluffing? The computer can compare this hand to every similar hand and assess the probability of a bluff at, say, 9 percent. If the pot odds justify it, call. If not, fold. It's following the same logic we use, but basing its decision on immeasurably better information.

Or consider the question, Should I semibluff now? Many people get glassy eyed when they read Sklansky's recommendations to add probabilities (e.g., 17 percent that you'll win the pot immediately, plus 23 percent that you'll draw out, plus 9 percent that you'll win if a scare card hits and you bet again, and so on). They insist that those numbers are just subjective assessments, but to a computer they're not subjective. In fact, it's easy to calculate many of them by just comparing this situation to every other one these opponents have played.

Using Imagination and Intuition May Not Be Necessary

The fact that computers have no imagination or intuition may make us feel comfortable about our uniqueness, but it is nearly irrelevant. First, imagination and intuition are not that important in most limit games, especially the smaller ones. They get the applause, but error-free, odds-based strategies win the money. Second, computers can be programmed to make imaginative moves at the optimal times. For example, they can be programmed to bluff at exactly the optimal frequency in a completely random manner. They will be much better at catching your bluffs than you will be at snapping off theirs.

Because of these advantages, I am confident that a computer will soon beat champions in limit games, especially the simpler ones. Greenstein and Sklansky agree. Greenstein is one of the world's greatest players, and he once worked as a programmer for Symantec, the company that makes Norton Anti-virus programs. He wrote: "It is likely that a computer could be programmed using concepts of noncooperative game theory to beat expert poker players."[3] Since he probably knows more about computers than any other top player, the odds are that it will be done.

Sklansky doesn't think it will take too long if a computer company decides to do it. In a comment posted on a twoplustwo.com forum, he said, "In games like single draw lowball, IBM could design a world champion computer in a year."

Beating no-limit champions will take considerably longer, and it may be impossible. No limit seems to require intuition that may be impossible to program. However, no-limit tournaments may be a different matter. In *Tournament Poker for Advanced Players*, Sklansky describes "The System" he developed for a casino owner's daughter to play in the $10,000 buy-in no-limit main event at the WSOP. The System had to be extremely simple because she had never played poker.

The father tested it in a smaller no-limit WSOP event, and "The System brought his chips from $2,000 to $35,000! He made the final table, and finished in about fifth place. But even that does not properly describe the result, because for some reason, with $35,000 in chips, he decided, for the first time in the tournament, to deviate from The System."[4] He quickly went broke. In other words, when he used no judgment, imagination, or intuition, he made the final table. Then, when he started to use his unique talents, he got busted.

Discovering Why It Hasn't Happened Already

I believe the primary reason that computers have not been publicly used is that nobody will spend enough money. IBM spent millions to defeat Garry Kasparov, the world's chess champion, to get some great publicity. However, because chess is much more "respectable" than poker, a computer company wouldn't get nearly as

3. Barry Greenstein, *Ace on the River* (Fort Collins, CO: Last Knight Publishing, 2005), 163.

4. Sklansky and Malmuth, *Tournament Poker for Advanced Players*, p. 126.

good publicity by winning a major poker tournament or defeating a champion heads-up.

Some of my friends insist that beating Kasparov is irrelevant because poker is different, but earlier chapters showed that this argument is baseless. It's been made about many, apparently unique tasks—from designing airplanes to making psychological judgments—but machines have repeatedly shown that they can outperform people.

A common objection is that poker is a game of incomplete information, while chess provides complete information. However, computers slaughter people in Rock, Scissors, Paper, another incomplete information game. The critical task is to assess the other player's move, which closely resembles reading another player's cards and intentions. Because computers can read people better than vice versa, they easily defeat people.

Learning What an Expert Thinks

Darse Billings is the primary designer of Poki, The University of Alberta's poker playing program. He played poker professionally for a few years after doing his M.Sc. on computer poker. In an e-mail discussion of this topic he commented:

> There have been lots of naysayers in other games, but they have been forced to accept computer dominance in checkers, Othello, backgammon, Scrabble . . . and the list continues to grow. . . .
>
> I am not overly optimistic by nature, or quick to make a pronouncement of this kind, but I see the dominance of computers in limit poker to be inevitable—it is only a matter of time.
>
> Lots of people will disagree—humans are especially proud of their mastery over the dark mysteries of poker, and are dismissive of what "stupid" computers are capable of. But to put it quite bluntly, they don't have a clue.
>
> [He jokingly concluded] I for one will not be the least bit sur-

prised when the top poker players in the world get spanked like little babies.

He put a :-) after that remark to make sure I didn't take it too seriously. They may not get spanked like babies, but they will be beaten.[5]

Who Cares?

I care about computers, and you should. You may never play against a computer directly, but the lessons learned from programming them to beat poker players will directly affect every serious player. Some people will use that research to gain an edge against the rest of us.

To survive, we have to stop denying reality and insisting that our game and we are unique. This research presents the same sort of threat to us that mathematical approaches once presented to the "seat of the pants" players. Many of them ignored or denied that threat, and they were busted. The ones who adapted, survived. That principle is the basis of all evolution, and only a fool would deny or ignore it.

---

5. Since this chapter was first published, a commerical version of Poki has appeared. It's too soon to tell how well it will do.

Darwin: Afterthought

In the four short years since I first published articles on this subject, many changes have occurred in poker, and there is no reason to believe that the next few years will be more stable. On the contrary, the pace of change will probably accelerate as it has done in so many other areas.

The social and psychological effects of the accelerating pace of change were analyzed in Alvin Toffler's *Future Shock*,[1] a huge best seller. He stated that life is changing so rapidly that some people react to new conditions the same way they do when they travel to a foreign country and experience culture shock. They become confused and disoriented. When people feel that way, they may cling to their old ways, even if they don't fit the new conditions. Since poker is brutally competitive, you can't afford to act that way.

Adjusting to Changes

This series of chapters has been quite long, but it just scratched the surface. It couldn't discuss all the changes that threaten your survival, especially if you don't adjust to them, but I hope the few we've discussed have convinced you of several points:

1. Your survival as a winning player is not guaranteed.
2. Changes will threaten your survival.

1. Alvin Toffler, *Future Shock* (New York: Bantam Books, 1984).

3. Your survival demands accepting, understanding, and adapting to change.
4. Poker is *not* different from other competitions.
5. The poker explosion did not end evolutionary pressures.
6. Your greatest enemies are your own attitudes.

Point No. 1: Your survival as a winning player is not guaranteed.

We all resist the idea of our own demise, either physically or in any other way. Young people almost believe they are immortal because death is so distant. Some players have the same sort of absurd beliefs about their skills. Since they see no immediate danger, they dismiss the idea that anything will become a serious threat.

Point No. 2: The changes will threaten your survival.

History proves that change is essentially constant and that it usually wipes out something. The dinosaurs are the most famous example. After dominating the earth for much longer than we have, they disappeared. So did every empire that preceded America's. So did many highly valued skills.

Talk to typesetters, tool and die makers, drafters, illustrators, or members of many other skilled occupations, and you'll hear the same story: they spent years learning a complicated, highly paid skill, but computers and other developments destroyed their worlds. If it can happen to them, it can happen to you.

Point No. 3: Your survival demands accepting, understanding, and adapting to change.

All three steps are essential. You must accept that change is inevitable, understand the implications of whatever changes occur, and then carefully adapt to them. You already adapt to rapid changes such as new cards and position, and you must use that same flexibility for the longer-term ones.

Poker is a very "now" game. We play about thirty hands an hour, and each one requires several decisions. We naturally focus on what we will do in the next few seconds, which can make us oblivious to longer-term developments.

Point No. 4: Poker is not different from other competitions.

Poker writers and players cling to an illusion that is baseless. As Billings put it, "Humans are especially proud of their mastery over the dark mysteries of poker," but there aren't any dark mysteries. Poker is a great game, but it does not demand skills or traits that are fundamentally different from other competitions. Set that illusion aside because it can prevent you from learning from history and research.

Point No. 5: The poker explosion did not end evolutionary pressures.

The "Darwin at the Poker Table" series was published in *Poker Digest* in 2002, a short time before the poker explosion. Since then there has been an incredible increase in the number of fish, and the games have become extraordinarily soft, but these developments just change the way evolution operates. You must never think that you and poker are immune from the forces that have driven many types of change.

Point No. 6: Your greatest enemies are your own attitudes.

Machismo, complacency, a short-term orientation, closed-mindedness, and many other attitudes reduce your ability to cope with change. Poker discussion groups and online forums have taught me a lot, but they have a serious limitation. Virtually every discussion focuses on short-term, narrowly focused issues. For example, how should I have played this specific hand? How should my strategy be changed if the game shifts from tight to loose? Should I choose this game or that one? These questions are interesting and worthwhile, but they do not deal with longer-term, more general issues. In fact, discussions of long-term development rarely occur.

Why don't we talk about longer-term developments? Because

most of us don't really care about them. We want to talk about a hand we played last night or adapt our strategy for the game we are playing now.

What Should You Do?

To change your thinking, you must take the critical step of shifting your attention from just the short-term issues to your longer-term development. If you're serious about poker, you should make a personal development plan. It does not have to be elaborate and detailed, but it should include several elements:

1. Take advantage of the vast array of resources. Don't just read books for fun; study them. Do the same with DVDs, magazines, and computerized instructional programs. And keep looking for reports—including very informal ones— about the research being done with pools of online hands.

2. Go beyond studying to active learning by joining a discussion group, posting hands and questions on forums, arguing with the other players and experts, and taking the risk of being criticized. If you do get criticized, your embarrassment will be temporary, but the lessons can be permanent.

3. Go beyond the narrow discussions you can get in these places and consider larger, longer-term issues. How is the game changing in your area? What skills and psychological traits (such as patience or emotional control) will you need to develop? Analyze your personal strengths and weaknesses. Discover ways to take full advantage of your strengths and overcome or minimize your weaknesses.

4. Get a coach. Some of my friends are successful pros. They are very good, but want to get better. Instead of resting on their success, they spend serious money for personal coach-

ing. If they can benefit from coaching, how much more value would you get from it?

5. Experiment with something new and different every month. For example, tighten up before the flop, or become more aggressive, or change the time and place you play. Of course, your experiment may fail, but even a failure can teach you something that improves your game. If you experiment and fail, you can try something else. If you never try anything new, you cannot develop your game.

6. Keep track of your results, and do it honestly and thoroughly. Keep the records that will let you see whether and why the changes are helping or hurting you.

7. Keep your mind open. Change is uncomfortable, even distressing. You naturally resist changing your game, even when the data say you should do so. Accept that temporary discomfort is necessary for any kind of growth.

8. Accept that you must progress or regress. Poker is constantly changing, and if you don't adjust, you will eventually move backward.[2]

Darwin was his era's most hated man. Hardly anyone wanted to believe his theory of evolution, partly because of its theological implications and partly because it emphasized the odds against surviving. But he was right.

We now know that the battle for survival is even harsher than he thought. Because many species could not adapt to the changing conditions, more of them are extinct than now exist. They are gone forever, and the same fate awaits poker players who refuse to keep learning and adapting.

---

2. The ways to develop yourself are the primary focus of my next book, *Your Best Poker Friend* (forthcoming).

Darwin's survival of the fittest principle suits our game perfectly. We must always struggle to survive, and our game and the competition are constantly changing. Our choice is brutally simple: we can use every tool available to adapt to these changes, or we will eventually be destroyed.

PART FIVE

Handling Stress

Introduction

Poker is an intrinsically stressful game, and many people do not handle its stresses well. Damon Runyon, who wrote frequently about gambling, said that there is no such thing as "a friendly poker game." Our goal is to take each other's money, and the game is based on deception and aggression, two very unfriendly qualities. Luck's huge short-term effects increase the stress. You can play extremely well, but still lose. You can even lose for weeks or months without knowing why.

Cardroom and online poker can be particularly stressful because the players are more serious, the action is faster, and the house takes a cut, creating negative-sum games: the players' collective losses always exceed their gains, and many people lose much more than they can afford, either financially or psychologically.

Reactions to these frustrations greatly increase the stress level. Some people complain, criticize, whine, curse, and occasionally throw chips or cards. These reactions have always been a problem, but the poker explosion has greatly aggravated them. World-famous players act like spoiled children on television, and many new players have copied their antics.

The Internet's anonymity increases the pressure. People who would not curse or threaten a player in a live game, can become extraordinarily abusive online. They learn from this experience that nastiness is "acceptable," and some of them act viciously during live games.

The new players have increased the good players' profits, but greatly increased the size of their swings. Because new players are so loose, there are more and worse bad beats. Since no-limit hold'em has become so popular, good players with premium cards often get busted by idiots playing trash.

The poker explosion has forced cardrooms to hire and promote inexperienced staff. They make terrible mistakes, and a few of them can't even speak English very well. They also don't know how to control nasty players, and they may let some of them get completely out of line.

All these factors make poker much more stressful than it has ever been. Since the stress level is so high, you must learn how to handle it. If you overreact, your game, disposition, and bankroll will suffer.

I'll start by discussing the game's intrinsically frustrating aspects, such as losing streaks and winning in home games, but losing in cardrooms. In addition to being harder to beat, cardrooms present a problem that rarely occurs in home games, vicious players.

I'll expand the points I just made about the poker explosion and other new developments in the chapter called "New Aggravations" (see p. 295).

Poker has become so frustrating that more than a few people have asked themselves: "Should I give up the game?"

I will end with, "Don't take poker too seriously." I have seen far too many people let poker destroy their lives to stand by silently while they do it.

Losing Streaks

Losing streaks really hurt, not just our bankrolls, but our moods and self-esteem. We may get angry or depressed, or wonder whether we are as good as we thought. This chapter will discuss two subjects:

1. Coping with losing streaks
2. Learning from them

This sequence of solving the immediate problem, then dealing with its causes is followed in every emergency room. For example, if you're bleeding heavily, they first stop you from bleeding to death. Only then do they deal with whatever is causing the bleeding. If you're on a serious losing streak, you're bleeding money, and you had better stop it quickly.

Coping with Losing Streaks

Losing streaks are often discussed on Internet forums as a way to cope with them. One request stated: "I am a winning player but . . . go thru periods where losing is more common than winning. . . . It is difficult to handle psychologically. Even though the losses are large, they are less than 25 percent of the bankroll so, at this point, money is not the problem, only my state of mind."

The replies to his post were so helpful that my first recommendation is: If you feel confused or upset about ANYTHING related to poker, discuss it—in person, by telephone or e-mail or at an online forum—but preserve your anonymity (except for a few trusted friends).

Some Don'ts

When you're losing, you may want to take several actions that can make the situation much worse. Here are a few things you should *not* do:

1. *Don't complain publicly.* Complaining publicly is a very human, but terrible mistake. You naturally want sympathy, but you usually won't get it. Poker is a predatory game, and all predators look for weak prey. Admitting you're on a losing streak has the same effect that blood in the water has on sharks: it creates a "feeding frenzy," and you're lunch. Even passive players may exploit your weakness because attacking vulnerable creatures is built into our natures.

2. *Don't blame bad luck.* Of course you have been unlucky. You have had terrible beats, and players' or dealers' mistakes have hurt you. But bad luck is rarely the only cause for a long losing streak.[1] The law of averages has not been repealed, even though you may feel that way. You are probably doing something wrong, and your long-term priority must be to correct it.

   When I talk that way to people, they often get angry. They want sympathy, but my job as a psychologist is to help you to cope with reality, and an essential step is accepting personal responsibility for your results. Unless you accept it, nobody can help you.

3. *Don't play when you're off balance.* That principle is always important, but it becomes critical during a losing streak. If you're on a losing streak, you may be off balance—even if you think you're okay—and it will probably affect your

---

1. Some authorities have stated that you can lose for thousands of hours just because of variance, but the odds are against it.

play. You will exaggerate its effects by playing when you're tired, angry, worried, or drinking.

Let's consider winning poker's most basic principle: always demand an edge, a positive expectation. Your edge has only one long-term source: your skill at playing your cards and selecting your games and seats, and your ego can take away that edge. You may think, "I don't have to play my A-game to win; I can beat these jerks even if my game is off."

That position is illogical because the difference between winning and losing is so small. The one big bet per hour that good players average is much less than 10 percent of the total amount wagered. If anything slightly weakens your game (and getting off balance often has large effects), your edge will disappear. Your expectation will become *negative*, meaning that you're probably going to lose.

4. *Don't try to get even.* A losing streak—and its underlying message that something is wrong—should make you more conservative, but you may become so desperate to get even that you take foolish chances. You may call or even raise with hands you would normally fold, chase with nearly hopeless hands, or move up to higher limits, despite knowing that the game is tougher. After all, your luck has to change, doesn't it?

Wrong! In fact, if you deny that something is wrong, become looser and more aggressive, or play for higher limits, you can easily destroy your bankroll and self-confidence. To win at poker you need a detached attitude toward money. It's just chips, and you must objectively assess your expectation and ignore irrelevant facts such as whether you are winning or losing or how much money you have invested in this pot.

Once you put a chip into the pot, it doesn't belong to

you, and your decisions must be based on your current expectation. Exactly the same logic applies to your past losses,
and it doesn't matter whether they came tonight or over the
past month. That money is gone, and your decision to play
this hand or in this game or at any stakes should be based
entirely on a realistic assessment of your expectation. If it's
positive, you should play; if not, you should look for better
alternatives, including taking the night off.

Some Do's

Your highest immediate priority should be to feel like a winner. If
you feel like a loser, you will play like one, give off negative vibes,
and encourage others to run over you. To avoid this situation, take
the following steps:

1. *Be realistic.* Unfortunately, you probably can't just psyche
   yourself into a winning attitude, no matter what some self-
   help books say:

   "The man who can't be beaten, won't be beaten."

   "When the going gets tough, the tough get going."

   "You can do anything if you want it badly enough."

   Nonsense! In fact, believing that sort of drivel can
   greatly aggravate the problem. Poker is a brutally realistic
   game; if you don't objectively assess and work within your
   limitations, you will often play in the wrong games at the
   wrong times in the wrong way.

2. *Put your recent losses into perspective.* The player who
   asked for help said he had lost 25 percent of his bankroll.
   That's a lot of money, but he said he was a winning player.
   If his bankroll came from previous winnings, he was still
   way ahead of the game. Positive thinkers see the glass as

half full, while negative ones see it as half empty. His glass was three-quarters full, but he was still whining!

The same principle applies to any long-term winner. Remember that it is all one long poker game, and try to ignore this week, this month, or an even longer period. The $500 or $3,000 or $50,000 you have lost during this streak sounds like a lot of money until you compare it to your total winnings. Then it may be one-tenth of a glass or perhaps just a few teaspoons. It is not enough to make you into a loser.

Besides, it's only money, and there are much worse disasters than losing money. You may know people who have suffered terrible tragedies such as dying children, ruined careers, bankruptcy, and incurable illnesses. Compared to them, you're lucky.

Overreacting can cripple you, not just at the poker table, but in more important places. Some people get so upset that they take out their frustrations on their families, friends, or co-workers, converting an essentially trivial loss into a real tragedy.

3. *Take a complete break from poker.* Don't play, read poker books, discuss, or even think about poker. Right now that losing streak may hurt so much that it damages your play and perhaps, more important, parts of your life. A break may ease your pain, restore your balance, broaden your perspective, renew your enthusiasm, and let you remember that it's only a game.

4. *Break the streak fast.* When you start playing again, you need to book a win, any win, even a tiny one. Of course, you shouldn't take desperate steps trying to convert a loss to a win. If you get behind and see that you're playing badly, go home. When you play again, become much more selective about your games.

Play only in the softest games. If there aren't any soft games, don't play. If the game gets tougher, quit. Accept that you aren't playing your best and find games you can beat.

One reply to that request for help that I mentioned earlier (see p. 265) stated: "The first thing you must do is step down to a lower-limit game immediately . . . if you still cannot win, then keep going down incrementally all the way to the $1–$2 game."[2] I agree, but let's go further: play until you're ahead, then run like a bandit. It doesn't matter whether you win $10 or a $100 or $1,000. The important thing is to go home a winner.

Many players know they should drop down, but they're too proud to do it. They essentially say, I'm a $20–$40 player, and I'd feel and look ridiculous in a smaller game. But that's their bruised ego talking, and they're denying the obvious fact that lately they've been a $20–$40 *loser!* Face that reality, and say to yourself, "Since I can't beat my usual game, I'll find one I can beat."

5. *Stay in the soft games until your confidence returns.* Don't just drop down, book a win or two, and then go back to your old game. Stay down there for as long as it takes to become and to feel like a consistent winner. Don't let your ego—that supremely destructive force—make you act stupidly. For some reason you can't beat your usual game, and going back to it too soon can destroy the confidence you gained by booking a few wins. It can also wipe out the rest of your bankroll.

After you build up your confidence and bankroll, slowly move up toward your old game. If it takes six months or a year to get back there—or if you decide to stay at a lower

2. Jim Brier, *Card Player* columnist and co-author of *Middle Limit Hold'em Poker*, posted that reply on a twoplustwo.com forum.

level—so what? Unless you must win a certain amount to pay your bills, the important things are enjoying the game, winning consistently, and feeling good about yourself. Don't let your ego force you to play in games you can't beat consistently.

Learning from Losing Streaks

I'll begin with a surprising statement: a losing streak can be very good for you! Now that I have your attention, I'll explain what I mean. The money you have lost recently may seem huge, but it's peanuts compared to your future possibilities, and you should focus on the long term.

Winning steadily often causes complacency, which can lead to disastrous losses. A losing streak can make you analyze your game, recognize your weaknesses, and make the painful adjustments that lay the foundation for much greater success. History contains many examples.

IBM was once so successful that it became arrogant and complacent. Competitors and customers said, "IBM stands for I'm Bloody Marvelous." When personal computers and other developments dramatically changed the market, management said, in effect, "We're IBM, the best in the world, and we don't have to change." They continued business as usual and lost billions.

Contrast IBM's arrogant complacency to the way the Japanese reacted to the loss of World War II. They analyzed what they had done wrong, carefully planned a new system, and made "Japan Inc." into an overwhelming powerhouse. It crushed the competition for decades until it became complacent and started to lose heavily.

A losing streak can make you take your game apart, put it back together again, and become a much better player, but only if you keep your mind open and act logically. That's right, I'm beating the same old drum. Don't just trust your instincts and your memory. Instead, take the following steps.

Step No. 1: Keep and use good records.

Without them, you can't learn much. You need to know how much you won or lost each night, how well you did in different kinds of games, how you played when winning and losing, and all the other subjects discussed elsewhere. Study those records to learn what is wrong and what you can do about it. The chapter called "How should you review logically?" (see p. 51) described the basic principles for using records, but take a much harder look at them and ask a friend or coach to do the same. He may see something you missed. Both of you should look for differences between your winning and losing sessions:

- How did you play differently?
- What different kinds of games did you play?
- What other differences were there between your winning and losing sessions?

But what if neither of you can see any differences? Don't assume that you have been terribly unlucky because bad luck rarely causes a long losing streak. You probably kept poor records. You have not accurately described your play and situations because good records should show you what you are doing wrong.

When I said that to a friend, he became furious and insisted: "I've never played better." He then told the same silly stories we have heard too often: bad beats, dumb players, idiotic dealers, and so on. I would have offered to observe and comment on his play, but he was too defensive to learn anything, so I mumbled condolences and walked away. Two days later he was flat broke, trying to borrow a stake and whining constantly.

It is worth mentioning again: if you can't see why you are losing, the most logical thing to do is have a coach or a friend observe and criticize your play. Tiger Woods has a coach videotape and analyze his swing. Are you more talented than he is?

Step No. 2: Play within your psychological bankroll.

A losing streak should teach you how much you can lose without getting so upset that your game deteriorates. Your records should indicate when your play began to crumble and how rapidly it fell apart. Malmuth, Sklansky, and others have published guidelines about the amount of money needed for various stakes, but little has been written about this psychological "bankroll." Yet it is almost as important as the objective one, and it is much smaller. You can be well within your financial limits, but be psychologically bankrupt.

Some people can afford to lose five buy-ins a night for months (or even forever), but can't handle a big losing session or losing for three nights in a row. It's not the money; it's the pain of losing it that matters. Most of us have this sort of limit, and we should learn how to recognize it before reaching it. Then, when we approach it, we should take a break or play for lower stakes or become more conservative so that we don't pass it and start playing stupidly.

Unfortunately, some people love to play for higher stakes than they can afford, either financially or psychologically. They need that adrenaline rush. If you have that need, learn how to control it before it destroys you. If a few losses or one big one greatly upset you and damage your game, you're probably playing above your psychological bankroll. You may be able to afford the losses, but you can't tolerate them psychologically. So put your ego in your pocket and play for stakes you can handle. One post on a twoplustwo.com forum put it more colorfully: "Only lose funny money. That is, maybe $100 a month, which does not affect your lifestyle in any way."

Step No. 3: Work on the basics.

You may think you're too advanced to work on the basics, but professional sports coaches run frequent drills on tackling, blocking, foul shots, and other "kid stuff." They know that everybody needs regular refreshers, even for the simplest skills. Since NFL and NBA players work on the basics, you should do it too.

Let's lighten up for a moment. Somebody told my poker discussion group, "It's terrible to forget the books you thought you'd mastered." I cracked them up by admitting, "It's worse when it's your own book." But I was serious; I'm just one of many authors who have forgotten or ignored what we have written. If authors can forget their own books, maybe you have forgotten some of the material you have read. So get out those books, and start again on page one.

Step No. 4: Remember, poker is only a game.

If you forget that fact and exaggerate poker's importance, you risk losing much more than money. The money at stake shouldn't affect your lifestyle, and your results—whether positive or negative— should not have much impact on your moods, feelings about yourself, or important relationships. If you let poker become the center of your life and if you feel euphoric when winning and depressed when losing, you're in grave danger of severely damaging your life.[3]

Step No. 5: Diversify your life.

One reason so many people take poker too seriously is that they have nothing else going for them. All intelligent investors diversify their portfolios, and mutual fund managers are required by law to do so. Apply that principle to your money, your time, and your emotions. "Don't put all your eggs in one basket" has been a cliché for centuries, and it still makes sense.

Don't let poker push out the more meaningful parts of your life— your family, career, friends, other hobbies, and, most importantly, your health. You may know people who have let poker take over their lives; none of them is mentally healthy, and some of them are seriously ill, physically, mentally, or both. In addition to messing up the rest of your life, overemphasizing poker virtually guarantees that you will have more frequent, longer, and more painful losing streaks. If

---

3. This point is so important that this book's last chapter is called "Don't Take Poker Too Seriously."

you have nothing else in your life, you will be on an emotional roller coaster, with your moods soaring when winning, crashing when losing.

Eventually, you will have a few losses in a row, and you can easily go on tilt, become desperate to get even, and play so badly that you convert a short losing streak into a catastrophic one. It has happened thousands of times.

Step No. 6: Don't take this losing streak too seriously.

It's not a tragedy, and you shouldn't make it into one. If you keep your mind and your life balanced, objectively analyze your game, work on the basics, and select your games wisely, you will soon start winning and feeling better about yourself.

Why You Lose in Cardrooms

You may be frustrated because you win regularly in home games, but often lose in cardrooms.[1] This chapter will analyze the major causes for losing and suggest ways to counteract them.

House Charges Eat Your Winnings

The first problem is that the house charges a lot of money. Even if your home game takes some money for expenses, it is probably much less than you pay in a cardroom, and you also tip the dealers. As I noted in this book's Introduction, "The house's charges dramatically change everyone's economics, especially at the lower limits (because they are proportionately larger). The average players will break even in kitchen-table games, but will lose in a cardroom."

Because the poker explosion has greatly improved their business, many cardrooms have increased their charges, aggravating the problem. In Las Vegas the rake varies from 5 percent to 10 percent, and the maximum varies from $3 to $5 per hand, which is much higher than it was just a few years ago. The percentage and the maximum rake are even higher in some other places. Many cardrooms also take a jackpot drop. Switching to a place wtih lower charges can seriously improve your bottom line. In addition to charging you a lot of money, many cardrooms have six important differences from home games.

1. An earlier version of this chapter was published in *Poker Digest* before online poker exploded. Although I use the term "cardroom," most points apply to both live and online games.

Difference No. 1: Many players are much more competitive.

Some home games are extremely cutthroat, especially in places that prohibit cardrooms; in fact, some of the world's best players— the famous "road gamblers"—won fortunes in them. However, many home games are essentially "cocktail parties with cards." People come to meet their friends, gossip, discuss sports and business, tell jokes, and so on. The poker may be primarily an excuse to get together socially. This chapter is directed toward players in these casual games. If you can beat the cutthroat games, you don't need my advice.

People go to cardrooms to play poker, and many of them take it very seriously. There are social players, of course, but many games have some serious players, including a few pros or semipros. They go there to play poker, and they play to win.

This desire to win affects even casual pleasantries. The answer to "How are you doing?" will not be "fine." It will usually be "I'm winning," "I'm losing," or "I'm about even." Almost everything—even pleasantries—relates to winning and losing. This competitiveness affects virtually everything, such as the speed of the action, the way people play their hands, and the amount of talking allowed.

Recommendation: Take the game more seriously.[2] If you cannot make this first adjustment, you are unlikely to make the others, and you will probably continue to lose.

Difference No. 2: The action is much faster.

You'll play far more hands per hour than in home games, perhaps twice as many. Professional dealers are one reason, but the players may be even more important. Home games have much more conversation and other distractions than cardrooms. If you talk too much, don't pay attention, squeeze your cards slowly, or do anything else

---

2. I mean that you should compete more intensively, but don't take the game so seriously that it affects your moods, self-esteem, work, and personal relationships.

that slows down the game, cardroom players will get annoyed and pressure you to hurry up.

This faster pace can significantly reduce your skills. Your opponents are playing at a pace they enjoy, while you may feel rushed or pressured. You may make decisions without thinking clearly.

Recommendation: Pay attention and be prepared to move more quickly.

Difference No. 3: The players are much tighter.

In casual home games, nearly everyone may stay in on third street or before the flop, and most hands may end in a showdown, often with several people still involved. In many cardroom games, half or more of the players fold on the first betting round, many hands do not go to a showdown, and only two or three people get to it. If you play too loosely in a cardroom, you will give the other players much more action on their good hands than they will give you on yours, and *you will have absolutely no chance to be a long-term winner.*

Recommendation: Tighten up on every street.

Difference No. 4: The players are much more selectively aggressive.

Some home games are extremely loose-passive: Everyone calls, and hardly anyone raises. In fact, raising too often can be seen as "unfriendly," and some people will even check a sure winner, especially if they are heads-up. Other home games are wildly aggressive. People will raise and reraise with garbage, sometimes without even looking at their cards. Enormous pots are won with extremely weak hands, and nobody cares that much. Since everyone is gambling wildly, nobody has much of an edge.

Those patterns work in home games because the players can keep out people who won't go along with the crowd. If they don't like the way somebody plays, they don't invite him back. In a cardroom you've got to play with anybody, including rocks and professionals. Since you can't keep out the controlled players, if you play too loosely and passively or gamble too crazily, you'll *certainly* be a long-term loser.

Recommendation No. 1: Be more selectively aggressive; attack ONLY when you have the edge.

Recommendation No. 2: Don't "be nice." Don't give free cards or check your winning hands.

Difference No. 5: The number of players changes frequently.

Since home-game players are guests who will see each other again, they usually feel an obligation to make the games enjoyable, but many cardroom players feel no such obligation to strangers. The number of players at the table is a clear sign of this difference.

Most people want a stable number of players. Because they feel an obligation to each other, home-game players usually arrive and leave at about the same time. After the "deadline" the number of players may dwindle, but the number at the table does not change rapidly. For example, if one or two players are away from the table, the others will stay until they return. If the game gets too shorthanded, everyone may take a break.

In cardrooms, people begin and stop playing whenever they like, and many of them feel no obligation to keep the table full. You may be annoyed by people who take a break—sometimes for an hour or more—when two, three, or even more seats are empty. In just a few minutes, a game can go from full to just a few active players. But unless it is breaking up, the game rarely stops.

If the game gets shorthanded and you don't know how to play in those games, you have to make a painful choice: If you play, you will probably lose. If you refuse to play until the table fills up, the game may break, and there may be no other seats available.

Some home-game players have another problem: they are used to playing five or six handed, and do not know how to adjust to the eight, ten, or even more players in cardrooms. Fortunately, several books recommend strategic adjustments for different numbers of players: Sklansky and Malmuth, *Hold'em Poker for Advanced Players*; Sklansky and Malmuth (with Ray Zee), *Seven-Card Stud for Advanced Players*; and especially, Ray Zee and David Fromm (with Alan Schoonmaker), *World-Class High-Stakes and Shorthanded Limit Hold 'em.*

Recommendation No. 1: Learn how to adjust your strategy for different numbers of players.

Recommendation No. 2: Carefully monitor the number of active players and make the appropriate adjustments.

Difference No. 6: The players turn over rapidly.

In home games you will play with the same people again and again, and the players will not change much (or at all) during the session. You can slowly learn how everyone plays and make adjustments, respecting the tight players' bets and calling the wild players' crazy raises and bluffs.

In cardrooms players are constantly joining and leaving the game, and you'll often find yourself against a complete stranger. He may have been playing for a while, but you didn't pay much attention to him. Suddenly, you have to make an important decision, and you don't know how he plays. Every cardroom player has misplayed hands and then becomes angry with himself for not paying attention sooner. We folded a good hand, and then realized that the opponent is an obvious maniac, but we just hadn't noticed. Or we raised with a marginal hand and then learned that he is a rock.

Recommendation: Start studying new players IMMEDIATELY, and be cautious until you know how they play.

Unfortunately, you may not know how to make quick judgments about other players. If you have always played in home games, you have no need to do it and you may not have much natural intuition. If so, you need some sort of category system.

My own system has been described in *The Psychology of Poker*, and there are many other published systems. The particular system you use is much less important than learning and using any simple system. You need a way to make quick judgments about people and then adjust to them. Several professionals have told me that my own system is too simple, and I always respond: "You're right. I didn't develop it for professionals because you don't need it. You know how to read players. But most people don't have your gifts, and they need some simple system that helps them to do what you do naturally."

A simple system provides general guidance about how to play against various types of players. It is a just a starting point, and you have to study many other dimensions. However, if you do not have a system, you will probably get confused and make costly mistakes.

Recommendation No. 1: Learn any simple system for classifying players.

Recommendation No. 2: Start putting players into categories as soon as possible.

Recommendation No. 3: Revise your assessments as you get more information.

Should You Play in Cardrooms?

If you cannot adjust and losing bothers you, don't play in cardrooms. Don't spend good money to have a bad time. Besides, unpleasant losers ruin the game for other people. If you're going to be unhappy, do everyone a favor by staying home.

If you can't make the adjustments, but don't mind the amounts you lose, yes. Cardrooms offer an excellent entertainment value. You can usually find a game, even several different ones, and you can meet people, get a drink or a meal, catch up on sports, and generally have a good time.

If you play well and can make the adjustments, definitely yes. You'll get those benefits, and you may win more than you would in a home game because you'll play more hands and can be more selective. If you don't like one game, you can change to another one. These benefits are particularly strong online. The games are much faster, and there are lots more of them.

The important point is to know what you are trying to do and pick the place that fits your priorities and abilities. If home games suit you better, and there are enough of them, don't go to cardrooms, especially if you'll be miserable and unpleasant.

Unfortunately, many people want the convenience of cardrooms, but not the differences in the games. Accept the fact that you can't have both. If you want to play whenever you like or if you're tired of your home game, you have no choice but to play in cardrooms or on-line, but make sure to adjust your strategy.

Vicious Customers

In addition to being harder to beat than home games, cardroom poker can be *much* more stressful. I've already discussed the pressures to play quickly and minimize socializing, but these pressures do not cause the most severe stress. A bigger problem is that some players are nasty, and a few are vicious.

You can easily keep such people out of your home game; if someone gets out of line, you just don't invite him again. But cardrooms are open to the public, and they often let customers act outrageously.

They needle us when we lose, criticize everybody, blow smoke in our faces, spread junk all over the table, and throw cards or chips at people. They slow down the game by arguing, squeezing their cards, slow rolling, and demanding deck changes. They often ruin games by driving away weak players, putting everyone on edge, and generally killing the mood and the action.

Fortunately, they are usually weak players. Most good players, but certainly not all of them, can control the rotten impulses that we all occasionally feel. *If* we keep cool, we can usually turn their nastiness against them, but we naturally want to punish them, a desire that can cost us dearly. This chapter will:

- Give a few extreme examples
- Analyze why some people get so nasty
- Analyze why we often react so foolishly
- Suggest ways to turn their nastiness against them

A Few "Horror Stories"

Anyone who has played regularly in cardrooms has encountered many nasty people and a few vicious ones. I've chosen a few extreme horror stories with a common element: management did nothing about them:

- A woman threw a chip and deliberately hit a female member of our discussion group. Our member complained to management, but nothing was done.

- In a cardroom years ago, I played with an extremely drunk man I'll call "The Tycoon." He became abusive toward anyone who told him to stop slowing down the game. At times he deliberately refused to act, telling us that we should wait until he had found his cigarettes, lighted one, and so on. He even left the table in the middle of a hand and then screamed at the dealer for mucking his cards. He also showed his cards to other players while they had live cards, tried to make impossible bets such as pushing in his stack (in a limit game), and challenged several people to play heads-up for much higher stakes. I complained to the floorman, but nothing was done.

- Someone reported on twoplustwo.com's Psychology Forum that a man was not drunk, but "was acting borderline psychotic. He was a huge man who would mutter about the joint cheating him, the particular dealer cheating him, etc.... When he'd lose at showdown, he'd just stare at his cards, shaking his head and gritting his teeth. Then, he'd explode, slamming the table and standing up, looming over the dealer (he was in the 1 seat). He'd turn as if to walk away, get one step behind the dealer, and sit down again. Then, he'd repeat the process. Seriously, he did this 4 times before I said something to the manager.... He really was

scary. . . . I believed there would be some violence in a public cardroom." Nothing was done.

If you have not spent much time in cardrooms, you may think I
am exaggerating. I assure you that I am not. You can read similar stories on many Internet forums, and some of the stories about remarks
on Internet websites are even worse.

Why Do They Do It?

Most people don't care *why* other people are vicious. They just
care about their own frustration. But to win at poker, you must shift
your attention from yourself to other people. Instead of trying to answer that question about a particular individual, most people make
meaningless comments: "Who cares?" or "He's just a jerk," or "He
loves to tick people off." (Note the word "he." I hate to admit it, but
nearly all the vicious players are men.)

Ignoring motives is foolish because we can cope more effectively
with people if we understand the forces that drive them. So, why do
they do it? The answer to my question is quite simple: they are nasty
because it *pays off*. Most of the rewards are psychological, but a few
of them are financial.

When they hear that, some people get angry. "What do you mean,
it pays off? It really costs him. He chases away weak players and
ruins the game. He makes everybody angry. He doesn't have a friend
in the whole place." These answers are examples of "the egoistic fallacy."[1]

Many people egoistically assume that vicious people have the
same motives they have. Since they want people to like them, they assume that everybody wants to be liked. Since they want weak players
to stick around, they think everybody would want them in their

---

1. The egotistic fallacy is the belief that other people think and feel just the way
   we do. It is discussed in my book *The Psychology of Poker* on pp. 49–50.

games. But vicious people's motives are often quite different. Most behavior is driven by a variety of motives, and hardly anyone has all the ones I will list, but here are a few of their motives:

First, they may get a big kick out of making people angry. You and I want people to like us, but they may crave a different kind of attention. The research on "problem children" shows that they *want* people to yell at, or even to hit them. We would regard these actions as punishments, but for some people they are rewards. They learned as young children that they could get extra attention and manipulate their parents and other people by throwing tantrums, swearing, hitting or biting people, and so on.

Second, they get relief, perhaps even pleasure, just from being nasty. Everybody occasionally has so much pressure inside them that they need the relief of expressing it. Vicious people may have more pressure than they can handle, and expressing their tensions makes them feel better. If you notice and react, you have essentially validated their feelings, even if you react negatively. You have given them the satisfaction of both expressing their feelings and making you share their misery.

Third, they may dislike or feel contempt for certain kinds of people such as women, different races, or weak players. A woman told me that men have asked her, "What's a pretty girl like you doing playing poker?" She resisted the impulse to reply, "I've been waiting for a fish like you." One sexist pig even said, "As long as you have chips in front of you, honey, I am not leaving this table." He finally left with about $50 ($450 less than his buy-in).

Fourth, they may become obnoxious only when they are losing. Getting vicious can be their way of coping with that frustration. Losing at poker implies that you are not only unlucky but that you play poorly. Instead of accepting responsibility for their poor playing, some people blame the "idiots" and "cheaters" who cause their losses.

Fifth, they may make others so angry that they play stupidly. This motive is particularly strong in the few nasty people who play well.

They want you to become so eager to beat them that you give away your chips. For example, angry people may make foolish raises and calls just to "get even" with a nasty player, and you may have done it yourself. At times one or more players can go on tilt, which is exactly what the nasty person wants.

As an industrial psychologist, I know that most businesses won't tolerate this sort of customer. So my natural question is, why allow it?

Why Does Management Let Them Get Away with It?

Here are three reasons why management allows poor behavior: First, management may not know what is happening or how people feel about it. Many dealers are reluctant to ask for help. They don't want to call the supervisors and be forced to complete an incident report. They rely on tips and know that disciplining a player can cost them money. It will stop the game, perhaps for quite some time, and they make tips only when the game is moving. In addition, some disgusting people tip well, almost as if their tips were buying them the right to be vicious. Many are so drunk or stupid that they build large pots that increase the dealers' tips.

Second, some managers do not closely watch their rooms, while others may think that nobody cares about nastiness as long as the hateful people are losing money. Of course, not all of them are losers; some winners—including a few famous professionals—are notoriously nasty. The solution to this problem is quite simple: *Send management an absolutely clear message.*

Tony Wuehle, a member of our discussion group, said that several people got so sick of one abusive player that, when he sat down, they *all* left the table. When the manager asked why, they told him they would not play with him. He was immediately barred.

Third, the vicious player might be a valued customer of the pits[2] or hotel. The Tycoon was holding a conference at the hotel, spending big bucks on rooms and meals for his people. Even if the poker room manager had wanted to eject him, he might have been afraid that the hotel management would intervene or retaliate.

The effects of this pressure were clearly communicated to me by a request to complete an incident report to protect a dealer. She had called the shift manager because a drunk I'll call "The Whale"[3] continually criticized her and the other players, slowed down the game, flashed cards deliberately, and did many other nasty things. Of course I completed the report, but I was appalled. Why should she need protection when she was just doing her job, and he had been odious for *hours?*

The shift manager told me that The Whale was a big loser in the pits. If he complained about the dealer and took his action to another casino, she would be blamed.

Why Do We Players Let Them Get Away with It?

I'm embarrassed to admit it, but hadn't objected forcefully to The Whale (but I had asked him tactfully and ineffectually to behave). He was losing lots of money, and I was getting my share. He wasn't as bad as the one I described in "A Few Horror Stories," but he did go on and on for hours. I'm sure he chased away some of the less greedy players.

I am usually much less tolerant than many players. I have made my share of complaints to management, and I have left many games to avoid abusive people. Other members of our discussion group will accept extreme nastiness if someone is losing enough. For example, we once debated whether a man should be thrown out because he

2. The pits are the games other than poker such as craps, roulette, blackjack, and slots. Most of a casino's gambling profits come from the pits, not poker.

3. In Las Vegas a "Whale" is a high roller, a big "fish" (aka "sucker" who loses lots of money).

had thrown a water bottle against the wall. He had $10,000 in front of him and was so completely on tilt that he would have lost all of it. Some others and I agreed that management was right to eject him, while others felt they should let him "throw a party."

Zero-Tolerance Policies

Only a few cardrooms have and enforce zero-tolerance policies. Because Linda Johnson, Jan Fisher, and Mark Tenner own Card Player Cruises and belong to our discussion group, I am most familiar with their rules. The pre-cruise newsletter says, "Because we want everyone to have a good time . . . we do not tolerate abuse in the poker room." This position is reiterated at the welcome-aboard party, and it gets appreciative applause. Players with nasty reputations are warned in advance and, in extreme cases, have been refused entry to the ship's cardroom. They have also told a few players, "You've got two strikes against you. If you get out of line, you will *not* get the benefit of a doubt. We will just bar you from playing on this and future cruises."

I once thought they could enforce this hard line only because they have a monopoly. If you get barred on a cruise, you can't go down the street to another game. But friends who have taken cruises said that there is also a different atmosphere. Because everyone is on vacation, relaxing and spending lots of time together for meals and excursions, the relationships become stronger and friendlier. People avoid abusing others, partly because of friendship bonds and partly because it could isolate them from everyone. In one sense there is almost a "home game atmosphere."

A few brick-and-mortar cardrooms have similar policies. They have realized that the nasty people chase away good customers and create more trouble than they are worth. I could not agree more.[4] In

4. I play almost exclusively at Las Vegas's Luxor and Excalibur. They and some other small rooms won't tolerate viciousness or even abusive remarks. I vividly recall a reply to someone who objected strenuously to being ejected: "Your only decision is whether you leave the casino by this door or that one."

fact, I'm embarrassed about the way I reacted to The Whale. Instead of waiting to be asked to file an incident report, I should have *demanded* that management tell him to act decently or leave. And if management refused, I should have left and taken some friends with me.

Management doesn't want to lose us. Given a choice between the nasty ones and us, they'll usually choose us. Let's all make sure management knows that they really must make that choice: let them know we won't stay if they don't insist that *everyone* acts decently.

The Worst Thing to Do

No matter how annoyed you are, *the worst thing you can do is to fight these nasty people openly.* I've heard and read long discussions of how to get even with them. I've even listened to "conspiracies." Mature, normally intelligent adults can get so angry that they make elaborate plans to get revenge. And all they're doing is rewarding the nasty ones, often at their own expense.

Making nasty remarks, being screamed at, or uttering challenges to step outside would embarrass you or me, but they often give him intense pleasure. He realizes that others are so upset that they have shifted their focus from playing well to getting even with him. He craves attention, and they are giving him lots of it, and they may also be so upset that they play badly.

As I mentioned earlier, the Chinese have a wonderful proverb: "When you plan revenge, dig two graves, one for your enemy, the other for yourself." Don't dig your own grave to punish an SOB.

Beware of Rationalizations

Although it's important to understand the nasty people's motives, it's *much* more important to understand and not to rationalize our own. In fact, a central poker principle is to *know why we are taking any action.* We usually do it when we make a bet or a raise. We think of pot odds, position, opponents, and so on, and then make a reasoned judgment about folding, calling, or raising. By knowing why we made a bad decision, we can avoid repeating it.

This principle is immeasurably more important and harder to apply when our emotions are involved. They can make us respond impulsively and then rationalize that we're just trying to "create a strong table image," "prove he can't run over me," or "protect other people."

Vicious people are an unavoidable part of life and of cardroom and online poker. If we let them affect us, they have essentially beaten us, even if they lose their chips. If we keep our heads, and play our cards well, we'll get the truly rewarding revenge of taking away both their chips and their pleasure.

How Should You React?

The first rule is to remember: *every time you play a hand differently because of your emotions,* THEY WIN. They have put you off your game and made you respond to irrelevant factors such as their nastiness or your emotions. Your reaction to these unavoidable people should be that you must beat them the same way you beat other players: by playing better than they do.

Their chips are worth exactly as much as any other chips. Their being in the game or this pot should not affect your decisions unless their play *affects* your expectation. Fortunately, they often make mistakes—and cause other players to make mistakes—which can dramatically increase your profits.

Exploit strategic errors.

Many of them play poorly. They get so emotional that they call or even raise when they should fold, make foolish bluffs, and do other silly things. They may also make other people act emotionally. Their games often resemble "King of the Hill" more than poker for real money. Some players may care more about dominating and punishing each other than they care about winning money. This foolishness creates highly profitable opportunities *if you can keep cool and rational.*

Exploit information management errors.

Since poker is a game of incomplete information, you can't win without managing information well. Because they are dominated by their emotions, many vicious players make two serious information management errors:

1. They don't read cards well.
2. They give away too much information.

Because they are so eager to express their anger, they may make extreme card-reading errors. For example, they tend to think that other people are trying to bluff them, and they are not going to let anyone run over them. They may focus primarily on their own hands instead of trying to interpret your signals. They respond, not to a rational analysis of the information, but to their inner tensions.

You must not assume that they are acting rationally. I coined a term for people who are acting foolishly, "DAI," meaning Don't Assume Intelligence. Don't assume that these players have the same hand that you or another player would have to make these bets. Let's say that there are three cards to a flush and three cards to two straights on the board. If you bet your small straight and get raised, do not assume that he must have at least a straight. He could have just two pair or—if he is really angry—even less.

DAI occasionally applies even to the few who can play well, and it is extremely obvious for the ones who play poorly. When people are dominated by their emotions, they do all sorts of stupid things. Their craziness may also cause other people to become so emotional that they make those same mistakes, increasing your expectation.

Study them (and others), especially when you are not in the hand. Their words and gestures contain a great deal of information, and it is often easy to "crack the code." You may see that this player throws his chips in forcefully when he is bluffing, but bets carefully when he has the nuts. Or that one says one thing when he is drawing and another when he has a made hand. Because other players are also emotional, they will also give away more information than usual.

Recognize that some of them are quite perceptive about emotions.

Although they are often poor at reading cards, some of them are quite good at picking up, and taking advantage of, emotional signals. Remember, they *want* to upset you. They may sense, for example, when you're angry, offended, or in danger of going on tilt, and they know just how to "push your buttons." You must therefore control your own reactions very tightly. Otherwise, you will give them ammunition that they will aim right between your eyes.

Beware of the other players.

Don't focus so intently on the nasty one that you ignore the other players or assume they are playing their usual game. Otherwise, you may beat him, but lose lots of money to the others.

They may be so eager to punish him that their games change. Some players will play poorly, but others will actually play better. They will become more focused and intent on playing their A-game. Instead of a relaxed, friendly game, it's war.

Some players will attack more aggressively; others will bluff more frequently; others will set traps to get revenge; and a few will become extremely tight. You must carefully study them, see how their games have changed, and make appropriate adjustments.

However, as I noted earlier, many of them are going to make the same sort of mistakes as their "enemy." They will make stupid plays for emotional reasons, give away lots of information, and fail to read you well. These people can put a whole table at or near tilt, creating very profitable opportunities.

If you can't stay cool, quit.

When one or more people are acting emotionally, the game can become a real moneymaker. However, because the tension level is so high, you can lose both your temper and your money. You must therefore monitor yourself closely.

Constantly ask yourself, "Am I taking this action to increase my expectation, or am I reacting to my emotions?" If you find that you're acting emotionally or if the potential profit is not enough to balance the irritation or, worst of all, if you're playing badly, are on tilt, or in danger of going there, you should quit *immediately.*

Ignore your desire to get even (either financially or personally), and leave the game before you lose serious money. If you stay for just a few more hands, you may take a bad beat (or have something else upset you) and go on tilt.[5] There will always be another game, and there is an endless supply of nasty people. Tomorrow when you feel and play better, you can get even or make some money.

5. See the chapter called "Preventing and Handling Tilt," p. 193 in this book.

New Aggravations

Because poker brings out the worst in some people, nastiness has always been a problem in cardrooms. Unfortunately, it has recently become much more serious. We now see an unprecedented amount of shouting, trash-talking, threats, and other forms of nastiness. At least five recent developments have aggravated the problem:

1. The poker explosion
2. Television
3. Online poker
4. Popularity of no-limit hold'em
5. Inexperienced dealers and supervisors

The Poker Explosion

The poker explosion has brought about an enormous number of new players, creating long waiting lists and crowding. You may have to wait for hours to get into a game, and some rooms have too many tables pressed closely together. If you push your chair back or walk around, you bump into someone. Waiting and crowding raise the tension level, causing some people to overreact to other frustrations.

Many of the newer players have no idea how they should behave in cardrooms. They take too long to act, play out of turn, show their cards to each other, give advice to other players, and so on. They essentially play the same way in cardrooms as they do in home games.

Some of them get really nasty when told to follow the rules. I've heard them respond to other players' very legitimate requests with remarks like this: "We're just having fun. Don't tell us what to do."

Television

Television producers encourage childish displays because they add "dramatic value." If someone acts wildly, the cameras focus on him, and the editors put it in the show. You may see far more outbursts in an hour of television than you will see in a week at a normal table. Far too many people play to the cameras. They know that acting stupidly can get a lot of attention, and some of them are too immature to resist the temptation.

When viewers—especially new players—see tournament players screaming, trash-talking, jumping up, pumping their fists, and giving high-fives, they naturally conclude that they can do the same. They posture, try to stare down opponents, count their chips, or ask, "How deep are you?" (even when playing limit poker). A dealer once told a young player, "If you're finished acting, it's your turn to act."

Online Poker

When you play at home, you can scream and swear at the computer because nobody can hear you. You can also use the chat feature to make extreme insults and threats without being embarrassed or afraid because nobody knows who you are or where you live. Some comments made in chat are extraordinarily nasty.

Some people needle losers after beating them out of large pots. Name-calling occurs frequently, especially on the large websites. Occasionally, someone even threatens to beat up another player. If people acted that way in poker rooms, fights would break out.

Since so many new players started online and they have seen such outrageous antics on television, they naturally copy in poker rooms what they have done at home and seen on television. They scream, curse, threaten other players, and so on.

Popularity of No-Limit Hold'em

No-limit games were once scarce, but now they are everywhere. Because you can play well for hours and lose everything in one pot, the tension level is much higher. When the inevitable "bust outs" occur, some people blow up.

Until recently most no-limit games had large buy-ins, and most players were experienced and emotionally controlled. Now most games have maximum buy-ins of $300 or less, and many players have hardly any experience, self-control, or idea of how to play or behave. These games have almost no resemblance to traditional no-limit games:

- If they play, they will find six or more opponents, which almost never happened before.
- If they learned how to play from watching those highly-edited television broadcasts, they will make outrageous moves such as all-in bets or calls with trash.
- If they win a huge pot, they may insult or needle the loser or scream, high-five, and do the other stupid things you see on TV.
- If they lose, they can get even nastier.

The first two differences greatly increase the good players' profits, but all of them escalate the tension and frustration.

The newbies' terrible play has also caused some experienced players to play for more money than they can afford to lose (in both limit and no-limit games). After expecting huge profits, they become enraged when they lose heavily. John Bushnell, a dealer and floorman, told me, "The tension is higher than ever because people are playing for their paychecks." When they lose the rent money, they erupt.

Because of six- or seven-way action, bad beats have become extremely common, and losing your entire stack to a trash hand is devastating. If the winner is screaming, trash-talking, and giving high-fives, the experience can be almost intolerable. Most of the really angry bad beat stories I have heard lately are about no-limit games.

Inexperienced Dealers and Supervisors

All over America new rooms have opened and old ones have expanded. As I mentioned earlier, there are not remotely enough well-trained and experienced dealers and floor people to staff them all. Many rooms have been forced to hire and promote inexperienced people, and some of them don't speak English well. They aggravate the problems in three ways:

1. They act slowly and make many irritating mistakes. We want to play, not to wait around, and we become frustrated when the dealer does not control the game and keep it moving.

2. They occasionally make big mistakes that cost people money. Players become furious when they are dealt pocket aces or kings, but a dealer's error causes a misdeal. When a large pot goes to the wrong player because a dealer burned and turned too soon, the loser can go ballistic.[1]

3. They are new hires who don't know how to handle nastiness. Repeatedly, I have seen dealers and even floor people freeze at exactly the time they should have taken charge. They don't have the experience to handle nasty situations tactfully, and they lack the confidence to insist that people act decently or get out.

---

1. In my entire life I have shouted only once at a dealer. She had burned and was ready to turn the river card when I told her to stop. I said that seat one had not acted, and she was going to foul the deck. She did not understand me and started again to turn that card. I had to shout, "Stop." A short time later she took a job at a bigger, more prestigious poker room.

They freeze, looking like a deer caught in the headlights, hoping the problem will go away, but it often just gets worse. I have seen many shouting matches, a few incidents in which men had to be forcibly restrained, and two players once left my table to go outside.

The Bottom Line

Because of all these factors, there is an unprecedented amount of nastiness and tension. A distressing number of people—including a few who would normally act better—blow up, and nobody stops them from going over the line.

This problem isn't going to correct itself. It is management's responsibility to take control. When the rules are clear and are firmly enforced, most people will obey them. Conversely, if they don't know the rules, or they sense that they can break them with impunity, some people will test the limits until they get stopped. Poker room managers *must* take two actions:

1. Clearly state and enforce a zero tolerance policy.
2. Definitely provide more training and supervision to their inexperienced people.

When a new dealer slows down the game or the action stops completely because of a dealer's inexperience, the casino loses serious money, and everybody gets annoyed. In purely bottom line terms, the time and cost of training people are justified.

Most importantly, managers *must train their people to prevent abusive language, threats, and violence.* If a dealer or supervisor sees threats or, worse yet, actual violence, he must *immediately* take firm action. Otherwise, the casino can lose a huge lawsuit.

A major Los Angeles casino lost a judgment of over $3,000,000 because a player who had repeatedly acted in a threatening manner hit and seriously injured another player. Because the casino had not reacted to the signals that he was dangerous, most of the award was for punitive damages.

That sort of incident will certainly occur again and again. Poker is frustrating, and some people just can't handle it. They get out of line, and somebody has to stop them before they get violent. If such a player injures somebody, the casino will be extremely vulnerable, and the manager will probably be held accountable, destroying his career.

The Regular Players Should *Demand* Better Behavior

There is no reason for us—the best customers—to tolerate abuse and other nastiness. We obey the rules, and there is no reason for us to accept harassment from others. When someone gets out of line, *insist* that management enforce the rules. They are often posted right there on the wall. Management just has to say, "There are the rules. If you don't obey them, you can't play here."

I'm Giving Up on Poker

Many people have said that they don't want to play anymore, but most of them didn't really mean it. They were just expressing their frustration. After a bad night, you may have even said it yourself. You got so sick of being card dead or having your good hands beaten, and you may also have recognized that you didn't play that well. Perhaps you tried to explain your feelings to your friends, but they didn't really listen. They just wanted to tell you their own hard luck stories. So you said, "Why should I let a stupid game mess up my life? I give up."

If you really don't enjoy playing and if your frustration is affecting your moods and relationships with other people, you should seriously consider quitting. Even if poker is your primary income source, you should quit if it's making you miserable. Life is too short to play at a game or work at a job that severely upsets you. But before making a final decision, let's analyze why you feel this way.

Some Players Really Want to Quit

Several posters on Internet forums have said they were quitting or close to it. Some of them were frustrated because they had overestimated their own skills and selected games they could not beat. This subject was discussed in a chapter called "Losing Steaks" (see p. 265) and other places. Now I will discuss just three problems:

1. Refusing to accept the game as it is
2. Playing above your psychological bankroll
3. Maintaining an unbalanced life

Problem No. 1: Refusing to Accept the Game as It Is

Because poker is gambling, swings and losing streaks are unavoidable. As Malmuth put it, a gambling game needs a proper balance of luck and skill to survive. If the game is too dependent on luck, the house edge will make everybody lose over the long run, as countless crapshooters and roulette players can confirm. If the game is mostly skill, people won't bet on it. For example, because the better player nearly always wins, hardly anyone bets on chess. Poker, especially hold'em, has an excellent balance of skill, and luck, which lets good players make serious profits.

Good players will win over the long term, but luck has enormous short-term effects. Players can make terrible mistakes, but still win, not just an occasional pot, but for an entire tournament or weeks of cash game play. The "long term" can be very long indeed, and it can be extraordinarily frustrating to watch helplessly as apparently inferior players take your money.

In addition, as I noted elsewhere, you probably don't play as well as you think. In chess and other games of skill, you'd know your limitations. There are very clear ranking systems, and you know that you'll usually beat the players with lower rankings and lose to the ones above you. Not knowing your limitations can dramatically increase your frustration. You may think you should win, but can't do it. However, we'll ignore that problem for the moment and assume you play well enough to beat your game over the long term.

Some authorities have stated that variance alone could cause a good player to have at least a 2,000-hour losing streak, about a year of full-time play. It may seem impossible, but it will happen to a few of us. You probably won't have such a long period of bad luck, but you'll certainly have some shorter ones. If you can't accept the swings that are an *inescapable* part of poker, it's probably the wrong game for you. You should play something else.

But don't expect to make significant money at it. Without luck there will not be large (or any) profits. As many authorities have argued, "the beauty of poker" is its huge luck factor. It deceives and seduces weak players so that they keep coming back to give us their money.

Reason No. 2: Playing Above Your Psychological Bankroll

Nearly everyone has this kind of bankroll; it's the amount of money that you can lose before your play deteriorates. Even if it's only a small fraction of your financial bankroll, you can't emotionally handle losing more than this amount. Far too many people deny this limitation, and they often go on tilt, sometimes without realizing it. Their desperate need to recover that money can make them take very foolish chances.

Both professionals and recreational players have this limitation. Smart ones—especially professionals—recognize and work within it, while fools ignore it or pretend it does not affect them. For example, a very smart professional wanted to move to a much larger game. He expected some losses at first and set aside part of his bankroll the way a businessperson would designate a specific amount to start up a new venture. If he lost all of it, he intended to move back down. After losing about 15 percent of his budgeted amount, he realized that stress was damaging his play. He wrote off the small loss and moved back to his old level. Because he understood and accepted his psychological limitations, his small loss did not turn into a catastrophic one.

You may think you can handle swings that are too big for you. You may also want the rush of big wins, but get extremely upset by the inevitable large losses. Because poker is a gambling game, there's an unbreakable link between the upside gains and the downside risks. If your psychological bankroll is too small for your current stakes, your emotions will harm your play, moods, and financial bankroll. If you can't handle the swings, move down or quit playing.

Reason No. 3: Maintaining an Unbalanced Life

If you get extremely upset by poker losses that you can afford, your life is probably unbalanced. Winning at poker may be too important to you because you have a great big hole inside you that you hope poker will fill. I will discuss this subject in the next chapter because it is a serious problem. If poker is too important to you, you are not just playing for money; you are literally gambling with your emotional stability, and those stakes are too damned high.

If your life is unbalanced, your wins and losses will have far too much impact on you. When you win, you will feel strong, smart, and confident. When you lose, you will feel like a loser, not just in poker, but in everything. You may find yourself overreacting to trivial losses or bad beats that do not really matter.

If you feel that way, don't quit poker because that hole won't go away. Instead, learn why you have that hole and find other things to fill it. Develop other hobbies, make a larger commitment to your job, or spend more time with your friends and family to make yourself feel more complete and balanced.

When poker is not the center of your life, you'll enjoy it more, and the inevitable losses won't have such a devastating impact. That is, if you have let poker dominate your life, don't give up just because you've had some losses. "Get a life" so that those losses don't upset you so much.

Don't Take Poker Too Seriously

Poker is just a game, and it should be played for pleasure. Of course, you should play your best, study, post on Internet forums, join a discussion group, and do whatever else will improve your results and skills, but don't let poker take over your life. That warning is valid even if you play for a living; don't let poker or any other job become an obsession.

The Problem

If poker becomes critically important to you, you're risking much more than your money. You can damage really important areas of your life such as your relationships with family and friends, education, work, and even your sense of personal worth. If too much of your identity or self-esteem depends on any one element of your life—such as poker, studies, athletic skill, career success, or a sexual relationship—you become vulnerable and fragile. If that element is damaged, you can fall apart.

Poker is a particularly bad foundation for your self-concept because luck has such huge short-term effects. When the inevitable bad beats and losing streaks occur, you may feel like a worthless failure or an angry victim.

This chapter was stimulated by several threads on twoplustwo. com's Psychology Forum. On just one day, May 1, 2005, there were six threads and one hundred thirty-two replies that related to taking poker too seriously. I have stated the thread's title, the original poster's screen name, and the number of replies on that date, plus a brief quotation from the original post. Some posts were edited for spelling or grammatical errors. You can read the entire threads by using the search function at twoplustwo.com.

So many people would not have written about this subject if they did not regard it as a significant problem. I excluded posts about losing money because my current focus is on poker's nonfinancial effects.

1. *Time consumption* (LetYouDown, 27 replies) "I think about it constantly. . . . Sometimes when I can't sleep at night, my mind starts going about poker, and I'm screwed. The amount of time it takes away from my social life (both family and friends) is a little absurd. . . . Poker just seems to make me socially numb. Not sure if that makes sense, but when I'm playing . . . I'm completely oblivious to the passing of time. . . . I rarely feel 'enough is enough,' even for an evening. I may be exhausted, but I don't want to stop playing."

2. *Leaving poker at the table* (NYPlayer, 29 replies): "I am looking for strategies on how to clear my mind and help me to lead a normal life away from the table instead of fixating on poker thoughts when I'm at the gym or dinner with my girlfriend or trying to fall asleep."

3. *Scheduling my way to a healthier life* (Sloth469, 12 replies): "I've . . . come to the conclusion that . . . poker online is not a fulfilling way to spend the majority of my time."

4. *Has poker killed my education?* (billyjex, 38 replies): "Poker has killed my education, basically. How sad is it? I'm going to get my degree, but I feel with every day I lose more interest in school."

5. *Finding a balance in your life* (Elektrik, 12 replies): "My fiancé recently pointed out to me that I have an addictive

personality. . . . Now I realize that, when I take up something, I pretty much focus solely on it."

6. *Feelings of guilt re: family* (carydarling, 14 replies): "I get
pains of guilt when spending too much time playing. . . . It
may mean all night Friday, all night Saturday and maybe
some Sunday."

Recurrent Themes

Several themes came up repeatedly, and they obviously overlap.
For example, if you spend too much time playing, you almost automatically neglect other activities. I will briefly discuss the most common themes in the preceeding six and a few other threads:

1. *Spending too much time:* This problem was mentioned
most frequently, and it affects the others. Many posters believe that they spend *far* too much time playing, thinking,
reading, discussing, and posting about poker. If they are
winning players, they may regard every moment away
from the table as costing them money. If they just love to
play, they may not care about studying, exercising, or even
being with their girlfriends. And some people play too
much without knowing why.

2. *Neglecting studies or work:* One thread was about "killing
my education," and posters in several threads reported that
their grades were suffering, or they were not working well.
Thinking constantly about poker and losing sleep over it
will usually damage performance and can destroy an education or a career.

3. *Thinking about poker while doing other things:* Several people said they thought about poker in class, while driving or
working, at parties, or even during intimate moments. A

few posts were funny. For example, several months earlier someone said that he saw a license plate with 4526 and thought, "Gut shot draw."

4. *Disrupting eating and sleep cycles:* Playing too much automatically disrupts these cycles. In addition, some people said that they did not feel hungry or sleepy while playing or that they played until they collapsed, then slept too long, even missing classes or work because they were exhausted.

5. *Showing concerns about mood swings:* Some people worried about poker's effects on their moods. When they won, they felt euphoric; when they lost, they became depressed, lethargic, or angry with themselves, other players, or the whole world.

6. *Having doubts about mental health:* Sometimes these doubts were explicitly expressed by remarks about "addictions," "obsessions," and "compulsive gambling." More frequently, people wondered whether their unbalanced lifestyle was a symptom of underlying pathology. They asked, directly or indirectly, "Is it healthy to spend so much time, neglect my family and friends, think so much about poker, and let it have such extreme effects on my moods?" The answer, of course, is *"No!"*

Clinical psychologists know more about mental health than I do, and two of them read this article and some of the posts. Dr. Dan Kessler e-mailed me:

> One way of defining any behavior as a problem or even a disorder is that it significantly interferes with some sphere of life. The three main spheres are work/school, love/relationships, and play/enjoyment. In fact, every mental health disorder requires either significant distress *or* significant interference in some aspect of life. Although not necessarily pathological gamblers, many posters have this interference.

7. *Damaging important relationships:* They believe that they are neglecting their families and friends, especially girlfriends. All the references to sexual partners related to girlfriends, including fiancés. That is, no women mentioned this problem on that date, which suggests that most of them don't have it (or won't admit it). Since ignoring girlfriends can easily destroy a relationship, some posters were clearly worried, but they felt unable to control themselves. They said, in effect, "I know I should pay more attention to her, but I can't help myself."

On May 9, 2005, a new thread (Losing at Love and Poker) told a painful story. "The love of my life is to marry someone else. She cited my poker playing as one reason why our relationship failed. She cited one particular occasion, where I chose poker over her as the moment it was over for her." He also stated that he was giving up poker because "I have a behavioral addiction when it comes to poker. For me it was an escape from the harsh realities of my life. . . . Poker . . . took up precious energy and time. It cost me the love of my life. Never again."

I am sorry that he paid such a high price, but appreciate his telling us about it. Perhaps his example can prevent some others from losing the love of their life or doing other irreparable damage.

Limitations of These Data

Some of these people clearly have a significant problem. Since all my data come from posters on the Psychology Forum, I cannot draw any conclusions about poker players in general. I think that the posters were fairly young, with a disproportionate number of male college students, but a few of them were in their thirties or older.

Dr. Eric Niler, the other clinical psychologist, said that a poll showed that many 2+2 posters were males in their late teens to midtwenties. In addition, posters are probably more interested in poker than most players. These sampling biases mean that I can't say how many people take poker too seriously. But I am not trying to draw general conclusions or to recommend social or legal changes. My only goal is to help people who have this problem. If some of these points apply to you, you may be letting poker damage more important parts of your life.

Of course, poker is not the only or the worst kind of addiction. In a comment posted on the twoplustwo.com's Psychology Forum Dennis Shaub, a regular poster, said it well: "It isn't poker, or drinking, or anything else, that's really the problem. It's an unbalanced life, where any one activity overshadows the other, more important things in your life."

Recommendations

We have seen a scary list of "symptoms." Nobody listed all of them, and most posts discussed only one or two. Even though I don't know how common these symptoms are, some people clearly have a serious problem. If you think you may be one of them, I recommend the following actions.

Remember this critical point: Don't take poker too seriously.

Please forgive my repeating the title, but it is the essential first step. You can't solve the problem without recognizing that poker is not that important. Never forget that—unless it is your livelihood—it is just a game.

Even if you play for a living, you should not let it take over your life. If you do, your attitudes and life are unbalanced, and "unbalanced" is a common euphemism for "crazy." All the other recommendations are just steps toward balancing your life and attitudes.

Clarify your priorities.

This step is also essential. If you don't know what you want out of life, you're not going to get it. Socrates once said, "The unexamined life is not worth living." Every so often you should ask yourself some searching questions, especially, "What is really important to me?"

If you seriously try to answer that question, you may be very surprised at what you learn. Some things that seem so important now may be revealed as utterly trivial, while others that you rarely think about may be critically important to you.

A reply to the poster who had lost "the love of his life" by playing too much said: "It's human nature to take things for granted when we have them, and when they're gone . . . clarity enters your mind, and you realize how much they meant to you." That's exactly what I mean. Make sure you understand what is really important to you before you have lost it forever.

Ask yourself: *Why* do I play so much poker?

This question is just another way to examine yourself and your life. You may find that your motives are unhealthy. For example, you may be full of anger, and poker lets you express it in socially acceptable ways. Perhaps you rely on poker to build your ego or to fill some sort of gaping hole in yourself. You may think. "I'm not worth much, but I can really play well." Or you may be using poker as an escape in the same general way that people use alcohol and drugs. Until you understand why you play so much, you have little chance of gaining control over your play or your life.

Ask yourself: Am I a compulsive gambler?

Some of you are compulsive gamblers, and others are in danger of crossing the line. Unfortunately, that line is not clear. A gambling addiction is not like AIDS or leukemia: you can't just take tests and be sure of the diagnosis.

If you think that you may be an addict, go to www.gamblers anonymous.org and take the test. It is *not* definitive, but it is suggestive: the higher your score, the greater the probability that you have a severe problem. You should also know that denial is a central characteristic of most addictions. People who are unquestionably addicted to gambling, drugs, or alcohol often insist, "I can handle it."

If your score is high enough to suggest that you're a compulsive gambler, consult a professional or attend Gamblers Anonymous meetings to get more information. If you are an addict or close to becoming one, get help before it destroys your life.

Set *rational* priorities.

Only you can say what is important to you, but you should also let your parents, spouse, teachers, friends, and others—perhaps even including professionals—help you with this step. They can probably help you see things more clearly.

"Rational" refers primarily to the long-term consequences of various choices. Some of the actions you take now—including playing too much poker or letting it harm your self-esteem, moods, studies, or important relationships—will have immense long-term effects. For example, if you lose your girlfriend, don't get your degree, or miss a promotion, you may regret it forever.

On May 6, 2005, Slimmah started a thread that illustrated irrational priorities. He wondered whether he should get psychotherapy to improve his win rate because he had "a serious problem with rage. . . . My emotions simply take over after taking too many beats in a certain timeframe."[1]

I told him that his problem with rage "has much more serious effects than costing you some money. For example, it is almost certainly damaging your relationships with family and friends, and it can easily ruin your career. Those effects are immeasurably more important than your win-rate."[2] He should get help with his rage to prevent much more serious problems than a low win-rate.

---

1. Slimmah, Psychology Forum, twoplustwo.com.

2. Schoonmaker, Psychology Forum, twoplustwo.com.

Put Your Education High on That Priority List

As a former professor, I naturally emphasize education. I have seen far too many bright young people severely damage their lives by not finishing their degrees. I have also seen many parents in their twenties, thirties, and forties struggling with jobs, mortgages, children, and night school, trying to get the degrees they could have gotten easily when they were younger.

If you are a student, your most important task is completing your education. Put in the hours, get whatever degrees and other credentials you need, and poker will still be here for you. Even if you think you can make a pile of money now, think of the longer term. With one or more degrees, you have *immeasurably* more options. If all you have done by the age of forty is play poker, you probably can't get a good job.

Even though we have never met. I'm confident that Barry Greenstein agrees with me. He is widely respected for three things:

1. He is one of the world's greatest players.
2. He wrote a great book, *Ace on the River.*
3. He has given millions of dollars to charities that he won in poker tournaments.

His son reported that Greenstein refused to play with him or to teach him how to play "until I—get this—actually got an education and accomplished a few things in life."[3] If you are wondering whether you should concentrate on poker or your education, ask yourself one question: "Do I know more about poker and life than Barry Greenstein?"

---

3. Joe Sebok. "All in the Family? A Chip Off the Old Block," *Card Player*, May 25, 2005, 30.

Compare your priorities to your actions.

If you spend much more time on low priority activities than you do on high ones, something is very wrong. For example, if poker is *really* a high priority for rational reasons, then spending a lot of time playing, studying, and talking about it is quite intelligent. However, if it is not important, but you are spending so much time on it that you neglect higher priorities, you have a serious problem.

Play within your comfort zone.

If you play for stakes above your comfort zone, the money may mean so much to you that poker damages your mind and body, even if you win. For example, a "therapeutic comment" posted on twoplus two.com's Psychology Forum about moving up in limits stated that a college student became extremely upset every time he moved up. He was literally ruining his health and life:

> I'm a pretty muscular guy. Yesterday I couldn't twist open the cap of a bottle. I had to let someone else do it. I'm tense all the time. I fall asleep at 6 a.m. . . . I feel like I'm getting older. Like I'm getting sick. Like poker is killing me. I've skipped lectures almost all week. I'm grumpy. Constantly I'm nervous. I haven't shaved. I haven't showered. It's worse then ever.

He was obviously playing far above his comfort zone, and he recognized that it was destroying him, *but he did not want to take the obvious action—move down.* He and many others love to play for higher stakes than they can afford, either objectively or psychologically. They need the same sort of rush that people get from skydiving and bungee jumping. If you have that need, you must learn how to control it (or give up poker) before it destroys you.

Diversify your life.

Even if you think poker is supremely important, investing too much time, energy, or emotion in it—or *anything*—is unhealthy, so diversify your life. All prudent investors diversify their portfolios because they know that any one stock, industry, or type of investment can go wrong. A diversified portfolio prevents one mistake from destroying them financially.

The same principle applies to your life as a whole. If your life and self-concept are too dependent on poker, work, a sexual partner, your grades, or anything else, you are vulnerable. Eventually, something will go wrong, and it can devastate you. So balance poker with work, studies, relationships, exercise, and so on.

Final Remarks

There is nothing original or sophisticated about these recommendations. I'm not an expert on compulsive gambling or personal counseling. Better-trained people, such as Dr. Niler and Dr. Kessler, could make other recommendations. I'm just trying to get you to think seriously about issues with enormous repercussions.

As countless poker experts have said, the only things you can control are your own decisions. Deciding how much time and energy you invest in poker is immeasurably more important than any decision you make while playing. Since these decisions can affect your entire life, I hope you make them wisely.

Afterthought

Poker is an intrinsically stressful game, and you must learn how to handle its frustrations. These chapters have discussed a few of them, and some people get so upset that they have vowed they would never play again. A few actually do quit, but they usually come back. It is an extremely exasperating game, but a wonderfully seductive one. We hate it, and we love it.

The poker explosion has made poker more nerve-racking than ever. Sometimes you have to wait hours for a game, and many of the new players don't know how to behave. From watching poker on television, they think it's okay to act outrageously. If they've played on the Internet, they've read disgusting comments in the chat box. Protected by their anonymity, they may have even threatened to beat up other players. When playing in casinos, they talk too much and too loudly, act out of turn, show their cards to each other, comment on other players' hands and personalities, get nasty when told to play faster, and do many other things we rarely saw before.

The popularity of no-limit hold'em increases the stress. Because you can lose your whole stack in one hand, the tension dramatically rises, and today's no-limit games are extremely different from traditional ones. Many pots have six or more players, and some of them will chase with almost anything, making bad beats *much* more frequent. Having your pocket aces cracked by 7-3 offsuit is extraordinarily frustrating, and it may become intolerable when you have lost your whole stack and the winner is screaming, trash-talking, and giving high-fives.

I've left early several times because it just wasn't fun to play, even though the games were very "juicy." I've never vowed to quit, and I never will. I love this game too much. But I often wish the new players knew how to behave. Perhaps greater tension is part of the price of the increased excitement and profits many good players are getting today. I wish that we could have them without the hassles, but it doesn't seem possible.

When the party ends, and the games get tougher—as will surely happen someday—we may look back longingly at today's exciting, chaotic, and very profitable time as the best we've ever had. When the dust settles, and we have to go back to dealing with the same old faces and problems, we'll probably miss having so many fish, despite their irritating ways.

But even after the new stresses go away, you will still have to deal with the same old ones: losing streaks, bad beats, annoying players, and so on. Your ability to handle them will be greatly increased if you develop a larger and longer-term perspective. If you compare your bad beats or losing streaks to the total amount you have won and lost, you will see that they do not matter that much.

If you recognize that poker is just a game, you will realize that getting too upset over whether you win or lose is just silly. In other words, keep your eye on the big picture. Then the losing streaks, bad beats, nasty players, and other frustrations will not bother you so much.

Recommended Reading

This list is organized first by skill level and then alphabetically within each level. Concentrate on the books that match your level. It is okay to read a book below your level because we all need to study the basics occasionally. Do *not* read books above your level for three reasons:

1. You need to *master* the simpler concepts to understand the advanced ones.
2. You should avoid studying advanced concepts because they can actually confuse you and make you indecisive.
3. You may try plays you don't understand and mess them up.

As I have stated repeatedly, most people overestimate their knowledge and skill. Try to resist this tendency. It is far better to master basic concepts than to gain a superficial knowledge of more advanced ones. If you are not sure that you are ready for advanced strategies, stick to the more basic books.

Incidentally, I believe that it is better to master one system than to take bits and pieces from several books. Every well-crafted book presents an integrated system. The actions fit together to reinforce each other. If you try to develop your own unique strategy, it will probably not hold together well. I therefore urge you to *study* just one or two books rather than superficially read many of them.

For Beginners and Near Beginners

Until you can break even at low limit games, don't read *anything* more advanced. You need to master the basics.

Caro, Mike. *Fundamental Secrets of Poker*. Las Vegas, NV: Mad Genius Info, 1991. A short, easy to read book with lots of ideas on strategy and psychology. Don't read it until after you have read at least one of the more basic books.

Hilger, Matthew. *Internet Texas Hold'em*. Suwanee, GA: Dimat Enterprises, 2003. This book is comprehensive and instructionally solid. He thoroughly explains strategies for both live and Internet games with over 200 hand examples.

Jones, Lee. *Winning Low Limit Hold'em*. A solid book for near beginners. Read it after *Getting Started in Hold'em* or *Quick and Easy Texas Hold'em*.

Malmuth, Mason, and Lynn Loomis. *Fundamentals of Poker*, 3rd Edition. Henderson, NV: Two Plus Two, 2000. This book is very basic.

Miller, Ed. *Getting Started in Hold'em*. Henderson, NV: Two Plus Two, 2005. This book is only for people who want to *begin* playing hold'em. His chapter on no-limit hold'em is the best I've seen for beginning players or ones making the transition from limit to no-limit.

Myers, Neil D. *Quick and Easy Texas Hold'em*. New York: Lyle Stuart, 2005. It's a basic guide for beginners.

Oliver, Gary. *Low Limit 7-Card Stud: Casino Strategy with Practice Hands*. Phoenix, AZ: Poker Tips, 1991. It proposes a very simple strategy for beginners only.

Percy, George. *Seven Card Stud: The Waiting Game*: privately printed, 1979. Since the most common and destructive mistake is being too loose, his "play very tightly" advice is well worth taking, especially for beginners.

For Players Who Can Beat Small Games

Do *not* read these books until you are at least breaking even. You need to master the fundamentals first. Once you are good enough to break even or beat low-limit games, you are ready for some more advanced material.

Caro, Mike. *The Body Language of Poker: Mike Caro's Book of Tells*. Hollywood, CA: Gambling Times, 1984. Distributed by Carol Publishing, Secaucus, NJ. This book has appeared with many different titles and publishers. Buy whatever one you can find; they all have nearly identical (and excellent) content. It can help anyone from this level upward.

Carson, Gary. *The Complete Book of Hold'em Poker.* New York: Lyle Stuart, 2001. It's for advanced beginners and intermediate players. His strategy is somewhat different from the conventional wisdom, but some people have had good results with it.

Ciaffone, Bob. *Improve Your Poker.* Saginaw, Michigan: privately printed, 1997. A solid book covering basic concepts that apply to stud, hold'em, Omaha, and other games.

Flynn, Matt, Sunny Mehta, and Ed Miller. *Professional No-limit Hold'em.* Henderson, NV: Two Plus Two, 2007. Some no-limit books are either too superficial or so detailed that they are hard to read. This book nicely balances depth and readability.

Hilger, Matthew. *Texas Hold'em Odds and Probabilities: Limit, No-limit, and Tournament Strategies.* Suwanee, GA: Dimat Enterprises, 2006. This book is *much* more understandable than the competing books on poker math. Most importantly, the focus is on how to apply the math to make better decisions.

Krieger, Lou. *Hold'em Excellence*, 2nd ed. Pittsburgh, PA: Conjelco, 2000. A well-organized, well-written, fairly basic book.

——— and Sheree Bykoffsky. *Secrets the Pros Won't Tell You About Winning Hold'em.* New York: Lyle Stuart, 2006. A compendium of a large number of tips that are not covered in many books.

Largay Angel. *No-limit Texas Hold 'Em: A Complete Course.* Toronto, Ontario, Canada: ECW Press, 2006. Angel focuses on "low-limit, no-limit" games and does a fine job of telling readers how to beat them.

Lessinger, Matt. *The Book of Bluffs.* New York: Warner Books, 2005. Some of this material may be too advanced for you, but you *must* learn when and how to bluff to continue your progress. Return to it again and again.

Miller, Ed, David Sklansky, and Mason Malmuth. *Small Stakes Hold'em: Winning Big Through Expert Play.* Henderson, NV: Two Plus Two, 2005. This book takes up where *Getting Started in Hold'em* leaves off. Its goal is to take you from being a small winner to someone who can *crush* small stakes and other loose games. I highly recommend it.

Othmer, Konstantin. *Elements of Seven Card Stud.* With Ekkehard Othmer. Cupertino, CA: Strategy One, 1992. This book is extremely well organized and provides more solid evidence than you will find in most books. However, some parts of it are hard to read.

Schoonmaker, Alan. *The Psychology of Poker*. Henderson, NV: Two Plus Two, 2000. This provides a simple system for categorizing players and games and then adjusting your strategy. It is also discusses some of the factors (such as your motives) that prevent you from playing well.

Sklansky, David. *Hold'em Poker*. Las Vegas, NV: Two Plus Two, 1976, 1989. The first serious book on hold'em. Read it after *Getting Started in Hold'em*.

————. *The Theory of Poker*, Henderson, NV: Two Plus Two, 2005. My own and many other players' favorite book. It is only for serious players. You may want to read it when you first reach this level and then study it more thoroughly when you become an advanced player. Instead of focusing on one game, Sklansky discusses theoretical issues that apply to all games. His chapter called "The Fundamental Theorem of Poker" contains the most original and useful material I have ever read about poker.

For Advanced Players

Brunson, Doyle (with many collaborators). *Super System: A Course in Power Poker*, 2nd ed. Las Vegas, NV: B&G, 1994. It's often been called "The Bible of Poker." It's a good book, but not remotely the best. He and his collaborators are champions, and they offer advice about all of the major games. The book is a little dated, but very worthwhile. However, people without great intuition can get into serious trouble trying to imitate Brunson's style in no-limit hold'em.

————. *Super System II: A Course in Power Poker*. With contributions by Crandell Addington et al. New York: Cardoza, 2005. It's a new edition of *Super System*, and some of the material has been dramatically changed. It also covers new games such as triple-draw lowball. The chapter on no-limit hold'em should have been updated because the game has changed enormously.

Ciaffone, Bob, and Jim Brier, *Middle Limit Holdem Poker*. Saginaw, Michigan: self-published, 2001. A well-organized and thorough book that clearly distinguishes between the strategies needed to beat small and middle-limit games.

Feeney, John. *Inside the Poker Mind*. Henderson, NV: Two Plus Two, 2000. It is a much more advanced book than my *The Psychology of Poker*.

It provides concepts that you need to beat larger games and tougher players.

Greenstein, Barry. *Ace of the River.* Last Knight, 2005. It provides a unique picture of the world of poker. As a psychologist, I was especially interested in his description of the "Personal Traits of Winning Poker Players." I believe he is the only great player to provide such a long list of them.

Harrington, Dan and Bill Roberti, *Harrington on Hold'em: Expert Strategy for No-Limit Tournaments,* Volumes I, II and III. Henderson, NV: Two Plus Two, 2004 and 2005. Dan Harrington was a decade's most successful player in the World Series of Poker championship. These books will help you understand how expert tournament players think. It is not as valuable for cash-game players.

Hayano, David. *Poker Faces: The Life and Work of Professional Poker Players.* Berkeley: University of California Press, 1982. The most thorough and scholarly book on this subject, but it is very dated. Anyone considering turning professional should definitely read it.

Malmuth, Mason. *Poker Essays,* Henderson, NV: Two Plus Two, 1991, and many other publishing dates. Also to be recommended from the same publisher are *Poker Essays, Volumes II and III* and *Gambling Theory and Other Topics.* They all contain some of his best columns on a wide variety of subjects. On many of these subjects, he offers the best advice you can get.

McKenna, James A. *Beyond Tells: Power Poker Psychology.* New York: Lyle Stuart, 2005. Even though it competes with this book and my *The Psychology of Poker,* and *Your Best Poker Friend,* I recommend this book. It provides a different way of looking at poker psychology.

Sklansky, David, and Mason Malmuth. *Hold'em Poker for Advanced Players: 21st Century Edition.* Henderson, NV: Two Plus Two, 1999. It is the best-selling book on limit hold'em. It includes extended discussions of general strategy and playing in loose and shorthanded games.

Sklansky, David, and Ed Miller. *No Limit Hold'em: Theory and Practice.* Henderson, NV: Two Plus Two, 2006. It is the most comprehensive book on deep-stack no-limit hold'em.

Sklansky, David, Mason Malmuth, and Ray Zee. *Seven-Card Stud for Advanced Players: 21st Century Edition.* Henderson, NV: Two Plus Two,

1999. The most advanced book on seven-card stud with the same strengths as their other advanced texts.

Tanenbaum, Barry. *Advanced Limit Hold'em Strategy: Techniques for Beating Tough Games.* Hassocks, W. Sussex, U.K.: D&B, 2007. Barry is a professional player and a great coach. His book describes a different and creative way to beat tough games.

Zee, Ray. *High-Low Split Poker for Advanced Players: Seven-Card Stud and Omaha Eight-or-Better.* Henderson, NV: Two Plus Two, 1992, 1994. I don't play either game, but my friends tell me it is the best book on them.

—— and David Fromm (with Alan Schoonmaker). *World-Class High-Stakes and Shorthanded Limit Hold'em.* Henderson, NV: Two Plus Two, 2007. You may have been baffled by some high-limit players' moves. We show how they think, and teach you how to use their advanced strategies to *crush* your game.

Index

About the Author

Alan Schoonmaker has a unique combination of academic credentials, business experience, and poker expertise. After earning a Ph.D. in industrial psychology from The University of California at Berkeley, he joined the faculties at UCLA and Carnegie-Mellon University. He then became a research fellow at Belgium's Catholic University of Louvain.

He was the manager of management development at Merrill Lynch before starting Schoonmaker and Associates, an international consulting company. He personally taught or consulted in twenty-nine countries on all six continents for clients such as GE, GM, IBM, Mobil, Rank Xerox, Bankers Trust, Wells Fargo, Manufacturers Hanover, Chemical Bank, Chase Manhattan, Ryan Homes, Sun Life of Canada, and more than two dozen others. His personal clients' annual sales exceed one trillion dollars.

He has written or co-authored three research monographs and has published four books on industrial psychology (*Anxiety and the Executive, Executive Career Strategy, Selling: The Psychological Approach,* and *Negotiate to Win*), one book on coping with college (*A Student's Survival Manual*), and *The Psychology of Poker*. His books have been translated into French, German, Spanish, Swedish, Japanese, and Indonesian.

He has published over one hundred articles in poker and business periodicals such as *Card Player, Poker Digest,* twoplustwo.com's *Internet Magazine,* Andy Glazer's *Wednesday Night Poker, The California Management Review,* and *Expansion.* He has written or played the leading role in four video series. Two were parts of multimedia training programs on industrial psychology. At one time his *Selling: The*

Psychological Approach was the world's best-selling computer-based program for business people.

He has served as an expert witness about poker psychology in both an administrative hearing and a lawsuit. He played online poker as a member of RoyalVegasPoker.com's team of experts. He has been interviewed several times on radio and television about both poker and industrial psychology.

He receives many requests for coaching. Most of them are referred to friends because he is not an expert on poker strategy. He accepts a small number of clients who need coaching *only* on poker-psychological issues such as controlling impulses, coping with losing streaks, going on tilt, and planning your poker career.

He welcomes readers' questions and comments at his e-mail address, alannschoonmaker@hotmail.com. His website is being constructed at www.alanschoonmaker.com.